T0138793

Walling Out the Insiders
Controlling Access to Improve
Organizational Security

Walling Out the Insiders
Controlling Access to Improve Organizational Security

Michael Erbschloe

CRC Press
Taylor & Francis Group
Boca Raton London New York

CRC Press is an imprint of the
Taylor & Francis Group, an **informa** business

AN AUERBACH BOOK

CRC Press
Taylor & Francis Group
6000 Broken Sound Parkway NW, Suite 300
Boca Raton, FL 33487-2742

Printed on acid-free paper
Version Date: 20160929

International Standard Book Number-13: 978-1-138-03160-9 (Paperback)

Visit the Taylor & Francis Web site at
http://www.taylorandfrancis.com

and the CRC Press Web site at
http://www.crcpress.com

Contents

Foreword

The need for security is not new. But the understanding that there is a need for security is new to many people, and that understanding is being driven by dramatic events and changing social conditions. The nightly news beams the message into people's lives on a daily basis. Although the message is loud, it is not always clear. News writers and newscasters instill drama into every twist and turn, and far too often oversimplify events and societal trends by attributing their causes to their usual list of scapegoats.

For security to work, nations, societies, and organizations need to take a deeper and more honest look at their dysfunctional tendencies. If they are honest, they can more rationally determine what drives events and creates conditions that lead to security threats. Without honest introspection, policies will be faulty from their foundation on up to the programs or mitigation efforts they propagate. In simpler terms, the current knee jerk, politically motivated blame passing has reached ridiculous proportions.

Further, the staged and manipulated denial that so many elected officials practice has also reached ridiculous proportions. This is most visible in the political response to mass shootings in the United States. Instead of admitting that gun control laws are weak and that crazy people should not have assault rifles, many elected officials hide behind the Second Amendment and will do and say anything to detract from their irresponsible inaction. They are more concerned about their lobbyist ratings and keeping those campaign contributions coming.

Scapegoating has been around for a long time as well. Power mongers stuck in their bigoted mentality will blame all who are different for all the problems of the world. They also expect that casting blame on a particular group will solve the problems and make it appear that they are doing something to protect innocent people. These denial and blame tendencies are destructive and costly.

Nations, societies, and organizations all need better security, but blaming, pointing at scapegoats, and denial are not the ingredients from which to build better security. It is way past time to get real, and not to build walls but to build better societies.

Preface

Much of the world's security focus is directed toward international terrorist attacks and high-profile corporate and government hack attacks. These are the events that nightly news is made from and for which politicians of one party blame politicians of the other party for not doing enough to prevent. The terrorist attacks have been both severe and heartbreaking. The corporate computer hacks have been embarrassing and costly. What may be more costly in the long term is that the focus of improving security efforts has squarely been on incidents perpetrated by outsiders.

Meanwhile, insider attacks and crimes continue to occur and continue to be very costly to the victim organization and to society in general. It seems that insider crimes and misdemeanors have become so commonplace that the world at large just ignores them and the victim organizations just suffer the consequences.

Protecting intellectual property and proprietary data from outside attacks is costly and time consuming, but it is not personal. Protecting intellectual property, proprietary data, and physical assets as well as the workplace from inside attacks can also be costly and time consuming. But the difference between protecting against outsider attacks and insider attacks is that protecting against insider attacks is a personal, often face-to-face process. When protecting against insider attacks, both managers and employees need to face the fact that many of their fellow managers and employees are dishonest or just plain careless and they cannot be trusted.

Walling Out the Insiders: Controlling Access to Improve Organizational Security is about accepting that fellow managers and employees are dishonest or careless and cannot be trusted. It is also about practical steps that can be taken to improve security against insider crime. This book recognizes that best practices are helpful, but it also recognizes that best practices can be very expensive and even unaffordable for many organizations. So the self-assessment steps included in this book are designed to help security planners and security staffs decide how much security they need and cope with the situation of how much security they can afford.

This book also does something that most security books will never do, and that is to clearly state that when managers avoid taking even simple steps to protect their organization because they do not want to deal with the face-to-face consequences of admitting they cannot trust their fellow managers and their employees, then the state of security for the organization is their responsibility. Blaming the perpetrator is always easy; admitting that an incident could have been easily avoided if managers would have taken preventive measures is yet another thing.

Introduction

The basic spirit of this book is practicality. It is about getting to the point about actions that can help an organization improve security policies and procedures as well as implement a wide range of appropriate security measures. So there will not be screams of panic, red lights flashing, or statements playing on fear, uncertainty, and doubt. Instead, there will be very fundamental issues addressed in a manner that does not alarm but also does not pull any punches. The best way to address security is by adopting a realistic perspective and pursuing solutions that an organization can both afford and implement.

A self-assessment method for the state of security in an organization is provided along with several other self-assessment lists for several issues covered in the chapters. Assessment tools and self-assessment questions to ask will help ascertain the perception of security and determine how well key employees think the organization is managing security. These tools are straightforward and are easy to use compared to many of the checklists available to evaluate security.

An overview of the security process is shown in Figure I.1. Security starts with the screening and background checks of all parties that come into a facility. Once approved, individuals are provided with an ID card/badge that is used to enter the facility through a physical access control system. The next step after gaining initial access is orientation and training on appropriate security policies and procedures.

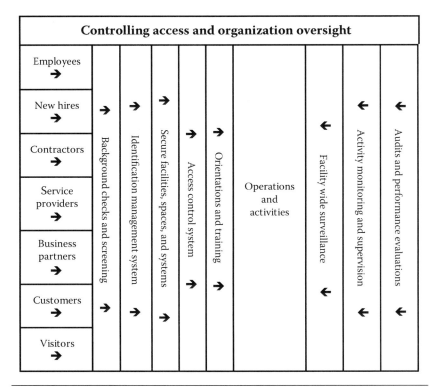

Figure I.1   Controlling access and organization oversight.

Upon completion of orientation and training, individuals are allowed to go about their authorized activities. During the course of those activities, all parties will be under surveillance, and their work will be audited and evaluated in a job appropriate manner. This will help control insider actions and prevent security violations.

Course material is also provided in each chapter and includes a case study relating to the topics in the chapter, key terms, course discussion questions, course projects, and short quizzes. The contents of the chapters are discussed next.

Chapter 1: How This Book Will Help to Build a Security Philosophy and Strategy—This chapter helps to establish a foundation for the understanding of security policies and procedures in an organization and introduces a self-assessment on the state of security. It also covers societal trends that impact security efforts within an organization.

Chapter 2: Identifying What to Protect and Who to Protect It From—This chapter provides methods to prioritize security efforts to ensure that important assets are adequately protected. It continues to elaborate on how to identify, or profile, those who may be most able or most likely to misuse or misappropriate various types of assets.

Chapter 3: Developing a Plan to Improve Security and Reduce the Insider Threat—This chapter covers the planning process as well as how to document security plans. It also examines the life-cycle management of security plans including conducting periodic reviews and audits. These areas are often weak points in achieving appropriate security against insider threats.

Chapter 4: Increasing Awareness, Diligence, and Vigilance—This chapter examines how to increase cultural awareness about security within an organization. It also covers methods to motivate employees to become part of ongoing security efforts. Increasing awareness and proper motivation are essential to achieving security goals and objectives.

Chapter 5: Developing Social Media Policies and Training Employees—This chapter explains how to develop social media policies, including when and who in an organizations should use social media. It also covers how to establish a practical training process and how to integrate security topics in other training programs as well as how to embed training into nontraining activities. Training is an expensive process and managers want to ensure that training efforts are effective.

Chapter 6: Evaluating Security Services and Security Products—Selecting and purchasing products and services before a thorough review is conducted is almost a universal occurrence. This chapter explains how to establish a critical review process and who should be included in the review process. The review process covers companies whose products are being considered as well as the products themselves.

Chapter 7: Establishing an Identification Program for Employees, Business Partners, Customers, and Other Visitors—This chapter covers the basics on how to establish an identification system for all of the people that may be entering a facility. It also covers how to determine who should be responsible for managing and operating the identification systems. A proper identification system helps to manage access to a facility by these part-time insiders.

Chapter 8: Implementing Strong Physical Access Controls—Managing and controlling access to facilities is a critical aspect of a good security program. This chapter examines how to design, implement, and manage access to control systems. It also discusses how to control knowledge of the systems and how to keep access systems secure.

Chapter 9: Managing Relationships with Vendors, Business Partners, and Customers—Working with other organizations is an essential part of the business process, but it is important stay in control of those relationships. This chapter goes beyond managing access by part-time insiders and covers methods that will help an organization maintain control over those relationships as well as the people or groups that employees may need to have interactions with.

Chapter 10: Developing Methods to Monitor Security Threats and Needs—Far too many organizations do not update their threat analysis and the steps they need to take to protect from those threats. This chapter explains how to establish a process of monitoring threats and what sources of information or expertise that should be utilized to develop a cost-effective monitoring process.

Chapter 11: Investigating and Responding to Security Incidents—Determining if and when a security incident has occurred may not be as easy as it sounds because many security violations go undetected for months or years. Some security violations may never be discovered unless staff members are vigilant. This chapter reviews straightforward investigative methods and useful steps to take when responding to an incident.

Chapter 12: Using Surveillance Technologies and Techniques—Surveillance of facilities is a very good way to detect and prevent security breaches. This chapter covers the basics of

installing and managing surveillance systems to prevent insiders from inappropriately accessing secure parts of facilities.

Chapter 13: What to Do When Hiring New Employees—
Turnover in the workforce is a natural process and organizations will frequently need to hire new employees. This chapter
covers ways to prioritize what to do when hiring various types
of employees including background checks and obtaining
references.

Chapter 14: Cyber Issues and the Insider—While much of the
world focuses on hackers and malicious forces attacking corporate information systems, many people forget that it is the
insider that most frequently does damage to computer systems,
cripples applications, and steals data. This chapter examines
cyber issues and the insider, and how to minimize damage
that insiders can do to information systems and networks.

Acknowledgments

I thank Richard O'Hanley, editor at CRC Press, and his publishing team for their support and assistance in getting this book from concept into print. There is a long list of people who have influenced this perspective on protecting organizations from both inside and outside threats. Working with many managers over the years has helped me to understand the struggle that organizations face when working to improve security. Many have had to address security issues on a limited and sometimes very slim budget. These managers helped shape the perspective that although best practices may be wonderful ideas, the reality of it is that most organizations will fall short of best practices and develop the best security measures that they can afford.

1

How This Book Will Help to Build a Security Philosophy and Strategy

People usually take security more seriously after an incident is discovered within their organization or when the nightly news reports crimes against companies, security breaches, or terrorist attacks. As a result, new security programs or fixes to existing security measures are often pursued in a panic. Unfortunately, panic is not always a good environment in which to make decisions about what security measures should be implemented. Many times quick fixes that are put into place often do little to improve the overall security profile of an organization. Approaching security with a well-thought-out plan designed to address security needs will result in longer lasting and often more economical mitigation methods being implemented.

Instead of being reactive and acting out of panic or desperation, this book approaches security from a balanced long-term and methodical perspective. It is not likely that all potential problems can be solved with one effort. However, an organization can effectively deal with security issues by keeping security in mind during all planning and management activities. In other words, build security in from the ground up rather than attempting to apply Band-Aids on a piecemeal basis. To do this may call for a philosophical and cultural shift in how an organization is managed.

The spirit of this book is practicality. So there will not be screams of panic, flashing red light, or statements playing on fear, uncertainty, and doubt. Instead there will be very fundamental issues addressed in a manner that does not alarm but also does not pull any punches. The best way to address security is by adopting a realistic perspective and pursuing solutions that an organization can both afford and implement.

1.1 Trends That Impact Security Efforts

Over the last couple of decades there have been several trends that have made organizations more vulnerable to insider offenses. Many organizations have gone through some sort of downsizing, reducing their headcount and often combining job functions with an eye on financial savings and without any specific regard for security. There has also been a trend toward having more *open organizations* and providing employees with access to more tools, resources, and data in the hope that the new leaner organizations will become more productive by empowering employees. In addition, the information technology industry has greatly focused on bringing products to market that are advertised to provide employees with more tools so they can have more access and be more productive. All of these trends were based more on hope than they were on proven results.

At the societal level, more people have greater access to *personal technologies* such as smart phones, flash drives, and other devices that better enable them to spy or steal intellectual property. The Internet allows insiders to quickly move data or information out of an organization's facility. The Internet can also provide a communications platform for insiders to stay in contact with outside coconspirators regarding their actions or the types of information they should look for and misappropriate. This communication can also aid insiders in providing outsiders with access to internal resources or make it easier to access physical properties or assets that could be the target of theft or destruction. Protecting against such threats is an absolute necessity in all security efforts.

In addition, there has also been an increase in gun sales and gun ownership in the United States, and those weapons can readily end up in the hands of disgruntled or angry employees. These weapons can be used to harm or threaten fellow employees, managers, or service providers. The debate on gun ownership in the United States is not likely to settle down any time soon, and thus it is likely that gun ownership will continue to increase. This means that guns or other weapons being brought into a facility is something an organization will need to protect against in the future. It is not a pleasant thought, but it is necessary to keep such protective efforts in the planning perspective.

There are other social trends that are a bit more ambiguous but nevertheless may increase current and future threats. The U.S. Federal Bureau of Investigation (FBI) lists several driving forces behind insider actions. As local and national economies shift, many people face financial need and excessive debt, while others may just view crime as an alternative means to increase their personal wealth. Such societal trends can foster anger and resentment on the part of employees, driving them to vengeful destructive behavior. Then there are other employees that may encounter problems with coworkers or managers, which increase their motivations for revenge and may very well seek the tools to do so.

Now we also face the threat of ideological differences and divided social or nationalistic loyalties that may align an insider with an outside cause or social group that advocates violence or economic espionage. These types of loyalties can drive an insider to seek adventures or strive to impress outside group members or leadership in order to raise their standing with a group that they want to be involved with in future life. In pursuit of recognition of the group of which they want membership, insiders may abandon all loyalties to their employer and turn into a major threat to security.

Other societal conditions that may impact insider behavior include drug abuse, family problems, and untreated mental illnesses.[1] It is difficult to predict all of the social trends or the impact those trends can have on insider behavior. Thus the best perspective is to expect that outside forces and social trends can always impact insider behavior. Monitoring employee behavior that could indicate future problems is probably the best route. This can be both time consuming and frustrating, but the easiest way to be alert is to watch for unusual, unexpected, or unnecessary changes in the behavior of an employee.

1.2 What Insiders Can Do to an Organization

Research conducted by the FBI shows that insiders commit a wide range of crimes against their employers. These include property crimes such as destruction or sabotage, financial crimes such as embezzlement, theft of property both physical and intellectual, misuse of property, and violence against other employees. The motivation of an insider to commit crimes against his employer can include greed or financial need, unhappiness at work, allegiance to another company or another country, vulnerability to blackmail, the promise of a better job, or drug or alcohol abuse.[1] The FBI also points out that people who commit many crimes against their employers are generally white males in their late 20s to early 30s, except for embezzlement, in which there is a higher proportion of females committing such offenses.[2]

There are numerous dynamics that can enable insiders to move forward on an intentional *premeditated malicious act* or change an employee's perspective about how easy it may be to get away with a crime against an organization. Planners should take these dynamics into consideration when evaluating security needs. These include the following:

- Situations that may increase the ease of thievery when supervisors are changed, departments are combined, mergers occur, or any other event that occupies the time and efforts of management and reduce monitoring of the work environment.
- Insiders are provided with greater access privileges than they had in the past resulting from organization restructuring or lax security efforts.
- Intellectual property or sensitive information is improperly labeled or not properly stored.
- Insiders discover weaknesses in security that allows them to remove property from a facility.
- Ambiguous policies about taking work out of the office or plant, which can result in misuse or misappropriation of information or equipment.
- A lack of training on procedures, which results in some employees unwittingly making it easier for culprits to access information or physical assets.

1.3 Categories of Security Measures

When working to improve security for an organization, people often become fascinated with the many and varied types of security products and services that are available on the market. These products and services can certainly be helpful in improving security. However, it is important to look at security from the ground up when deciding how to address insider threats and reduce insider opportunity to commit offenses. When strong measures are appropriately implemented, the need for add-on security products can be reduced. Security measures can be sorted into four main categories: physical, procedural, mechanical, and spontaneous. Explanations and examples of the four categories are as follows:

- *Physical security measures* are barriers that control entry and access to building areas by unauthorized employees or contractors, and that prevent materials or information from being physically accessed or removed from a controlled area. Examples include fences, traffic barriers, tamper-proof doors and windows, moats, and open areas that are easily monitored for intruders.
- *Procedural security measures* are structured processes or steps that employees must follow when entering or exiting secure areas, when handling and working with sensitive or proprietary materials, or when transferring products or data from one controlled area to another controlled area. Procedural security measures can also apply to how materials are ordered, received, or shipped, as well as how information or data is transferred to a different division or building.
- *Mechanical security measures* include all of the various devices or protective systems that can be installed to prevent unauthorized movement and monitor the movement of people, materials, products, supplies, or data. These include surveillance systems, devices requiring a pass code to get into restricted areas, and radio frequency identification (RFID) tags installed on important items.
- *Spontaneous or situational security measures* are those that are put into place when out-of-the-ordinary events are taking place at a facility. Such events can include major building repairs or remodels, construction of new facilities, disruptive weather, or visits by corporate dignitaries or delegations from business partners or customers. Examples include special security details, designated escorts, or specialized identification badges.

The decision as to which type of security measure to deploy in specific areas of a facility will depend on several factors including available financial resources, difficulties in deployment of a security measure, or existing security measures such as surveillance systems and secured access doors. A sound analysis of threats and security needs can help in selecting an appropriate measure for a specific situation or for specific areas of a facility that need protection. Analyzing security needs from the ground up can help reduce the costs of deploying security measures as well as the long-term maintenance of a security measure.

1.4 Obstacles to Developing and Implementing Appropriate Security Measures

It is important that there is a security champion in any organization. In some cases this may be the security director, if, in fact, there is one in the organization. However, it is more effective if there is a C-level manager that champions security and is willing to spend the time to speak up at management meetings and planning sessions about security. It is also helpful that there is a security champion that will advocate budgeting appropriate resources for security and advocate for security reviews and improved policies and procedures.

Developing security programs and implementing security measures does not take place in a perfect world where all people agree on the need for high levels of security or the need to spend the money to achieve appropriate security. Conversations with security managers indicate that one of the biggest obstacles is getting upper management to provide sufficient financial resources. The willingness to spend money on security is often tied to the perception of threat. The willingness to spend money goes up during or after security incidents and goes down in the extended absence of security incidents.

One now-classic example is airport security screening funding. Soon after the events of September 11, 2001, security spending increased in both the public and private sectors. As security incidents declined, in part due to the success of security measures, funding for the Transportation Security Administration (TSA) was reduced. The U.S. Congress slowly chipped away at the TSA budget. The impact of the reduced spending became obvious in the spring and summer of 2016 as air travel increased and TSA screening efforts did not correspondingly increase. Thus, Congress may have saved money by not spending it, but the traveling public suffered long waits, missed flights, and a high level of toxic stress as a result of Congressional actions in budget reductions, followed by Congressional inactions to address increased budgets to meet security needs.

In addition to management resistance to funding security, the fact that security is often inconvenient and time consuming makes managers and employees view security efforts in a negative light. A negative view of security intensifies when it is perceived that threats have subsided but inconvenience still lingers. The perception then shifts in the direction that the value of security has declined and budget increases are not necessary and spending can even be decreased. The impact of this dynamic is often denied or at least ignored. Ultimately excessive shifts in spending and fluctuating dedication to security are likely to result in negative consequences as efforts are initiated and halted on a frequent basis.

Finally, this is the age of downsizing, shifting business models, mergers, acquisitions, globalization, and tumultuous political dynamics. In such an environment, investors, business owners, and legislative bodies often lose focus on what is needed in the long term to achieve and ensure sustainability. The short-term desire for flexibility, fluidity, and profits or savings can easily overshadow the long-term need for security.

When security is reprioritized and relegated to a lower level of interest or action, security can easily be denied, neglected, or, in so many cases, just simply ignored. As high-level decision makers rationalize away the need for security, they do not eliminate the threat. Those behind the threat can wait to strike when defenses are down and security capabilities are diminished.

1.5 Researching Industry and Government Input on Security

One way to overcome management sluggishness in addressing the need to maintain appropriate security is to step out of the organizational context and review what other organizations are doing about security. This can be facilitated by examining the work and recommendations of industry groups and industry associations regarding threats and security needs. Reviewing the work of standards organizations can also be helpful.

Since the events of September 11, 2001, many governments have supported the implementation of stronger security measures in their country as well as in the countries of their treaty or trading partners. In the United States, the Department of Homeland Security (DHS) has provided a leadership role in promoting threat analysis and security efforts.[3] The DHS and the Office of the President have identified 16 critical infrastructure sectors whose assets, systems, and networks are important to sustaining national interest including economic stability and sustainability. Presidential Policy Directive/PPD-21 lists the *critical industry sectors* and assigns responsibility for monitoring threats and fostering the growth of improved security to specific federal agencies or departments.[4] The sectors and corresponding federal agencies are shown in Figure 1.1.

Critical industry sectors and federal agencies charged with security leadership	
Critical industry sector	**Sector specific agency**
Chemical	Department of Homeland Security (DHS)
Commercial facilities	DHS
Communications	DHS
Critical manufacturing	DHS
Dams	DHS
Defense industrial base	Department of Defense (DOD)
Emergency services	DHS
Energy	Department of Energy (DOE)
Financial services	Department of the Treasury
Food and agriculture	Department of Agriculture (USDA) and Department of Health and Human Services (DHHS)
Government facilities	DHS and General Services Administration (GSA)
Healthcare and public health	DHHS
Information technology	DHS
Nuclear reactors, materials, and waste	DHS
Transportation systems	DHS and Department of Transportation (DOT)
Water and wastewater systems	Environmental Protection Agency (EPA)

Figure 1.1   Critical industry sectors and federal agencies charged with security leadership. (From The White House, Presidential Policy Directive—Critical Infrastructure Security and Resilience, February 2013, retrieved May 18, 2016, from https://www.whitehouse.gov/the-press-office/2013/02/12/presidential-policy-directive-critical-infrastructure-security-and-resil.)

The sector specific agencies provide guidance regarding security for the sectors for which they have been designated. The agencies can provide very good technical assistance and their recommendations may be helpful in justifying budget decisions in an organization.

Another organization that can provide helpful guidance is the National Institute of Building Sciences, which supports the Whole Building Design Guide (WBDG). The WBDG focuses, in part, on how to design and create integrated security into new building construction and in the remodeling of existing buildings.[5] The Building Security Council's (BSC) Building Rating System (BRS) and certification for professionals has also been established with the goal of integrating security into the design and construction of buildings.[6] The BSC also provides a certification for building design professionals.

The American National Standards Institute (ANSI) facilitates and fosters the creation and implementation of numerous standards and guidelines to help organizations manage and implement security measures. The ANSI also works on a wide variety of standards that impact almost all industries. The standard setting process is fluid and ongoing. Membership in the ANSI is comprised of government agencies, private companies, nonprofit organizations, and academic institutions. The standards can be purchased from the ANSI website (www.ansi.org).

The websites of the aforementioned organizations provide a wealth of information that can help planners evaluate security efforts that are already in place or to build security in from the ground up when you construct a new facility. Thus, planners do not need to invent security on their own because there are many helpful resources to explore.

1.6 Checking in with Your Insurance Company

If risk managers do not already conduct an annual insurance audit with an insurance company and review changes that impact the cost of insurance coverage, then such a process should probably be initiated. During the periodic audit it can be determined why insurance costs as much as it does. Security planners may also find ways to reduce insurance costs without reducing coverage by discussing which security measures you have implemented and the types of physical, mechanical, procedural, and spontaneous or situational security measures that have been put into place or are being considered for the future.

Insurance coverage can, at times, be highly debated in an organization. Many organizations want sufficient coverage to maintain sustainability in the face of security incidents, natural disasters, and industrial accidents. On the other hand, insurance costs are sometimes hotly debated, especially during times when austerity measures are being implemented or cutting costs is necessary to keep an organization afloat in the short term.

When considering insurance options, all organizations should evaluate fidelity bonds, which are commonly known as commercial crime policies. They are specifically designed to protect organizations from the financial impact of dishonest acts committed by employees. This includes the following:

- Theft by employees
- Deposit fraud or alterations of deposit instruments
- Misappropriation, disappearance, or destruction of money and securities
- Robbery, or safe or secure storage burglary
- Computer crimes (theft, funds transfer fraud)

The insurance audit is a process that should involve many people in an organization. They can include legal counsel, upper management, functional area managers, planners, and, of course, those responsible for security. Insurance audits can be very lengthy and boring processes, but they can also render very favorable results as well as new knowledge on which to build security upon as an organization strives for sustainability.

1.7 Addressing Cyber Security Issues

Cyber security issues are never ending because the threat is constantly evolving. Protecting information systems from outside attacks and intrusions is a specialty that is best handled by the IT security staff or department in conjunction with the security staff or department. Protecting information systems, data, and business processes from outside attacks is not directly addressed in this book. This book does focus on protecting those systems, their content, and purpose from insider attacks or misappropriation of data or disruption of business processes.

Protecting information systems from insider attacks is at least as equally important as protecting them from outsider attacks. There have been numerous incidents of insiders attacking information systems. Some attacks occur for revenge or out of anger against the organization or managers and staff. Other attacks involving theft of data or trade secrets often happen for financial gain. The FBI contends that insiders do not need to know how to hack information systems from the outside because they already have some knowledge, and at times extensive knowledge, of an organization's information systems. They also may have very few restrictions to their access privileges and can cause extensive damage to the system or steal system data.[7]

Insider attacks on information systems have been as numerous as they have been varied. A review of investigations conducted by the FBI illustrates this variety. There have been police officers perpetrating unauthorized access to data on victims and posing as an attorney to offer their services. There have been information technology staff members accessing systems and doing damage or stealing data as an act of revenge against their employer. Employees in medical facilities have accessed systems and stole data regarding the general health and medical conditions of individuals. Information systems have enabled embezzlers to readily steal millions of dollars from a wide variety of organizations. The list seems endless. More detail on the specific security incidents can be found in cases on the FBI website (fbi.gov). Chapter 14 covers cyber security issues related to insiders.

1.8 Adopting a Philosophy of Security

An organization is obliged to protect the security and privacy of customer data, which it generates through the process of doing business or is collected from customers to fill orders, responding to requests for information, or providing a management function for a customer. There has been a rash of insiders inappropriately accessing and disseminating data and information that companies or customers consider private. Protecting data against privacy violations committed by insiders is an ongoing challenge.

When organizations exchange information to help facilitate business processes, the importance of privacy has been fairly well established and has become customary. An organization wants its information kept confidential to prevent damage that may occur if the information was obtained by competitors or other parties that could use the information to negatively impact the competitive position or the well-being of the information providing company. The provider of the information has a public image to protect and the misuse of confidential information could result in bad publicity. In the case of publicly held companies, improper dissemination of proprietary information could negatively impact stock value.

Individuals who provide information to businesses or government organizations can also be negatively impacted by the misuse of information. Such misuse may impact their job, career choices, and lifetime earnings. An individual who is gay or lesbian may choose to keep this information private in order to not have to deal with potential social or financial negative consequences. People who are making investment decisions, who are considering changing jobs, or who have decided to get divorced may suffer damages from the release of information related to their life or their plans.

The common thread between the security of proprietary corporate information and personal data provided by individuals is that the improper dissemination and use of their information can cause damage. In some cases, such damage could be financial and in other cases it could damage reputations. Because there is a lack of universal definitions as to what constitutes the ownership of information and the privacy of information, the privacy security contract is essential to establish an agreement between the information provider and the information recipient as to the use of the information exchanged.

The example of a business-to-business exchange of information to facilitate business processes is done under specific conditions with agreed upon procedures and rights to use the information. Likewise, the exchange of information between a consumer and a business needs to be governed by a similar contract that establishes rights and expectations.

When information is exchanged there must be a contract between the parties that are giving and receiving information as to the scope of use of that information. It is not reasonable, or prudent, to expect both parties to share a common view for the rights to use the information. Where there are local or national laws governing the use of information, the contract should of course be in compliance with such laws. Where there is a lack of specific laws, the exchange of information should be governed by a contract that both parties can understand and which binds them.

Having appropriate policies to protect customer privacy and training employees to help protect that privacy is a challenge that is addressed over time. Key is that employees understand that an organization takes privacy seriously and expects all employees, contractors, and business partners to understand the need to protect the confidentiality of information used in the business process.

1.9 Assessing an Organization's Perception of Security

Introspection and self-assessment can be challenging because people generally do not want to admit that they are less than perfect regarding important management functions or activities. They especially do not want to admit that their organization is doing a flat out horrible job in implementing appropriate security measures. It is also difficult to assess something in your head without rationalizing away answers. Sometimes it is best to do a pen-and-paper exercise and that can be done with little extra effort.

One way to go about this is to develop a brief survey of how various managers in an organization view security efforts or specific security measures. If security planners decide to do such a survey, have as many managers and employees complete the survey as possible. This will help capture the perceptions of people that view an organization from different vantage points. Sample questions for managers and staff are provided in Figure 1.2.

Once the planning team has collected the perceptions of various managers, it is time to compile results. As you may suspect, the more questions that are answered with a no answer, the more likely it is that security planners and managers have considerable work to do in developing and documenting security policies and procedures as well as training managers on security policies and procedures. Keep in mind that this survey is only a starting point. Security planners may want to follow up with survey respondents so that they can elaborate

Sample questions for managers on their perception of security		
Sample questions	**Circle yes or no**	
Do you know who in the organization is responsible for security?	Yes	No
Do you know what the security policies and procedures are for your organization?	Yes	No
Have you been trained on security policies and procedures?	Yes	No
Has your department employees been trained on security policies and procedures?	Yes	No
Do you discuss security policies and procedures in management meetings?	Yes	No
Do you discuss security policies and procedures in departmental meetings?	Yes	No
Have you been asked about the potential effectiveness of security policies and procedures?	Yes	No
Have you worked with security staff to improve the effectiveness of security policies and procedures?	Yes	No
Do you know who to call if you know or suspect that security policies or procedures have been violated?	Yes	No
Have security violations in your department been appropriately dealt with by the organization?	Yes	No
Do you feel that security policies and procedures are adequate to protect the organization?	Yes	No

Figure 1.2   Sample questions for managers on their perception of security.

on their perceptions or experiences. Security planners also may want to survey managers on specific areas covered in later chapters of this book.

1.10 Developing and Gauging an Organization's Philosophy of Security

Another approach to examining how security is addressed in an organization is to review areas like those covered in the survey questions and summarize perceptions in forms of a philosophy. A corporate philosophy toward security is not a rationalized perspective. Look at it as a summary of the actual actions that have been taken on security and what those actions may indicate about the real-life philosophy toward security. The responses to the survey questions may be helpful in determining what the philosophy is, but reality checks on what has or has not been done regarding security will help make the assessment more realistic.

The graph in Figure 1.3 is set up so that survey takers can apply a ranking of how an organization performs in managing key areas of a security program. The organization is ranked on a scale of 1 to 10 for each of the key areas. A score of 5 or under indicates weaknesses in asset protection and a score of 6 or above indicates that asset protection is stronger. When completed, survey takers should tally the scores in the bottom row by adding the scores respondents have circled for each area.

Indications of an organization's philosophy toward security											
Inconsistent philosophy						Pro-security philosophy					
Rank how your organization manages security issues on a scale of 1 to 10 for each area											
It is **not clear** who is responsible for security in the organization						There is a **clear delineation** as to who is responsible for security in the organization					
1	2	3	4	5	←	→	6	7	8	9	10
Security policies and procedures are generally **poorly understood**						Security policies and procedures are generally **well understood**					
1	2	3	4	5	←	→	6	7	8	9	10
Training on security policies and procedures has **not occurred** or is uncertain						Training on security policies and procedures **has occurred** throughout the organization					
1	2	3	4	5	←	→	6	7	8	9	10
Security policies and procedures are not **discussed** or rarely discussed or reviewed						Security policies and procedures are **frequently discussed** or reviewed					
1	2	3	4	5	←	→	6	7	8	9	10
Department managers are **not involved** in developing security policies and procedures						Department managers are **often involved** in developing security policies and procedures					
1	2	3	4	5	←	→	6	7	8	9	10
It is **uncertain** if or how security violations are dealt with by the organization						It is **clear** how security violations are dealt with by the organization					
1	2	3	4	5	←	→	6	7	8	9	10
Budget requests for security are frequently **denied** or reduced						Budget requests for security are frequently **approved** or encouraged					
1	2	3	4	5	←	→	6	7	8	9	10
There are **ambiguous** feelings about the state of security in the organization						People in the organization feel that security is **appropriate** and well managed					
1	2	3	4	5	←	→	6	7	8	9	10
___	___	___	___	___	Tally scores on this line	___	___	___	___	___	

Figure 1.3 Indications of an organization's philosophy toward security.

The lower the scores are, the more likely it is that security planners should pay more attention to the areas with low scores. The tally in the bottom row will provide a measure of overall security functioning from a high level. The low tallied scores are an indication that security planners should either work on the security program or put more effort into security training and education. The ranking of 1 to 5 should be made on based on how weak you feel the organization is on that particular aspect of security. If respondents feel the organization is stronger in this area, the ranking of 6 to 10 should be made based on how strong they feel the organization is on that particular aspect of security. More detailed analysis of specific areas is provided in later chapters.

1.11 Summary

This chapter has helped to set a foundation for moving ahead on improving security in an organization. It also provided a method to review the philosophy with which an organization approaches security issues and designs and selects security measures. Key areas covered include the following:

- Societal trends that impact security efforts now and some of those trends that will impact security in the future
- The type of crimes insiders commit, including theft, destruction of property, violence against others, and embezzlement
- The four major categories of security measures: physical, procedural, mechanical, and spontaneous
- The type of obstacles that you face in designing and implementing appropriate security measures, including financial and cultural obstacles
- Organizations that provide guidance for developing appropriate security measures, including government agencies, private nonprofit organizations, and insurance companies
- The importance of developing strong cyber security measures to protect from insider inappropriately accessing information and computer systems
- How to begin assessing an organization's attitude and philosophy toward security and how to begin to develop or change those attitudes and philosophy

COURSE CASE STUDY THE JAMES MARTIN MANUFACTURING COMPANY

The James Martin Manufacturing Company is a family-owned business that has been in operation for over 80 years. It became a viable company in World War II, supplying the United States military and allies with defense products. The founder, James Martin Sr., ran the company for many years and eventually turned it over to his son, James Martin Jr., who remains the president and CEO. James Martin Jr. developed health problems about 10 years ago and entrusted the company operations to a long-time manager Harold Smith.

As fate would have it, Harold Smith died a sudden death three months ago. Tonya Martin, the daughter of James Martin Jr., has taken over the management of the company until the family can decide its future. Tonya has a BA in business and an MBA. She worked summers in the company for much of her life. After some life-changing events coincided with the death of Harold Smith, the former corporate manager, she returned to manage the company.

Tonya is familiar with virtually every aspect of the company and had worked in several positions in the company from secretary to production line supervisor to part-time accounting specialist. Through the years Tonya became discouraged by her father's hands-off approach of ownership and by the lack of informal structure of the company. Her father was not much on structure because, following in his father's footsteps, he preferred an intimate day-to-day management approach and knew everything that was going on inside the company. He also had a good understanding of the various industries he manufactured, parts, and equipment.

After Tonya said hello to all of the people in the company she knew from the past and introduced herself to some new supervisors, she started digging into her new responsibilities. She was in Harold Smith's old office and going through whatever documents she could find. One of her pet peeves about Harold

Smith's management approach was that he kept almost every-thing to himself. There had not been an external audit of com-pany financial accounts in over a decade. Her father felt he had everything under control and Harold Smith maintained the tra-dition. James Martin Jr. trusted Harold Smith with everything and did not require any outside audits or oversight.

One of the first things Tonya looked at were tax returns for the last few years. She noticed that sales revenue grew slowly since her father left day-to-day involvement in the company, but during the same period profits steadily decreased. This finding prompted Tonya to look back at tax returns for the few years just before her father retired up to the present day. The rev-enue growth trends and the decline in profit trends followed a pattern. There was slow growth in revenue and steady decline in profits since Harold Smith had taken over the company management.

The manufacturing aspects of the company along with order processing and shipping and receiving were running smoothly enough to allow Tonya time to review what had happened in the company over the last 10 years. Fortunately, the in-house accountant kept meticulous and orderly records of everything. The accountant, however, merely processed whatever Harold Smith asked her to process and never questioned anything.

Tonya started digging and the more she found, the more she would dig. She suspected that Harold Smith had been stealing money and rerouting purchased items for his own use. It did not take her long to confirm her suspicions. It was clear that with every year that passed, Harold Smith stole more and more from the company. He would minimize pay increases for the workers while he was stealing, and the less the workers were paid, the more money there was to steal.

Tonya was now in a quandary as to what to do about the thefts. She concluded that there was little chance of recovering any of the money or equipment that Harold Smith stole, so she called her father's attorney, James Davis, to discuss the situa-tion. James welcomed Tonya back and they sat to discuss the situation. After discussing various strategies, they agreed not to report the crime to the police just yet, but James Davis said he would chat with Harold Smith's widow, who still lived in town. He once again offered Mrs. Smith his condolences about her late husband's death and informed her that Tonya Martin was, at least for the time, running the James Martin Manufacturing Company.

Mrs. Smith had met Tonya on many occasions at various holiday events and summer picnics sponsored by the company. Then Mrs. Smith told the attorney that Tonya may be able to help her with something. She said she had a garage full of stuff and that Mr. Smith was always bringing stuff home from the plant and that she had no idea what to do with the boxes and boxes of stuff that had accumulated over the years. James Davis set an appointment for he and Tonya to visit Mrs. Smith the next day.

Tonya and James Davis arrived at the home of Mrs. Smith brining her a dozen roses. Tonya had recalled how Mrs. Smith used to grow roses before she developed arthritis. Mrs. Smith was more than gracious and told them to go look in the detached garage, which was always unlocked. It took only a few minutes to confirm Tonya's suspicions because the garage was filled with boxes marked James Martin Manufacturing Company. Upon inspection they found the boxes full of almost everything that they could imagine, including tools, machine parts, finished products, and even stationery from the James Martin Manufacturing Company.

Tonya and James conferred for a few minutes and returned to the house to speak with Mrs. Smith. Mrs. Smith was always pleasant and she had prepared a pot of tea. Tonya and James were treading lightly because the last thing Tonya really wanted to do was add misery to Mrs. Smith's life.

Mrs. Smith asked Tonya and James if the stuff in the garage belonged to the James Martin Manufacturing Company. Tonya and James told her yes, much of it does seem to but they could not be sure about everything. Mrs. Smith reiterated to them that Harold had always been bringing things home but she never really knew what it was. She said that Harold was always a good provider and she felt that what was in the garage was his business.

Mrs. Smith said that Harold had always taken good care of her and when she needed in-home assistance including having a housekeeper that Harold always had the money to pay for whatever she needed. She then asked Tonya if she could take care of all of the stuff in the garage and apologized for any problems Mr. Smith may have caused. She also asked James if there were any legal issues, to which he replied no.

Tonya did not want to create an issue for gossip at the plant and arranged for the stuff in the garage to be picked up over the weekend and put into the warehouse at the James Martin Manufacturing Company. On the way back to the office, Tonya and James talked about what to do next. Tonya felt she could not do much about the past and wanted to focus on the future and get the company back to a sustainable state of affairs.

Tonya decided that security was one of the biggest issues that the James Martin Manufacturing Company was facing at this time and felt strongly that she needed to make sure that the stealing was stopped no matter who might be involved. She considered hiring a consulting firm to help her assess security, but before she did that she wanted to find out as much as possible on her own. One thing she had just found out that morning was that the security guard that the James Martin Manufacturing Company had for several years died two years ago and had not been replaced.

Tonya found the entire situation depressing and was pondering telling her father about it. Soon she concluded that it would do little if any good to discuss it with her ailing father and decided to move ahead on her own. She needed to get a better grasp on how well any security that was still in place was working and determine what she would do about securing the company's facilities and she felt she needed to do that quickly.

Before she did anything else, Tonya wanted to know what the remaining supervisors and key staff knew about security at the James Martin Manufacturing Company. She wanted to know what their perceptions were about either how good or how bad security was and what they thought should be done. She set up meetings with 10 people she wanted input from. Nine of them had been with the company for several years and one was a recent hire who had been laid off when a similar company closed down a few towns away. He had about 20 years of experience and had worked in a company that was far more formally managed than the James Martin Manufacturing Company.

Tonya had thought about distributing a questionnaire, but she wanted to have personal conversations with the 10 people she selected. She drafted a set of questions to ask the 10 selected people and she filled in their answers and comments as she interviewed them. She put her questions on a single sheet of paper and took notes from each discussion and attached them to the question sheet so she could review them later. The questions she asked and the answers provided by the 10 interviewees are shown Figure 1.4.

Tonya was a bit disappointed after the interviews, but she was not surprised that she gained little information about existing security. She was pleased that there was a consensus from the answers that security was lacking in the company. The most recent hire reported that his past employer had rather strict security and offered to help Tonya by telling her what he knew about security at his previous employer.

Tonya's next challenge was to convince her key staff to be supportive of the upcoming efforts to improve security. She intended to share the responses to the questions with them but also wanted to have a graphic impact with which to display her analysis. She also found Mr. Smith's files on security and discovered that there were security policies and procedures documented, but they had basically been sitting in the file cabinet for a long time. Tonya compiled the graphic presentation shown in Figure 1.5.

Tonya was preparing to meet with the 10 people she wanted involved in working toward better security. But she wanted to be able to show where James Martin Manufacturing stood relative

Interview questions and answers for security assessment at James Martin Manufacturing Company on perceptions of security		
Security assessment questions for James Martin Manufacturing Company	**Yes**	**No**
Do you know who in this company is responsible for security?	2 (Mr. Smith)	8
Do you know what the security policies and procedures are for this company?	3 said a little bit	7
Have you been trained on security policies and procedures at this company?	1	9
Has your department employees been trained on security policies and procedures at this company?	0	10
Do you discuss security policies and procedures in company management meetings?	2	8
Do you discuss security policies and procedures in your departmental meetings?	0	10
Have you been asked about the potential effectiveness of security policies and procedures in this company?	2	8
Have you worked with security staff to improve the effectiveness of security policies and procedures?	0	10
Do you know who to call if you know or suspect that security policies or procedures have been violated?	2 (Mr. Smith)	8
Have security violations in your department been appropriately dealt with by the company?	2	8
Do you feel that security policies and procedures are adequate to protect the company?	0	10

Figure 1.4   Interview questions and answers for security assessment at James Martin Manufacturing Company on perceptions of security.

to another company. She asked the new hire, Samuel Davis, to fill in the philosophies graph based on what he knew about his previous employer. His answers are displayed in Figure 1.6.

Tonya was able to use Samuel Davis's graphic to show contrast between James Martin Manufacturing and the similar company that he had worked for in the past. This was an easy way for Tonya to relay the message to her team of 10 people about what security was like in their company compared to what it was like in another similar company. The contrast was striking

James Martin Manufacturing's philosophy toward security												
Inconsistent philosophy						**Pro-security philosophy**						
Rank how your organization manages security issues on a scale of 1 to 10 for each area												
It is **not clear** who is responsible for security in the organization						There is a **clear delineation** as to who is responsible for security in the organization						
	2					←	→					
Security policies and procedures are generally **poorly understood**						Security policies and procedures are generally **well understood**						
	2					←	→					
Training on security policies and procedures has **not occurred** or is uncertain						Training on security policies and procedures **has occurred** throughout the organization						
	2					←	→					
Security policies and procedures **are not discussed** or rarely discussed or reviewed						Security policies and procedures are **frequently discussed** or reviewed						
	2					←	→					
Department managers are **not involved** in developing security policies and procedures						Department managers are **often involved** in developing security policies and procedures						
	2					←	→					
It is **uncertain** if or how security violations are dealt with by the organization						It is **clear** how security violations are dealt with by the organization						
		3				←	→					
Budget requests for security are frequently **denied** or reduced						Budget requests for security are frequently **approved** or encouraged						
	2					←	→					
There are **ambiguous** feelings about the state of security in the organization						People in the organization feel that security is **appropriate** and well managed						
				5		←	→					
	8	*3*		*5*	Tally scores on this line							

Figure 1.5 James Martin Manufacturing's philosophy toward security.

and the message was well received. The group readily concluded that security could and should be improved.

Tonya drove her message home and explained the downward trend in profits (without discussing the issue concerning Mr. Smith). She informed the team of 10 that there have been some security breaches and she had determined that things have gone missing in the past. The team was not surprised. Tonya pointed out that the sustainability of James Martin Manufacturing depended in part on improving security. She

Similar company's philosophy toward security												
Inconsistent philosophy							Pro-security philosophy					
Rank how your organization manages security issues on a scale of 1 to 10 for each area												
It is **not clear** who is responsible for security in the organization							There is a **clear delineation** as to who is responsible for security in the organization					
					←	→				*9*		
Security policies and procedures are generally **poorly understood**							Security policies and procedures are generally **well understood**					
					←	→		*7*				
Training on security policies and procedures has **not occurred** or is uncertain							Training on security policies and procedures **has occurred** throughout the organization					
					←	→	*6*					
Security policies and procedures **are not discussed** or rarely discussed or reviewed							Security policies and procedures are **frequently discussed** or reviewed					
					←	→	*6*					
Department managers are **not involved** in developing security policies and procedures							Department managers are **often involved** in developing security policies and procedures					
					←	→		*7*				
It is **uncertain** if or how security violations are dealt with by the organization							It is **clear** how security violations are dealt with by the organization					
					←	→				*9*		
Budget requests for security are frequently **denied** or reduced							Budget requests for security are frequently **approved** or encouraged					
					←	→			*8*			
There are **ambiguous** feelings about the state of security in the organization							People in the organization feel that security is **appropriate** and well managed					
					←	→			*8*			
				Tally scores on this line		*12	*14	*16	*18			

Figure 1.6   Similar company's philosophy toward security.

won them over and built a consensus that the effort to improve security was worth the time and expense. The 10 people offered their support and promised to provide any assistance they could.

Her next challenge was to dig deeper into security policies and procedures, and work to ensure that proper security, or at least better security, was implemented. She decided her next step would be to focus on securing the company's assets. She also wanted a security person in place to act as a deterrent to theft.

COURSE DISCUSSION QUESTIONS

1. What experiences have you had with insider threats or insider violations of security policy?
2. Have you ever known anybody that was fired for a security violation?
3. Do you know what your employer's security policies and procedures are and can you elaborate on some of them?
4. In The James Martin Manufacturing Company case study on page 18, do you think that Tonya made the right decision by not calling in law enforcement when she first verified that Harold Smith stole money as well as materials and supplies?
5. In the said case study, do you think that Tonya should hire a security consultant instead of working to improve security at James Martin Manufacturing on her own?

COURSE PROJECTS

1. Design a 20- to 30-question questionnaire that you would use to survey all employees at James Martin Manufacturing on how they view security.
2. Research and report best security practices that you think would be appropriate for a company like James Martin Manufacturing.
3. Create a PowerPoint presentation covering 10 to 15 points about security that you think all employees in James Martin Manufacturing should know and understand.

COURSE TEST QUESTIONS

1. The industries and business sectors that provide essential infrastructure support for the economic activity that enables a country to function economically, politically, and socially are known as _____.
2. The various devices or protective systems that can be installed to prevent unauthorized movement and monitor movement of people, materials, products, supplies, or data in a facility are _____.
3. Barriers, locked doorways, and access-controlled doors that prevent entry and access to building areas by unauthorized

employees or contractors, and that prevent materials or information from being physically accessed or removed from a controlled area are considered to be _____.

4. Structured processes or steps that employees must follow when entering or exiting secure areas, when handling and working with sensitive or proprietary materials, or transferring products or data from one controlled area to another controlled area are called _____.

5. Societal conditions that may impact insider behavior and result in security violations or crimes against an employer include _____.

6. People who commit many crimes against their employer are generally _____.

7. Crimes of embezzlement are generally committed by _____.

8. Examples of spontaneous or situational security measures that are put into place when out-of-the-ordinary events are taking place at a facility include _____.

9. The role of a security champion in an organization is to _____.

10. The Whole Building Design Guide (WBDG) focuses on how to _____.

Key Terms

Critical industry sectors: are those industries and business sectors that provide essential infrastructure support for the economic activity that enables a country to function economically, politically, and socially.

Mechanical security measures: include all of the various devices or protective systems that can be installed to prevent unauthorized movement and monitor movement of people, materials, products, supplies, or data.

Open organizations: tend to be more informal and not highly structured; they often lack strict hierarchal communication structures, project teams are fluid, information flows freely, and employees have extensive access to information, systems, and people.

Personal technologies: include employee-owned devices such as cell phones, tablets, laptops, and digital media that can be used to inappropriately record and remove propriety information from an employer's facilities.

Physical security measures: are barriers that control entry and access to building areas by unauthorized employees or contractors, and that prevent materials or information from being physically accessed or removed from a controlled area.

Premeditated malicious act: is an action that an insider deliberately plans and executes that is intended to do harm to their employer or their fellow employees.

Procedural security measures: are structured processes or steps that employees must follow when entering or exiting secure areas, when handling and working with sensitive or proprietary materials, or transferring products or data from one controlled area to another controlled area.

Spontaneous or situational security measures: are those that are put into place when out-of-the-ordinary events are taking place at a facility.

2

IDENTIFYING WHAT TO PROTECT AND WHO TO PROTECT IT FROM

This chapter provides methods to prioritize security efforts to ensure that important assets are adequately protected. It elaborates on how to identify, or profile, those who may be most able or most likely to misuse or misappropriate various types of assets. Making the decision as to what to protect from insiders and then deciding what level of security to put into place to protect it can be a complex process. This is especially true when resources are limited because of budget constraints. That decision may also be influenced, if not dictated, by the size and type of organization that needs to be protected. In some cases the type of organization, industry sector, product offerings, or customer base may very well dictate the extent that an organization goes to protect assets.

In other cases, where there are no external pressures or requirements for high levels of security, the decision as to what to protect and how much to spend to protect it can be based on a number of factors, including the societal makeup of the workforce, the geographical location of facilities, and the perceived value of assets relative to the overall business plan and long-term goal of an organization.

Organizations in the financial and defense sectors need to contend with a variety of standards and practices that are expected, or are customers, for those sectors. In many cases, *security requirements* can be rather stiff and costly. The financial sector faces almost obvious requirements to secure assets from insiders because in many cases those assets belong to the individuals or organizations that entrust financial services organizations with their assets and have a reasonable expectation that a service provider will protect those assets from all threats.

The defense industries also face an expectation to protect assets from their customer base. When a company is producing or servicing items for the military or for other defense contractors, their customers generally expect and very often absolutely require a level of security that exceeds those in organizations in less sensitive environments. Likewise, the critical industries sectors designated by the White House and Department of Homeland Security are under considerable pressure to deploy strong security.

Smaller organizations with few direct ties to any sensitive industry sector do not necessarily face the same expectations or requirements that organizations in sectors like financial services or defense face. This usually translates into less expensive security. However, since there is a lack of requirements on the part of the customer base, such organizations face another challenge. They must make security decisions without strict requirements in place, which leaves them open to more security options while simultaneously requiring them to make security decisions pretty much on their own volition.

However, all organizations face some level of threat from insiders and the possibility that an insider may collaborate and conspire with an outsider to steal, sabotage, or humiliate the organization in which they are employed. Thus there should be a minimum level of security in almost all organizations to deter or prevent violations by insiders.

2.1 Starting with Basic Security for Data and Information

One constant about security that planners will almost always hear is to start every program, project, expansion, contraction, partnership, contract, and anything else an organization is doing by keeping security in mind from the very beginning. The U.S. Federal Trade Commission (FTC) reiterates this in several publications.[8] The reason for this is simple: Insiders can often abscond with data or information used in the business process. This asset has value because it can be sold or misused. Insiders love to steal data, customer lists, information about business plans, and details of contracts with suppliers or customers.

Insiders who do steal data or information usually have an idea of what they will do with it or who outside the organization considers the data to be valuable enough for somebody to steal. There are numerous potential scenarios that can lead the insider to steal data and information. They could already have a buyer and are conspiring with an outsider to illegally transfer the material. They also may be seeking a new job and can use the information and data as leverage to gain new employment by offering it to companies that may hire them. In some cases, they may want to make an organization's data and information public by posting it on the Internet and reveal things about the business that may disrupt processes, jeopardize business relationships, or attract people that may want to embarrass an organization or expose activity that they and others consider unethical or illegal. No matter why the theft occurs, organizations need to take steps to ensure that they are protected.

The FTC contends that *sensitive information* pervades every aspect of many organizations. It will save time later and may very well reduce pain if planners first think about why an organization collects data. The FTC recommends not collecting any data an organization does not really need and not to keep it longer than needed in order to conduct business.[8] The same can be said about data and information an organization compiles to support a business process. An informal survey of records managers and data custodians showed that this philosophy is becoming a standard operating procedure in many types of organizations around the world.

The second axiom of data and information security is to control access and ensure that only people in an organization that need to have access to data in order to perform their job duties are the ones that have access to the material. This may take considerable effort. First, the data and information must be in a secure area. Second, access to computer systems with data and information must be restricted to those people that need access in order to perform their job functions. Finally, steps must be taken to ensure that instruments such as flash drives or laptops containing the protected data and information cannot be removed from the facility in any way or form.

The *Code of Federal Regulations* Title 16—Commercial Practices requires that organizations maintain security of customer data including protecting that data from *unauthorized use* or dissemination by insiders.[9] Figure 2.1 shows the elements of the data protection process that should be in place. More specifics about how to protect data and

---

Federally required elements of a data security program

In order to develop, implement, and maintain your information security program, you shall:

(a) Designate an employee or employees to coordinate your information security program.
(b) Identify reasonably foreseeable internal and external risks to the security, confidentiality, and integrity of customer information that could result in the unauthorized disclosure, misuse, alteration, destruction or other compromise of such information, and assess the sufficiency of any safeguards in place to control these risks. At a minimum, such a risk assessment should include consideration of risks in each relevant area of your operations, including:

    (1) Employee training and management;
    (2) Information systems, including network and software design, as well as information processing, storage, transmission and disposal; and
    (3) Detecting, preventing and responding to attacks, intrusions, or other systems failures.

(c) Design and implement information safeguards to control the risks you identify through risk assessment, and regularly test or otherwise monitor the effectiveness of the safeguards' key controls, systems, and procedures.
(d) Oversee service providers by:

    (1) Taking reasonable steps to select and retain service providers that are capable of maintaining appropriate safeguards for the customer information at issue; and
    (2) Requiring your service providers by contract to implement and maintain such safeguards.

(e) Evaluate and adjust your information security program in light of the results of the testing and monitoring required by paragraph (c) of this section; any material changes to your operations or business arrangements; or any other circumstances that you know or have reason to know may have a material impact on your information security program.

Figure 2.1   Federally required elements of a data security program. (From *Code of Federal Regulations,* Title 16—Commercial Practices, Chapter I, Subchapter C, Part 314—Standards For Safeguarding Customer Information, §314.4 Elements, United States Federal Trade Commission, May 2016, retrieved May 25, 2016, from http://www.ecfr.gov/cgi-bin/text-idx?c=ecfr&sid=1e9a81d 52a0904d70a046d0675d613b0&rgn=div5&view=text&node=16%3A1.0.1.3.38&idno=16.)

information from insider theft or misappropriation is provided in corresponding chapters later in this book.

When it comes to data security, issues of social responsibility are certainly important, but the most important things an organization needs to be concerned with regarding data privacy and security issues are the potential for litigation and the possible damage to its reputation for ignoring or blundering on a privacy issue. This does not mean that individual people are not important in the myriad of privacy and security concerns. In fact, just the opposite is true. It is because people are so important that an organization may face litigation or reputation-damaging public relations disasters if it does not adequately address privacy and security issues for customer data and information.

The social nature of privacy and data security along with rising concerns among citizen groups and governments will likely keep privacy issues at the forefront of social concerns. This will be fueled in part by a desire to deal with many of the issues that have emerged because of the Internet and the portability of data on devices such as an insider's cell phone or flash drive.

It is important to develop a strategy to keep an organization out of the line of fire when investigations of privacy or data security violations become wider spread or as governments attempt to grapple with data thieves whether they are inside an organization or outside the organization. As with past social issues, such as environmental protection and equality in human resources, practices labeled as "bad" are not going to be good for a company. The best possible strategy is one of risk avoidance.

There have been several relatively high-profile data security and privacy problems during the last few years. Enterprise problems with alleged data security and privacy breaches will eventually fade away. However, the process of dealing with the public relations aspect is emotionally draining, physically tiring, and has a negative impact on productivity. Overall, it is best to avoid privacy-related incidents.

Every company is always at risk of having trade secrets compromised, intellectual property stolen, and business plans revealed in an untimely manner. Industrial espionage and spying remain at a high level and are practiced on an international scale. An organization's data security and privacy planning process needs to take these threats into consideration. However, theft of propriety information is only part of an organization's vulnerability in the security wars. How it uses the information it collects about its customers or even its suppliers can increase its vulnerability.

One of an organization's greatest points of vulnerability internally is a lack of knowledge about what types of data it has and how it is being used. Far too many organizations do not know all the data they collect and how it is being used. Those companies without a data security and privacy plan in place are the most vulnerable. Although those companies with a track record in collecting and using a wide variety of data may be better versed in privacy issues, they may still not understand what is happening with the data that may create privacy problems.

2.2 Protecting Cash, Bank Accounts, and Credit Tools

Most organizations operate with some level of trust of their employees. Background checks, references from former employers, a reference from a trusted employee of the organization, solid work ethics, and years of dedicated service are often used as an indicator that an individual can be trusted in sensitive positions that have access to financial systems or tools. In practice, it is actually those people that are entrusted to manage money in an organization who are the ones that end up stealing the money or misappropriating it in some way. This goes to show that diligence may not always work in preventing malicious acts by insiders.

Among the most favorite targets of insiders are cash, checks, credit cards, and an employer's online accounts. Because a high level of access to accounts and accounting systems is required to perpetrate an insider financial crime, it is the trusted insider that is most often the thief or the embezzler. A review of Uniform Crime Report data shows that men and women are equally likely to commit such crimes. A search for the word "embezzlement" on the FBI website in May 2016 revealed the following examples of headlines about financial crimes against private companies and nonprofit organizations:

- Former employee pleads guilty to embezzling more than $5.1 million from nonprofit over an 8-year period
- Former president of federal credit union charged with embezzlement
- Woman pleads guilty to embezzling $1 million from credit union
- Former hospital payroll director convicted in embezzlement
- Woman guilty of embezzling from state bank
- Tribal executives indicted in embezzlement scheme
- Former bookkeeper sentenced to a year in prison for embezzlement and signing a false tax return
- Former union officials plead guilty to embezzlement
- Bank senior vice president sentenced for embezzlement

- Woman allegedly embezzled $653,000 from state senator
- Man pleads guilty to embezzlement and making false entries in credit union records
- Man imprisoned for embezzlement and bank fraud
- Former county employee pleads guilty to embezzlement
- Medical office receptionist pleads guilty to embezzlement
- Former bank employee sentenced to 27 months in prison for embezzlement

There are many off-the-shelf recommendations to help secure financial instruments and prevent fraud and abuse. However, these steps within themselves will not guarantee that an organization is safe. The U.S. Small Business Administration (SBA) provides a list of recommendations that are generally consistent with those provided by several different organizations. Those recommendations include the following:

- Conducting background checks when hiring employees
- Protecting bank accounts and credit cards by limiting and auditing their use
- Securing information systems and computers
- Using a dedicated computer for banking
- Educating employees about security
- Having *appropriate separation of duties* for financial processes and instruments
- Having adequate insurance coverage against insider theft[10]
- Having fidelity bonds or commercial crime policies that are specifically designed to protect organizations from the financial impact of dishonest acts committed by employees

These suggestions will be helpful in protecting against financial crimes, but the fact remains that it is the insider who has some degree of trust and access to these systems and assets that commits financial crimes against his employer. So, it is logical that an organization will need to take further action and implement additional safeguards. The key thing is to monitor and audit as frequently as possible. Some of the offenders mentioned in the FBI material had been committing their crimes over a period of years.

Auditing and monitoring the financial aspects of an organization take time and costs money. However, without the audits and monitoring, ongoing criminal activity on the part of an employee may go undetected for years. Audits should focus on the systems or processes where the most is at stake and should occur at least annually. Monitoring activity on accounts on a continuous basis may be more effective, and setting limits on the type or frequency of transaction that an employee can execute will help minimize damage. Then, of course, the person who is monitoring will be in a trusted position and may be able to commit financial crimes against the company. There is no one foolproof way to stop such crimes, and constant diligence and prevention efforts are required to protect financial instruments.

2.3 Securing Processes, Inventions, and Trade Secrets

Many organizations have some sort of trade secret that can include processes they have invented to conduct business or manufacture products, a secret formula for the production of a substance or consumer good, or a plan for a new product or process. All of these things are sensitive in that they provide a competitive advantage for the owner. If they are compromised, there could be a loss of revenue, a loss of market leadership, and even the loss of existing or renewed contracts with customers seeking those protected products.

There are several legal means to claim and protect trade secrets, including the Economic Espionage Act of 1996 (18 USC 1831-39), which defines *trade secrets* as any form or type of "business process, scientific formula, technical specification, economic data, or engineering designs that the owner has taken measures to protect and which economic value can be derived."[11] In addition to providing economic value, a trade secret is generally not known by or discoverable by legal means by people other than those who were its creators or those who currently own legal the rights. The Economic Espionage Act of 1996 provides penalties for the theft or misappropriation of trade secrets.[12]

It can cost considerable sums of money and take years in some cases to develop products, processes, or formulas. This expenditure makes a trade secret worth protecting. The FBI has been actively involved in fighting against trade secret theft both domestically and internationally. The FBI recommends several methods to help protect trade secrets including the following:

- Recognize that a threat exists and prepare to protect trade secrets from that threat.
- Determine what trade secrets an organization owns and determine the value of the trade secrets.
- Deploy specific measures to protect and safeguard trade secrets.
- Limit access to and knowledge of trade secrets.
- Engage in ongoing employee training on how to protect the trade secrets.
- Design and deploy a specific program to protect trade secrets from insider theft or compromise.
- Engage with law enforcement and report suspicious activity regarding trade secrets to the FBI.[13]

Many organizations take precautions to protect their trade secrets by terminating employees who have accepted positions with other organizations or who have had job interviews with other companies. This reduces the chance that the insider will help themselves to data, information, trade secrets, or equipment on their way out the door. Using this method to protect trade secrets is generally determined by the individual employer.

2.4 Protecting Equipment, Parts, and Maintenance Supplies

Things always seem to go missing. Although exact dollar amounts are not known, there is a consensus that equipment theft costs hundreds of millions of dollar each year and may well exceed $1 billion. In 2012, the Uniform Crime Report published by the FBI showed that just over $13 billion worth of property was reported stolen nationwide, with only 20.5% being reported as recovered. The FBI reports cover a wide range of property for commercial enterprises as well as private individuals.[14]

Equipment and related parts and supplies have considerable value and are relatively easy to sell. That, combined with ready insider access to such items, makes equipment and parts a handsome target for the insider thief. In some cases, the insider may have a garage full of stolen items and in others the insider may have a list of people that are instant customers when the price is right. It is also amazing what can end up for sale on online auction sites, in garage sales, and at flea markets. Some local police departments check online auction websites for items reported stolen. If an investigator finds items that have been stolen listed for sale on these websites, they should report that to the police.

There are many organizations involved in helping equipment owners reduce theft and recover their stolen equipment. The National Equipment Register provides recovery and risk management services for equipment owners, insurers, equipment dealers, and equipment manufacturers. These include IRONwatch®, which is a GPS tracking and recovery device designed to track and recover equipment for construction, agriculture, and other industries that use heavy equipment. HELPtech® provides a service where owners can register and mark their equipment. Finally, IRONcheck® supports dealers in the used-equipment market to obtain an equipment history report before finalizing a transaction.[15] An allied organization, the National Insurance Crime Bureau, provides services that help in the recovery of stolen equipment.[16]

Other technology solutions to reduce theft and aid in recovery include permanent equipment tags and the use or *radio frequency identification (RFID) tags*, both of which are attached to equipment to help identify the proper owner. There are several companies that offer these types of products.

Of course not all equipment thefts are committed by insiders. But in general, insiders have a better knowledge of where and how equipment is stored and may even know the various security measures that are in place to protect the equipment. They may have also figured out how to get past those security measures without being detected. There are several straightforward steps that can be taken to reduce equipment theft:

- Maintain an accurate record of equipment and its location, and keep the record updated.
- Tag and track equipment so it can be easily identified and be more likely to be recovered.
- Keep equipment under surveillance using security cameras and/or alarm systems.

- Conduct a periodic inventory of equipment to determine if any equipment has gone missing but the theft has gone unnoticed.
- Report thefts to local law enforcement as soon as the theft becomes apparent.
- Design storage facilities in a manner that makes it physically difficult to remove equipment.

It may be difficult for many people to steal large pieces of equipment. On the other hand, equipment parts and supplies are smaller and far easier to move. In some cases, these items can still be made more secure by using inventory tags or RFID tags. In addition, access to parts and supply storage facilities should be limited only to those who need the items to perform their job functions. These are all very sound steps, but remember it is the trusted insider with access to parts and supplies that can do the most damage.

2.5 Keeping Track of Production Materials and Supplies

Employee pilfering is rather widespread and costs millions of dollars per year. An exact figure as to what smaller things that employees steal is impossible to calculate. Many crimes are not reported to the police and there are many thefts that go on undetected. Insiders who steal will steal just about anything they can get away with stealing. This type of pilfering is especially damaging when it comes to the theft of materials and supplies that are needed in the production process. These losses increase overhead and increase the cost of manufacturing or operations and ultimately increase the cost of a product or service for the consumer. It does not take long to have a negative impact on a company's competitiveness.

The main tactic to reduce the theft of production materials is to maintain strict control on access to the materials and supplies. This requires keeping materials and supplies in a secured area until they are needed in the production or business process. When needed, just move a usable amount of material out of the secured area into the manufacturing or assembly area.

Surveillance of production areas is helpful. But because many parts or supplies are small and can be easily pocketed or stashed into somebody's lunch box or purse, surveillance in and of itself is not sufficient security. Many companies inspect employees' personal belongings as employees depart the facility. In addition, employees are not allowed to bring large personal conveyance devices, such as backpacks, into secured areas. As unfriendly as it may seem, there is little choice but to have tight physical control over all work areas and work to minimize opportunities for employees to steal.

There has been a movement toward employee education about the negative impact of employee theft and toward developing a culture within a company that encourages honesty and dedication. Those who believe in this approach are very evangelistic on its behalf. This approach may work very well in some environments but in other settings. The idea sounds good but there is not any widespread proof that it is effective. Try such programs if desired. But do not let down the guard against employee theft. It is also wise to make sure that there is adequate insurance coverage to minimize the economic impact of employee theft.

2.6 Controlling Inventory In-House and in the Supply Chain

Inventory control in this case means protecting the finished products that are ready for sale on a wholesale or retail basis. Inventory can be items an organization manufactures, distributes, or purchases for resale. Inventory can be stored at an organization's own facilities or in warehouses or distribution centers somewhere up and down the supply chain. It is necessary to protect finished inventory against employee theft just as a company does with production materials, supplies, and equipment used in production or maintenance. Protecting finished inventory is more complicated because not only does it need protection from insiders (direct employees) but also protection from part-time insiders, those employees of logistic services companies and supply chain partners that have an insider capability of stealing inventory.

Protecting inventory within an owned facility has the same basic challenges as protecting equipment and parts, and production materials. However, finished products may very well have a broader theft appeal because it is easier to tell what the item is and how it can be used. The theft of equipment and production materials may be less appealing to more people than the theft of finished products because equipment and production materials require some sort of knowledge as to what to do with them or how to sell them in order to realize their value. On the other hand, finished products require less knowledge about resale value and in many cases may have a *souvenir value* that motivates the insider to steal the product.

Once in the distribution and supply chain systems, finished products may have less of a souvenir value because handlers lack familiarity with the product. However, products in the supply chain have far greater exposure than they do when they are in an organization's own facility. Again, people will steal just about anything.

There are two main paths organizations can take to protect inventory once it has entered into a supply chain system. The first option, and the easiest, is to contract with a logistics company with a known reputation for integrity and effectiveness in protecting products in transit. The second option is to try to manage the many complex aspects of logistics and distribution with company staff. This is more complex the larger the supply chain and is especially complex when a supply chain extends beyond international borders.

The United States Customs and Border Protection Agency published "The Supply Chain Security Best Practices Catalog: The Customs-Trade Partnership Against Terrorism (C-TPAT)" in 2006.[17] The partnership has over 6,000 members who adhere to several sets of standards to create a more secure supply chain. The "Best Practices Catalog" covers security practices in great detail and on an end-to-end basis. The best practices listed next provide an indication of the many aspects of security that will need attention if an organization attempts to navigate the global logistics system without the support of a qualified logistic provider including the following:

- Risk analysis
- Business partner requirements
- Container and trailer security
- Conveyance security
- En route cargo tracking
- Physical access control
- Personnel, procedural, and physical security
- Information technology security

2.7 Protecting an Organization's Public Image

Public image is an asset that needs to be protected just as physical assets are protected. Protecting the public image asset from insider sabotage or irresponsible actions is part of that challenge. An organization's public image must also be protected from carelessness as well as embarrassing non-work-related acts of employees. Years ago, the impact of employee misbehavior was mostly localized. However, the emergence of social media has created an environment where local acts can become globally known overnight and sometimes in minutes.

Protecting an image from negative social media is a twofold process. The first is to protect social media tools and accounts on the various Internet platforms. The second is to protect the public image from harm that can be caused by employees using their own social media accounts. Special attention is given to this issue in Chapter 5.

2.8 Protecting against Lone Insiders and Insider Groups

As discussed earlier, controlling access to facilities, proprietary information, equipment, materials, and even supplies is the first step in protecting against an insider threat. Surveillance and monitoring of movement and activity to ensure that an insider has not exceeded their approved access is essential to making certain that the physical barriers and restrictions are being observed and are functioning properly. These mitigation steps need to be an ongoing part of efforts to neutralize the individual insider threat.

More in-depth checks of what an insider has done can be achieved during regularly scheduled reviews of the insiders' activities and audits of their work. Such steps are just a routine part of security and of protecting an organization from damage by an insider. Bear in mind, of course, that the greater the access insiders have to systems and facilities, the greater the negative impact they can have on an organization. Although they are in a trusted position, the more access insiders have, the more damage they can cause. This really means that insiders must be monitored more closely and if necessary they should have in-depth reviews more frequently, including very thorough audits of their work.

It is important to keep in mind that insiders do not always work alone. They sometimes work in teams or groups to execute more complex violations of security and to accomplish more damaging criminal actions against an organization. Monitoring group activity is a more difficult process. Of course, security staff or managers must first monitor or audit the individuals. Then ascertain if in fact an individual is working with others as a team or a group. This is where solid investigative work comes into play.

The insider team conspiring to commit a crime against a company may be difficult to discover, but there may be indicators that the team members have an affiliation and can be prepared to perpetrate a joint crime. One sign that the individuals can come together as a team is if they have a relationship outside of the workplace. Are they related by family or by marriage? Have they worked together for a long period of time? Are they involved in outside activities together? Do they share a philosophical perspective against society or against an organization? Long-term observation can yield a considerable amount of intelligence about the individuals and about their potential team actions.

A big part of being able to catch a criminal is being able to think like a criminal. It may sound like a cliché, but it is nonetheless true. Attempting to ascertain the potential impact that a team of people could have on an organization is more of an art than a science. If security staff does determine that individuals have some sort of ongoing relationships with each other and supervisors or managers become suspicious for some reason, continued observation is called for to prevent the insider team from being successful.

Constructing a potential scheme or scenario is easy when staff members have practice in doing so. One way to measure the potential impact that the team could have is by summing their individual access and abilities, and modeling what their combined efforts could accomplish. This is, of course, time consuming and requires long-term dedication to task.

If supervisors or managers become convinced that the individuals are forming a team and conspiring against the organization, then they can certainly take steps that could mitigate the potential perpetrator's efforts. This includes limiting or changing team members' access from what it was to a status that could make it more difficult for them to accomplish anything significant; and if they did accomplish anything, it could be less damaging with their new limited access.

Visible security can serve well as a deterrent. When people know they are under surveillance and that their work will be monitored and audited, they will likely feel that it will be more difficult to get away with stealing something. In some cases, this may just make them more cautious and clever about how they actually execute their criminal intent. However, spying and intelligence gathering will better enable security staff to determine if an insider plot is afoot.

It is important to keep in mind that many security efforts and especially steps to strengthen security will not be welcomed by everybody. There are organizations that advocate that workers' privacy is sacred and workers should be relatively free of surveillance. In some cases, labor unions or other employee organizations will resist surveillance and monitoring, and declare it intrusive. This resistance can end up being part of future contract negotiations. In other cases, labor union representatives will take an organization's manager's time as they complain and protest the efforts. They will do so in an effort to try to convince their members that they are standing up for their rights.

2.9 Protecting against Insider-Outsider Teams

Protecting against insider threats is challenging in any situation but even more so when the insider that can do the most damage is generally already in a trusted position. Defending against the insider team is also challenging, but protecting against an *insider-outsider team* may be the most difficult of all situations when it comes to maintaining security.

Insiders may recruit outside help if they need to supplement their capabilities. If the insider needs a truck, needs to have some heavy lifting done, or needs to augment their computer skills in order to perpetrate a fraud scheme, then they may team with an outsider. Outside help may be seen as safer for the insider because they do not need to reveal to other employees that they are working on committing a crime.

Conversely, the outsider may recruit the insider if the outsider is attempting to increase their access to a facility or to a computer system and the insider can provide assistance in that effort. The insider can provide the outsider with physical help or just with information that makes it easier to enter a facility and perpetrate a crime. The deliberate actions on the part of an insider-outsider team can cause considerable damage or cost large sums of money.

The insider-outsider relationship may be even more complicated if either the outsider or the insider is unaware of the intention of the other. If any insider, for example, can get after-hour access to a facility without being noticed or with little chance of getting caught, they are in the position to steal and do so perhaps without consequences. The outsider may not even question the insider as to the legitimacy of their actions. The insider can act as if everything is normal and never let the outsider know that a crime is being committed.

The outsider may also dupe the insider to thinking that the outsider is on a legitimate mission. This could be fixing the plumbing, repairing a piece of equipment, or performing maintenance on a building. The insider may fall for such a guise on the part of the outsider and let them walk right in and right out a facility without question.

The other outsider scenario that can be difficult to detect is when a legitimate outsider (part-time insider) attempts to expand their access. This could be the regular photocopier repairman or a member of the janitorial service. The insider may be very familiar with the outsider and even know them by name and have had chatted with them over time. The insider is less likely to question somebody they are familiar with and has often seen coming and going from the facility.

Protecting against the insider-outsider team scenario requires adherence to access policies and procedures. It is likely that those procedures are already being violated, so the next line of defense is surveillance and monitoring. This sort of team will be less likely to engage in a crime if they know that they are being watched.

2.10 Assessing an Organization's Perception of Asset Protection

As discussed in Chapter 1, introspection and self-assessment can be challenging. The goal of this self-assessment survey is to simplify the process of collecting people's perceptions of security processes, procedures, and methods. The questions are designed to be nonthreatening.

If security planners decide to do such a survey, have as many managers and key employees complete the survey as possible. This will help capture the perceptions of people that view the organization from different vantage points. Sample questions for managers regarding their perception of asset protection are provided in Figure 2.2.

Once survey takers have collected the perceptions of asset protection from various managers, it is time to compile results. As planners may suspect, the more questions that are answered with a no

Sample questions for managers on their perception of asset protection		
Sample questions	Circle yes or no	
Do you know what assets in your organization need protection?	Yes	No
Do you know what the security policies and procedures are to protect assets in your organization?	Yes	No
Have you been trained on security policies and procedures to protect assets?	Yes	No
Have your department employees been trained on policies and procedures to protect assets?	Yes	No
Do you discuss policies and procedures to protect assets in management meetings?	Yes	No
Do you discuss policies and procedures to protect assets in departmental meetings?	Yes	No
Have you been asked about the potential effectiveness of policies and procedures to protect assets?	Yes	No
Have you worked with security staff to improve the effectiveness of policies and procedures to protect assets?	Yes	No
Do you know who to call if you know or suspect that policies or procedures to protect assets have been violated?	Yes	No
Have asset protection policy and procedure violations in your department been dealt with appropriately by the organization?	Yes	No
Do you feel that security policies and procedures are adequate to protect assets for the organization?	Yes	No

Figure 2.2   Sample questions for managers on their perception of asset protection.

answer, the more likely it is that there needs to be considerable work done in developing and documenting security policies and procedures covering asset protection. The answers may also indicate which areas managers should develop additional policies and procedures. Keep in mind that this survey is only a starting point. Planners may want to follow up with survey respondents so that they can elaborate on their perceptions or experiences.

2.11 Developing and Gauging an Organization's Philosophy of Securing Assets

An expanded means of examining how asset protection is managed in an organization is to review areas like those covered in the survey questions and summarize those perceptions in forms of a philosophy. This approach will serve as a summary of the actual actions that have been taken to protect assets and what those actions may indicate about the real-life philosophy toward asset protection. The responses to the survey questions may be helpful in determining what the philosophy is, but reality checks on what has or has not happen regarding asset protection will help make the assessment more realistic.

The graph in Figure 2.3 is set up so that survey takers can apply a ranking of how their organization performs in managing key areas of a security program. Rank the organization on a scale of 1 to 10 for each of the key areas. For each area on the grid, a score of 5 or under

Indications of an organization's philosophy of securing assets											
Inconsistent philosophy						Pro-security philosophy					
Rank how your organization manages security issues on a scale of 1 to 10 for each area											
It is **not clear** who is responsible for asset protection in the organization						There is a **clear delineation** as to who is responsible for asset protection in the organization					
1	2	3	4	5	←	→	6	7	8	9	10
Asset protection policies and procedures are generally **poorly understood**						Asset protection policies and procedures are generally **well understood**					
1	2	3	4	5	←	→	6	7	8	9	10
Training on asset protection policies and procedures has **not occurred** or is uncertain						Training on asset protection policies and procedures **has occurred** throughout the organization					
1	2	3	4	5	←	→	6	7	8	9	10
Asset protection policies and procedures **are not discussed** or rarely discussed or reviewed						Asset protection policies and procedures are **frequently discussed** or reviewed					
1	2	3	4	5	←	→	6	7	8	9	10
Department managers are **not involved** in developing asset protection policies and procedures						Department managers are **often involved** in developing asset protection policies and procedures					
1	2	3	4	5	←	→	6	7	8	9	10
It is **uncertain** if or how violations of asset protection policies and procedures are dealt with by the organization						It is **clear** how violations of asset protection policies and procedures are dealt with by the organization					
1	2	3	4	5	←	→	6	7	8	9	10
Budget requests for asset protection are frequently **denied** or reduced						Budget requests for asset protection are frequently **approved** or encouraged					
1	2	3	4	5	←	→	6	7	8	9	10
People in the organization feel that asset protection is **not** well managed						People in the organization feel that asset protection is **appropriate** and well managed					
1	2	3	4	5	←	→	6	7	8	9	10
___	___	___	___	___	**Tally scores on this line**		___	___	___	___	___

Figure 2.3 Indications of an organization's philosophy of securing assets.

indicates weaknesses in asset protection and a score of 6 or above indicates that asset protection is stronger. The ranking of 1 to 5 should be made based on how weak planners feel the organization is on that particular aspect of security. If security planners think the organization is strong in this area, then the ranking of 6 to 10 should be made based on how strong they think the organization is on that particular aspect of security. When completed, they should tally the scores in the bottom row by adding the scores circled for each area.

The lower the scores are, the more likely it is that planners should pay more attention to the areas with low scores. The tally in the bottom row will provide security planners with a measure of overall asset protection efforts from a high level. The low tallied scores are an indication that there should either be work on asset protection policies and procedures or more effort put into asset protection training and education. Later chapters will include a similar detailed analysis of specific areas.

2.12 Summary

Chapter 2 examined issues regarding asset protection and established a foundation for improving asset protection in an organization. It also provided a method to review the philosophy with which an organization approaches asset protection policies and procedures. Key areas covered include the following:

- Basic security steps for protecting data and information focusing on access control and monitoring
- Protecting cash, bank accounts, and credit tools by limiting access to financial tools, monitoring transactions on accounts, and routinely auditing financial accounts
- Securing assets including trade secrets, proprietary information, equipment, parts, materials, supplies, and inventory, and what steps to take to secure inventory in supply chains
- Protecting assets from insiders, insider groups, and insider-outsider teams through access control, surveillance, monitoring, and intelligence gathering
- How to assess perceptions of asset protection policies and procedures, and gauging and developing a philosophy on asset protection

COURSE CASE STUDY THE JAMES MARTIN MANUFACTURING COMPANY (CONTINUED)

Tonya assumed the executive management position of the James Martin Manufacturing Company, a privately owned company that had been in her family for over 80 years. The founder, James Martin Sr., ran the company for many years and eventually turned it over to his son, James Martin Jr., who, about 10 years ago, entrusted the company operations to long-time manager Harold Smith. As fate would have it, Harold Smith died three months prior.

Upon review, Tonya had discovered that the late Harold Smith had been embezzling and stealing equipment and supplies from the company for the last decade before his death. Tonya and her attorney James Davis met with the widow of Harold Smith and with her assistance recovered truckloads of items stolen from James Martin Manufacturing.

Tonya had also worked with 10 people she selected in the company to assess the state of security. She interviewed them and gathered their opinions about several aspects of security. Tonya discovered that security at James Martin Manufacturing was in dismal disarray. Her 10-person panel concurred that security was not what it should be and pledge their support in improving security and hopefully improve the company's sustainability.

One of the first things Tonya did was to fill the security position that had been vacant for almost two years. She decided that she needed more than just a security guard and recruited a retired police officer who her father had known for several years. Ronald Thomas had been a police officer most of his life and since his retirement had worked in security for several companies in the adjoining counties. He became James Martin Manufacturing's new director of security.

Tonya set up a meeting with Ronald Thomas and Samuel Davis, the new hire with experience in a similar company. One of the immediate concerns she had was the security of assets. Equipment and tools recovered from Mrs. Smith's garage alarmed her and she wanted to prevent further theft of those items as well as production materials and finished products. She asked them to access the security of assets but urged them not be ad hoc in their approach. They agreed that they would review the following:

- Determine the assets that need to be protected from theft and where those assets were located.
- Review the security policies and procedures for asset security and determine if they were adequate and in fact if they were actually in practice within the company.
- Render an opinion as to what if any training program on asset security they should implement.
- Determine if there are documented action steps to be taken if it is discovered that an employee has been stealing and if those steps are adequate.

They decided that Ronald Thomas, the new director of security, would take the lead in speaking with supervisors and line employees, and compile a brief report. They also decided that Samuel Davis's role in the process would be behind the scenes and that he would help Ronald Thomas with the report and provide any input on the topics that he could provide. They planned on meeting again in a week or so to review and discuss the report.

The following week Tonya, Ronald Thomas, and Samuel Davis met to discuss what they had determined about asset security at James Martin Manufacturing. The key findings from the informal study were as follows:

- Equipment and supplies are what needed to be most protected. There are five locations where supplies are stored and three locations where equipment and tools not in use are stored. The storage areas are all equipped with locks and can be secured, but the common practice is to leave those areas unlocked for ease of access by all employees.
- The review of the security policies and procedures for asset security found that for the most part the policies

are adequate but the procedures need to be updated and enforced.

- The conclusion about training was that supervisors and midmanagement staff should be trained relatively soon but training of line employees could wait for a while, and that they could integrate what they learned from training managers and supervisors into the training for other personnel. In addition, there should be a campaign to increase security awareness and stress the importance of securing assets to better ensure that the company would remain sustainable.
- The review of documented action steps to be taken if it is discovered that an employee has been stealing showed that the steps are relatively standard and straightforward but the team did not know if anybody had been caught stealing during the last few years. Harold Smith would have handled such incidents, but his files contained no documentation of incidents or actions.

During the meeting, the three-person team decided that Ronald Thomas, the director of security, would develop and implement a plan to make the storage areas more secure. He would also further review the existing security policies and procedures, and recommend changes and additions. Samuel Davis said he had some training material that had been used at his former company that covered security and that he would find it and bring it in for them to review.

COURSE DISCUSSION QUESTIONS

1. In the case study, what options do you see to make the equipment and supply storage areas more secure?
2. Have you ever been trained on security policies and procedures by an organization at which you were employed? What did you think of the content of the training? Can you elaborate on any aspects of the training?

3. Have you ever read security policies or procedures? What do you think about any of the security policies and procedures you may have read?
4. Discuss any experience you have had in developing security policies or procedures for protecting assets.

COURSE PROJECTS

1. Identify any security checklists that could be used on a daily basis in James Martin Manufacturing to help guide employees on the security task that they should perform every day. Write a brief report on your findings and compare your findings to others in the class.
2. Identify surveillance technology and equipment that could be useful in securing the equipment and supply storage areas at James Martin Manufacturing. Write a brief report on your findings and compare your findings to others in the class.
3. Develop a statement that all employees should be required to sign regarding their adherence to security policies and procedures at James Martin Manufacturing. Compare your statement to others in the class.

COURSE TEST QUESTIONS

1. An organization structure that prevents individual employees or agents from having access to or control of work functions in a manner that would allow them to independently misappropriate corporate assets with little chance of detection is called _____.
2. Two or more people that jointly conspire to act maliciously against an organization with which one of them (the insider) is employed or has privileged access and the other does not have a relationship with the organization is known as _____.
3. Radio frequency identification (RFID) tags are _____.
4. Any form or type of business process, scientific formula, technical specification, economic data, or engineering design that the owner has taken measures to protect and which economic value can be derived are known as _____.

5. Unauthorized use is _____.
6. Audits should focus on _____.
7. List four of the FBI recommended methods to help protect trade secrets.
8. Equipment and related parts and supplies have considerable value to an insider thief because they are _____.
9. The insider thief may find finished products have a broader theft appeal because _____.
10. Visible security systems such as locked doors, surveillance cameras, and security guards can _____.

Key Terms

Appropriate separation of duties: is an organization structure that prevents individual employees or agents from having access to or control of work functions in a manner that would allow them to independently misappropriate corporate assets with little chance of detection.

An insider-outsider team: is two or more people that jointly conspire to act maliciously against an organization with which one of them (the insider) is employed or has privileged access.

Radio frequency identification (RFID) tags: are very small electronically detectable and readable marking tags that can be read via radio frequencies when they are in a defined proximity of an electronic reader that does not require direct contact with the tag.

Security requirements: are the levels of and types of security required for an organization by law or because of the nature of the work performed, assets held, or research conducted on behalf of other organizations that depend on security provided by the service organization.

Sensitive information: is that information held or created by an organization that, if revealed to the wrong party, would cause harm to the organization owning or creating the information.

Souvenir value: is the perceived noneconomic value an item has for a person who steals or misappropriates an item.

Trade secrets: are any form or type of "business process, scientific formula, technical specification, economic data, or engineering designs that the owner has taken measures to protect and which economic value can be derived."[11]

Unauthorized use: is the reading, recording, transmitting, or storing of data that belongs to a specific party and is meant for a specific and restricted use by the owning or custodial organization or its designees.

3

DEVELOPING A PLAN TO IMPROVE SECURITY AND REDUCE THE INSIDER THREAT

This chapter covers the security planning process as well as how to document security plans. It also examines the life-cycle management of security plans including conducting periodic reviews and audits. These areas are often weak points in achieving *appropriate security* against insider threats.

Lots of people develop a security plan, but most do not develop a good security plan that covers security threats in a comprehensive manner. A security plan is not just a paper document; it is a well-thought-out set of policies and procedures that is tailored to an organization's security needs and is designed to cover its unique set of facilities and business processes.[18]

In addition, a plan is not just a document. The policies must be put into action and clearly delineate who in the organization is responsible for enforcing the policies and training employees on the policies as necessary. The security procedures must also be covered in detail as well as whom in the organization is responsible for each procedure and specify who will train employees on the procedures. It also covers who will monitor compliance with the security procedures.

In the management of data security there are two types of threats within an organization. The first is the deliberate misuse or theft of information. This can range from incidents where employees deliberately remove proprietary information including trade secrets, customer lists, or financial data and provide that information to unauthorized parties. The second type of internal threat stems from ignorance or carelessness in how proprietary data and information are used. This can result in information being unnecessarily compromised, putting an organization at risk or having a negative impact on its ability to function or compete. In addition, improper disclosure can result in civil litigation by the parties who believe their privacy rights have been violated.

A lesser threat has to do with how professionals interact with one another at conferences, workshops, scientific, or engineering meetings and now even over the Internet in communities and chat rooms. Professionals like to network, share ideas, and learn from one another. They like to help one another solve problems and accomplish research or advance their profession in some way. This, of course, may be good for society as a whole or for the professionals involved in the networking activity, but it may not be the best thing for an organization. It is essential that the data security plan define appropriate behavior in these circumstances.

Chapter 2 discussed how to identify what needs to be protected and whom it needs to be protected from. That is a management decision that should be made before the planning process goes off in a wrong direction. Once the threats to assets are identified that the organization faces in protecting those assets are determined, the planning team is ready to get into a detailed security planning process. Perspectives vary, but identifying the assets before starting to develop the plan provides the planning team with an actual goal and focuses its efforts. Assets can always be reevaluated throughout the planning process, and the importance of the asset can be modified along with the necessity to protect the asset.[18]

3.1 Selecting a Security Planning Mode

There are several possible modes in which an organization can mobilize a security planning effort. The planning process will be relatively the same and the same standards of thoroughness apply to each mode. The difference in the modes is the scope of the security that is being planned.

The first mode is a *comprehensive security plan* encompassing as many security threats and issues possible, and it is most often adopted when an organization is constructing a new facility or complex or has no security at all. In the case of a new facility, security is being built in from the ground up, and every aspect of design, planning, and construction of the new facilities will integrate security technologies and security methods. This mode may also be useful when remodeling an existing facility or when an organization takes occupancy of an existing building or complex for which security must be planned and implemented.

The second mode involves all the aspects of a comprehensive planning mode, but the intention of the planners is that security measures will be implemented on a piecemeal basis with the most important assets and most critical threats addressed first. The remaining elements of the security program are implemented one at a time or a few at a time as resources are made available. The organization eventually moves toward a comprehensive security program but does it one step at a time.

The third mode is a considerable departure from the first two: when an organization does not have the resources to implement a comprehensive program but still deems it necessary to have strong security to protect selected assets or designated parts of a facility. In this mode, the organization has no real intention of developing comprehensive policies and procedures but instead focuses on what it deems the most necessary. This approach may be effective in protecting a specific asset or areas of a facility but leaves a lot be desired in that a secure area or item could be surrounded by weak security, which makes protecting the isolated asset more difficult.

Another approach to planning and implementing security measures is *ad hoc security management*. An organization may decide, for example, that stronger locks on the doors may help in improving security. However, if the windows are not secure, the stronger locks may provide little if any improvement to security. Likewise, if the front door is kept locked and visitors must be buzzed in to keep people out of the building but the back door is unlocked, then there is little if any improvement in security. However, some organizations have little choice but to take this approach because they lack resources to initiate a comprehensive security effort.

3.2 Organizing the Security Plan Development Team

Deciding how and why an organization selects specific team members for the security planning effort is an important first step. The selection of members will reflect the organization's commitment to the security planning process and demonstrate just how serious the effort is being addressed. Team member selection can also demonstrate that an organization will take the input from seasoned staff members who know the organization's operations and facilities. It also shows that the organization wants real security, not just a paper document.

To show commitment on the part of the organization, a C-level executive is often appointed to the security plan development team or to an annual security review team. The role of the high-level executive is not necessarily to tell the team what to do or how to do it. The high-level executive can support the team by ensuring that the team gets the resources necessary to properly achieve planning goals and develop appropriate procedures. Second, the high-level executive can assure that the development team gets access to the records, reports, and other documents the team may find helpful. Finally, the executive can be used as leverage to get managers, supervisors, and technical specialists employed by the organization to provide the development team with the information it may need as well as access to areas of the workplace that may otherwise be off-limits to employees other than the ones working in those areas.

The next critical team member is the director of security (DOS) or, if there is not a director, then the lead person for security in the organization. The DOS will play several roles in the planning process. The first is to bring security expertise to the planning process. The second is to help other team members understand security and how to evaluate the need for new security policies and procedures, or to evaluate the effectiveness of existing security policies or procedures. Finally, as the DOS works with team members who are from various departments or functions of an organization, the DOS and other team members will build trust and commitment to the planning process as well as the ongoing management of security.

It is also important to have representatives from the various departments and functions in the organization. If there is a legal department, there should be a representative to identify and help address potential legal issues. The director of human resources can be a very valuable team member who can provide input on new-hire screening processes, documenting security violations, and dealing with individual employees who have committed security violations. The facilities manger can also play an important role because he or she knows and understands how the facility is designed and the physical layout and infrastructure systems of the various buildings. The facilities manager can also contribute to an understanding of how buildings could be remodeled in order to achieve better security.[19]

Other important security planning team members will depend on the organization. For example, if there is a vehicle fleet, the fleet manager can provide insight into security needs for the fleet and the appropriate use of company vehicles. Second, the manufacturing director can provide insight into the manufacturing process and help identify areas that need improved security. Do not forget to include representatives from shipping and receiving, accounting, sales, marketing, or public relations if the organization has such departments.

Each department can bring insight to the development of the security plan, and the policies and procedures needed to ensure appropriate security is implemented. Some organizations do not include a variety of departments in the planning process. This is a choice but not a good one, because no one person, even a security expert, can know everything about an organization. An example of how departmental responsibilities could be divided to implement a security plan to guard against insider security breaches and violations is shown in Figure 3.1.

It may not be prudent for all department representatives to have specific details about security methods, surveillance systems, monitoring plans, or audit schedules. Generally that level of detail comes later in the planning process; the DOS and a high-level executive can decide when the planning process goes into a secure mode and development team members who do not need to know details can be excluded from the later phases of plan development.

Once the team members are identified, a team leader should be designated and it may be prudent, depending on the size and nature of the organization, to have two people leading the team in a coleader arrangement. If one leader leaves the team or terminates employment, the organization will be able to maintain some continuity in the planning process.

Last, planners need to decide who will be responsible for assembling and maintaining the security documentation that supports security policies and procedures. This person does not need to be a management-level employee. However, they should be assigned to the task until the planning process is completed and all documents have met with final management approval. The documentation manager will need

Assignment of planning and implementation responsibilities for the enterprise-wide protection against insiders	
Department	**Examples of implementation tasks**
Security planning team	• Oversight and direction, monitoring implementation
Public relations department	• Corporate communications, internal awareness campaigns • Preparation of material to send to customers and business partners
Human resources department	• Developing and managing the employee training process • Creating orientation process for new employees
Central information technology department	• Setting standards for application development and maintenance to improve computer security • Implementing improved computer security procedures • Training employees on computer security • Setting standards and selecting more secure computing and software products
Security department	• Implementing new procedures to protect the security of physical records • Work with other departments in an advising capacity
Facilities management department	• Implementing new procedures for the disposal of obsolete and used computer equipment and magnetic media • Work with records management to implement new procedures and improve storage facilities
Records management	• Implementing new procedures for the management, storage, or records • Implementing new procedures for the disposal of enterprise records, files, and customer data
Sales department	• Work with the PR department on implementing awareness campaign for customers • Work with marketing and legal counsel to revise materials
Legal counsel	• Interpret new laws and regulations • Review customer notices and contract language for accuracy and compliance
Marketing department	• Work with sales and legal counsel to revise materials about security awareness • Create new material or modify existing marketing material and campaigns to incorporate security policies
Customer service department	• Work with PR to develop material covering the security policy for use in the customer service process • Work on security awareness campaign with customers

Figure 3.1   Departmental responsibilities for security planning and implementation.

the appropriate computer skills such as word processing, some graphic capabilities, and possibly spreadsheets or databases, all depending on the complexity of the plan and the supporting documents.

3.3 Security Planning and Implementation Workflow

The process of developing security policies and procedures, and selecting methods to ensure that those policies and procedures are adhered to requires several steps. Policies must be established, then procedures designed to support those polices. Then it is necessary to select and deploy the technologies that will enable security goals to be met. Figure 3.2 illustrates how the process works.

The steps of security planning and implementation process		
Planning team		**Staff specialists**
Makes initial decisions on what to protect and forward to specialists for review	⟲ ⟳	**Review and comment on decisions on what to protect and return to planning team**
Drafts policies to protect selected assets and forward to specialists for review	⟲ ⟳	**Review and comment on draft policies and return to planning team**
↘ → →	**Jointly develop procedures to protect assets** ← ←	↙
Reviews methods or technologies to support procedures	⟲ ⟳	**Select methods or technologies to support procedures and send to planning team for review**
Create final policies and procedures documentation and forward to specialists for review	⟲ ⟳	**Review final policies and procedures documentation and return to planning team**
	⟲ ⟳	
Implement plan and deploy methods and technologies		

Figure 3.2 The security planning and implementation process.

The planning and development process for security is an interactive process between the planning team and the specialist the team deems necessary to achieve the goals. Figure 3.2 provides a very basic example of how the process will work and the interaction between the planning team and the selected specialists.

The security planning process should be very interactive with the planning team consulting with as many specialists or managers necessary to do a thorough job. Once the planning begins, there should be lots of interaction between planning team members and various departments. Later chapters cover many aspects of security that an organization will encounter during the development phase as well as when the security plan goes into the maintenance phase.

When implementing a new security plan or updating outdated plans, there is often an awareness campaign component. Increasing and maintaining security awareness is a continuous process, and the security planning team should use any and every communication tool available. This could include company newsletters, a poster campaign, frequently mentioning or discussing security in staff meetings, and discussing security during annual employee reviews. The key thing is to keep security in the forefront and on everybody's mind. Chapter 4 discusses how to increase awareness about security and build a diligent and vigilant workforce.

Companywide policies covering access, protection of proprietary information, and facility security are essential elements of a good security program. There is also a need for policies covering employee actions, and it is prudent to train employees on the policies and any related procedures. This process is covered in greater detail in Chapter 5. What to do when hiring new employees including background checks, new-hire training, and employee signatures on appropriate documents covering facilities and equipment is covered in Chapter 13.

As the planning team develops policies and procedures that are supported through technology or outside services, they will probably be dealing with a variety of vendors, service firms, and technology companies. Some of this interaction will occur while the security plan is in the development stages and many times the interaction will be ongoing through the process. Evaluating security services and security products is covered in Chapter 6.

Many organizations utilize an identification process, which can include security key cards and identification badges for employees along with representatives from service providers, business partners, and customers. These identification programs can help control who comes into a facility and when and where they are allowed to be within the facility. This is covered in more detail in Chapter 7. More detail on managing relationships with vendors, business partners, and customers is covered in Chapter 9.

A security plan will probably have access control as a key element. As previously mentioned, controlling access is essential for good security. Access control systems can become rather detailed and involve an identification system as well as surveillance and monitoring technologies. This is covered in more detail in Chapter 8. Deployment and utilization of surveillance technologies and techniques is covered in Chapter 12.

3.4 Post-Security Planning and Maintenance Activities

A word of caution: Far too many people get their security plans finished and implemented, and then file the work away in a cabinet and forget about it altogether. This is a serious mistake and can lead to problems in the future. There are several activities that are necessary to accomplish after the security plan is in place including the following:[8]

- Investigating and responding to security incidents including enforcing policies and procedures and dealing with employees who have security violations (this is covered in Chapter 11)
- Monitoring changing security threats to ensure that the security plan is still capable of addressing emerging threats (this is covered in Chapter 10)
- Periodic reviews of deployed security measures including technology-based systems as well as procedures achieved by human actions (this is covered in Chapter 10)

The security plan and all of the elements that comprise a security program will not likely remain stagnate and very often be in flux. The world changes and security measures must evolve to meet new and different threats. *Periodic reviews of existing security measures* and the evaluation and implementation of new security methods or technology can help keep an organization more secure from insider threats in the future.[10]

3.5 Management Oversight of Security Planning Progress

Once the security planning process is initiated, upper management needs some way of monitoring the progress of the planning and implementation efforts to ensure that they do not get stalled. It is great to have faith in project teams, but as many managers have found out in the past, management cannot always count on project teams to maintain their own momentum. At the very least, upper management should get periodic reports of the progress that the planning team is making and at what point they are in the planning process.[20]

The team leaders can provide a written report to declare the status of the project, but far too often written status reports do not reflect the reality of the circumstance. In addition, many people do not bother to read written reports. A face-to-face meeting between upper management and the team leaders is more conducive to determining how the project is moving along.

All projects hit some sort of bump in the road and sometimes elements of the projects get stalled and can even fall right off the edge of a cliff. So the team leaders should not only report on aspects of the planning process that are going well but also report on elements that may have become stalled and never got restarted. They should also report on elements that got stalled and eventually restarted. It is also wise to determine just what caused problems and how the obstacles were overcome. This should be done earlier rather than later in the planning schedule to ensure that too much time is not lost.

Conducting a brief survey of people who have participated in the security planning or implementation process can help identify problems and the source of those problems. Some helpful questions to ask participants in the security planning project are shown in Figure 3.3.

The survey of security planning participants can be administered in a manner that keeps respondents anonymous if the team decides to do so. The security planning team can also collect the same information from team participants during short interviews. Once collected and tallied, the responses should provide an indication as to the necessity of changing team members or providing more time for members to

Suggested survey questions to determine security planning progress	
How many hours have you spent working on the security planning project? (Circle answer that best describes hours spent.)	<10 11–20 21–30 31–40 >40
Describe your role in the security planning and implementation process. (Circle all that apply.)	**Advise Research Procurement** **Installation Review Writer**
How do you feel the security planning process is working? (Circle answer that best describes your perspective.)	**Very well Fairly well Just okay** **Not very well Very badly**
From what you know, is the security plan development on schedule or running behind? (Circle answer that best describes your perspective.)	**On schedule Ahead of schedule** **Slightly behind Somewhat behind** **Way behind schedule**
How well are the security planning team members working together? (Circle answer that best describes your perspective.)	**Very well Fairly well Just okay** **Not very well Very badly**
What suggestions do you have to improve the functioning of the security planning team?	

Figure 3.3 Suggested survey questions to determine security planning progress.

work on the project during the week rather than work on their daily assigned tasks and functions.

3.6 Writing and Reviewing Security Policies

Writing security policies need not be difficult. Most people have very little experience writing, and thus it is not just writing a security policy that is the challenge because writing just about anything challenges many people. So, not surprisingly, it is at the stage, when it is time to document security policies, that the security planning process can slow down. If the security planning team does not have sufficient writing skills, there are several ways to overcome the obstacles of having less than great in-house writing skills.

One way to not get bogged down at the security policy writing phase is to hire an outside technical writer. There are numerous websites that can provide a matchup between writers and clients, and some websites have references and comments about the writer's past work. For-hire writers have various skill levels and their fees can vary greatly. So it is important to screen the potential writers to make sure there is a good match. It is advisable to offer the writer a small amount of work in the beginning to test their skills and their timeliness in completing the work.

Another source of writing talent can be a local college or university. There are often job boards at the school where outside organizations can post a notice of the work they need to have done. One advantage of having a local person provide writing assistance is that they can readily have face-to-face meetings with the security planning team. This can make a for-hire writer more effective and make it easier for teams to communicate about the work they need to have done. It is also handy to have a person that can come to face-to-face meetings during the review and modification of the draft policies. There are a few basic rules that apply to writing security policies including the following:

- Security policies, like all policies, need to be very clear and understandable. Ambiguous rambling language can make the policy difficult to understand, which may make enforcing the policy more challenging when people cannot readily understand the intent of the policy.
- For the sake of clarity, security policies should be written in a very straightforward business style without complex sentences or paragraphs.
- Security policies should be reviewed by as many members of the security planning team as possible and eventually be reviewed by an upper level manager who can sign off on the policy or endorse the policy.
- Planners should have at least a few employees in the organization read the security policies before they are finalized. It is important that the security policy is clear enough for the average worker in the organization to understand.

- If a security policy is to be enforced by a specific department, then it is important that the managers and/or supervisors in that department understand the policy. If the department staff cannot understand the policy as it is drafted, then the policy will need to be rewritten in a manner that the department staff can understand the documents.
- Once there is a final draft of the policies, it is important to have a final copyedit review. This is best done by a person who has not been involved in writing the policies. The job of the final reviewer is to proofread the document to eliminate any serious areas in grammar or spelling.

3.7 Writing and Reviewing Security Procedures

Writing security policies and writing security procedures present their own unique and different challenges. The intent of a security policy must be clearly stated and easy to understand. A security procedure, on the other hand, will have more detail and will most often provide step-by-step instructions on how to implement or manage a specific procedure designed to protect an organization's assets. This means that the person who writes the security policies may not be the right match to write the security procedures. As when hiring any writer, it is prudent to give the security procedure writer a small amount of work as a test to see how well they do.

Some procedures that are designed to secure an organization's assets may be relatively complex compared to just making sure the door is locked when everyone leaves for the day. This means that the process of reviewing the security procedure may involve additional steps to those used to review the security policies. The most obvious aspect of having security procedures reviewed is to make sure that the procedure is thoroughly tested and walked-through during the review process.

A procedure should document step-by-step instructions as to what an employee should do to protect an asset. If, for example, material is to be stored in a locked filing cabinet, the specific filing cabinet or group of filing cabinets and their location should be included in the procedure. If the filing cabinet has a key, then the procedure should document what the employee should do with the key after locking or unlocking the filing cabinet. The key to writing an effective procedure is to leave nothing to chance and document exactly what needs to happen.

There are two types of procedure reviews that the security planning team can conduct. The first is a desk review, where a reviewer reads through the procedure to determine clarity and thoroughness. The second is a walk-through, where one or more employees, using the documented procedure, actually execute all of the steps in the procedure. This will help to determine if the procedure is thoroughly documented and that the procedure actually accomplishes the desired goal.

After the walk-through exercise, the procedure testers should have a mechanism with which they can report the results of their test. The procedure can be approved because it works or comments can be made by the tester as to what did not work using the documented procedure. A sample form to be completed by the testers when the procedure is being tested is shown in Figure 3.4.

The procedure test reports should be returned to a designated security planning team member and successful tests should be logged and

Sample procedure test results form	
Procedure tester(s) name(s): Tester #1: _____ Tester #2: _____	Date of test:_____ Location of test:
Procedure title	Procedure number:
Purpose of the procedure(s):	**Circle Yes if test shows procedure worked** **Yes positive test**
Circle No if test shows procedure did not work. **No test did not work** Explain what did not work during the test:	

Figure 3.4   Sample procedure test report.

filed. Tests that indicate that a procedure needs to be rewritten or redesigned should be logged and a copy of the procedure along with the test results report should be sent to the team member responsible for that particular procedure for a rewrite or redesign of the procedure. Then the revamped procedure needs to be tested again.

3.8 Creating and Maintaining the Final Security Plan Documents

The final security plan document and accompanying procedures should be a very formally prepared document with a title page, names of the authors and/or security planning team members, dates of completion, dates of review, and other relevant historical information included in the front matter of the document(s).

Each section, policy, or procedure should have a place to indicate the date it was written, the dates last reviewed or tested, and the dates last revised. Each section should be maintained as an electronic stand-alone file to make it easier to change or modify one section without having to work on the entire plan.

The security plan documentation should be kept in a specifically designated place, and access to the plan documentation should be limited only to those people that need to have access in order to manage security, develop security training, copy policies as necessary, and other security related activities. An additional off-site secure backup is also recommended.

3.9 Summary

Chapter 3 examined issues regarding security plan, policy, and procedure development. It also covered security policy and procedure writing, and managing security-related documentation. Key areas covered include the following:

- When and how to select a comprehensive ground-up security planning mode, or planning and implementing ad hoc security
- Establishing a security planning development team and who in the organization should be members of the team; and the importance of having good representation from across the organization and how to select team members

- The importance of managing the workflow during the security planning process in order to ensure that security is designed from a multidisciplinary approach and the importance of monitoring security planning team progress
- The importance of ensuring that the team has planned for post-planning activities, including security plan maintenance; monitoring for new threats; and updating the security plan, policies, and procedures to meet new threats
- The steps necessary to draft, finalize, and document security policies, procedures, and important security plan material

COURSE CASE STUDY   THE JAMES MARTIN MANUFACTURING COMPANY (CONTINUED)

It had been an eventful night for the management team at the James Martin Manufacturing Company. The previous evening, Ronald Thomas, the director of security (DOS), was making his final rounds of the facility about 6:30 p.m. when he found a car backed up to the loading dock at the rear of the building. The back door of the building was propped open and there were two wheeled carts sitting on the dock. They were full of boxes.

Ronald took up a position not far from the back door but out of sight. In a few minutes a white male in his mid- to late 50s came out of the building with a box full of tools. Ronald confronted him and found out his name was Larry Jacobs, who claimed to have worked at the company for several decades. The man said he was just taking home some stuff that Harold Smith had given him. Not a very good lie, thought Ronald Thomas, who then called the police.

It took only a few minutes for the police to arrive. They photographed the stuff Larry Jacobs was trying to steal and took him off to jail. Later in the evening Ronald briefed Tonya and the company's attorney, James Davis. They decided that Larry Jacobs would be fired and be provided with written notice of his termination in the morning. They would leave the rest of the matter to local law enforcement and the courts.

They also decided to tell the police about the incident with Harold Smith and informed them as to their resolution of the matter. The police agreed to search Larry's garage and got a warrant. When the police searched the garage they found boxes of tools and other items, much of which were marked as belonging to James Martin Manufacturing. The police hauled the tools and material off as evidence.

Tonya's new role as top executive for James Martin Manufacturing came with the responsibility for making much needed improvements to security. It was becoming increasingly clear that security issues need to be addressed sooner rather than later. She began to wonder just how many people were stealing and how much stuff they were stealing from the company.

Tonya had been working with Ronald Thomas, the new DOS, and Samuel Davis, the new hire with experience in a similar company, to assess and improve security. One decision they had to make was just how far and how fast they would move to improve security, including having a security plan that covered all of the security needs of James Martin Manufacturing. After much discussion, they decided that they would work toward a comprehensive security plan, but for the time being they were going to focus on the areas that need the most protection and work to develop solid security measures for those high-priority areas. Once better security was in place for the most important areas or assets, they would move forward one step at a time toward the comprehensive security plan.

The new DOS had reviewed the existing security documents and found that many of the basic policies were sound, but the documented procedures were poorly written and outdated. He started with the updates and revisions of policies and procedures that focused on the financial management of the company, including central accounting records, accounts payable and accounts receivable processes, payroll, and banking and credit card account security. Meanwhile Samuel Davis, the new hire with experience in a similar company, was going to spend some time focused on examining security for physical assets.

COURSE DISCUSSION QUESTIONS

1. Do you agree or disagree with the decision to move ahead on improving security measures for the high-priority assets and leave the development of a comprehensive security plan for later after security has been improved in the high-priority areas?
2. Discuss the pros and cons of the approach Tonya selected for improving security.
3. What is your experience developing documentation of security policies and procedures? What is your opinion of the methods outlined in this chapter for writing security polices and security procedures?
4. What is your experience in testing security procedures? What is your opinion of the methods outlined in this chapter for testing security procedures?

COURSE PROJECTS

1. Draft a security policy that covers access to central accounting records for the James Martin Manufacturing Company. Compare your draft to those of other people in the course and see how similar or different your drafts ended up being.
2. Draft a security procedure for corporate credit cards at the James Martin Manufacturing Company. Compare your draft to those of other people in the course and see how similar or different your drafts ended up being.
3. Develop and document a step-by-step process for testing security procedures and processes for the James Martin Manufacturing Company. Compare your testing procedure to those of other people in the course and see how similar or different your procedures ended up being.

COURSE TEST QUESTIONS

1. A set of mitigation mechanisms or steps that can protect against known security threats an organization faces because of its activity, location, or value is known as _____.
2. An approach to security planning and management that is piecemeal and has several uncoordinated and unrelated elements is known as _____.

3. A plan that covers all security needs of an organization from the ground up and is designed to mitigate known security threats is referred to as a _____.
4. The purpose of periodic reviews of existing security measures is to _____.
5. The benefit of having two people leading the security planning team in a coleader arrangement is _____.
6. Why is a structured face-to-face meeting between upper management and the security planning team leaders important?
7. What impact does ambiguous rambling language have on the clarity of security policies?
8. A security procedure has considerable detail and will most often provide step-by-step instructions on _____.
9. A walk-through of a security procedure by one or more employees, using the documented procedure to actually execute all of the steps in the procedure, helps to _____.
10. When a person reads through a draft security procedure to determine the clarity and thoroughness of the procedure, the review is known as _____.

Key Terms

Ad hoc security management: is an approach to security planning and management that is piecemeal, and has several uncoordinated and unrelated elements.

Appropriate security: is a level of security and set of mitigation mechanisms or steps that can protect against known security threats an organization faces because of its activity, location, or value.

Comprehensive security plan: covers all security needs of an organization from the ground up and is designed to mitigate known security threats.

Periodic reviews of existing security measures: are an examination or evaluation of existing security measures to determine if they are adequate to continue to protect an organization from ongoing or new threats.

4

INCREASING AWARENESS, DILIGENCE, AND VIGILANCE

This chapter examines how to increase cultural awareness about security within an organization. It also covers methods to motivate employees to become part of ongoing security efforts. Increasing awareness and proper motivation are essential to achieving security goals and objectives.

One of the keys to achieving better security against insider threats is to increase security awareness, diligence, and vigilance in employees. An organization certainly needs security policies or procedures in place to help deter insiders or prevent insiders from malicious acts. However, this will have limited impact unless there is the support and compliance of a large percentage of employees. Gaining that support takes time and effort, but it will be worthwhile.[1]

Getting everybody on board with security has been a challenge for many organizations. Even those organizations with long-standing security programs have to keep working with employees and their service providers to make sure employees do not become complacent and let security standards deteriorate. Organizations that are implementing new security measures or just renewing old security plans also face the challenge of fostering awareness and vigilance necessary to support compliance with security policies.

4.1 Past Trends in Achieving Organizational Change

Achieving social or cultural changes in an organization can be very difficult. There has been a rash of methods proposed or utilized to get both managers and line employees to make changes or implement new ways of working or communicating. But no matter what the goals of a change effort have been, past efforts to change have been met with various levels of success. Many change efforts have been failures relative to the success that the implementer was hoping to achieve.

There have been many approaches to promoting cultural change. Organization development, leadership training, and reengineering have all had more popular days. These types of efforts have been very costly. When the economy was better and when these efforts were popularized by gurus, book authors, magazine coverage, and conferences, many organizations pursued change through these approaches. Some were successful, but years of observation show that not all such efforts did well and lived up to their advertised promise.

Less complex efforts to achieve change have included internal media campaigns, extensive employee training, and various levels of employee engagement including team building, circle programs, and quality improvement. These efforts were also met with some success. But years of observation show not all such efforts always yielded desired outcomes.

The philosophies supporting past change programs ranged from desperation portrayed in last-ditch efforts to save an organization from going under all the way to humanistic pop psychology programs to build employee loyalty and compliance. Hundreds of conferences, seminars, management trainings, and introspection sessions were hosted across the country and around the world. As the global economy worsened, upper management became very discouraged about funding such efforts. With the outcomes of these programs being so ambiguous it was no wonder that so many ended up on the corporate scrap heap.

Polling of several hundred graduate-level management students over several years showed that middle managers and technical specialists very often viewed these efforts as a waste of time. The polling was focused on a scenario of what happens when your boss goes off to Orlando or Palm Springs for a management training program. The responses were almost universally negative. Comments included, "Well the boss comes back and needs to justify the junket so we have meetings and spend time discussing how to improve how well we function, and then that fades away after several weeks and all we achieved was wasting time."

One of the main reasons so many past efforts have failed is because there was not a clearly stated goal and readily measured outcomes.

The cynicism toward the boss going off on a junket was sometimes shrouded in humor and at other times expressed in angry tones. Start-and-stop fad efforts do most often end up wasting time but can also derail or delay ongoing projects or workflow. Thus the lesson is to be careful with what an organization experiments with and be conscious of the financial costs and the impact on productivity and employee morale.

4.2 Focusing Efforts to Develop a Culture of Security

Successful organization change can be better achieved if organizations are very clear about what they want to accomplish and they have a method to measure the success of their efforts. In addition, it is important to realize that the type of program that will work with upper managers may not be applicable to line workers. Middle managers and technical specialists also have their own way of thinking and of viewing the world.[13] This makes creating a *culture of security* all the more challenging.

So one of the first steps a training team needs to take is to decide what they want to achieve with each type of employee and gear those efforts to meet the communication and *learning styles* of that group. Part of what will determine how to approach each group is determining how trainers and security planners want them to view and support a security program. One of the main things to focus on is behavioral changes that will occur, in part, from changes in attitude and the development of a sense of responsibility for security.[17]

Employees can contribute to security in many ways. Sometimes these contributions impact the entire organization and at other times may only have an impact on a small part of the organization. The various roles that employees can fulfill in security efforts are shown in Figure 4.1.

Each level of employee involvement in security efforts can help to improve and maintain security against insider threats. The level of involvement should closely correlate with an employee's job functions within the organization. However, job functions do not always dictate an employee's participation in security efforts or their support of security policies and procedures. It does take a variety of attitudes and behaviors to maintain security against insider threats.

How employees can contribute to security efforts		
Employee involvement in security efforts	Characteristics of role in security efforts	Contribution of role in organization security
Leadership	Demonstrates commitment to the organization and to security needs	Requires that security is taken into consideration in all organization activities
Vigilance	Monitors security efforts and security problems, provides input and feedback	Reports security problems and works to improve security
Evangelism	Always dedicated to security and promotes security efforts	Supports security programs and encourages others to support security efforts
Performance	Complies with policies and specific security procedures	Executes security directives and procedures
Awareness	Understands the importance of security and consequences for failure	Cooperates with security efforts and directives
Familiarity	Knows that security is important to organization	Follows instructions associated with security

Figure 4.1   How employees can contribute to security efforts.

Each of the roles and contributions employees make to security shown in Figure 4.1 can help build stronger security. A well-executed campaign of indoctrination and training can help develop employees so they can contribute in at least one if not multiple capacities when maintaining security against insider threats. The following sections discuss each role in greater detail and discuss how to foster attitudes and transform employee behavior into a security-conscious culture in an organization.

4.3 Developing Leadership to Support Strong Security

The debate as to whether leaders are born or leaders are developed will never come to a conclusion because nobody really knows the answer. Some people do seem to be natural-born leaders and some people have been educated, trained, and cultured to become leaders. Regardless of their origins, a security program can benefit from having a *security leader* or leaders that philosophically and financially support security efforts.

Somewhere in an organization there are probably people who are leaders and they may be in a leadership position. Hopefully, security planners and trainers will find that many of the top managers or executives not only hold a high rank in the organization but also have leadership abilities and have the personalities of leaders. It will be fortunate if the people in leadership positions have an inherent appreciation for security and believe that strong security contributes to the sustainability of the organization. That will make training relatively easy. If leaders do not have an appreciation for the role of security, then the organization faces another set of challenges all together.[21]

Experience shows that working with and training high-level executives and managers can be challenging because many of them may feel that they already know everything the need to know. They most likely feel that their knowledge and skills contributed to their ability to hold their positions. Regardless of the egos or narcissism of the upper-level executives in an organization, it is likely that they will still need some preparation to help tackle security issues.

One key to successfully training top management people is packaging the security message in a manner that will make them more receptive. A little research on the part of security managers and trainers can help set the stage for briefing and/or training top managers. It may take some digging around and questioning a variety of people about the top managers but try to answer the following questions:

- Has there been past training or briefing events that included or were focused on top managers in the organization?
- What type of briefings do top managers in the organization routinely have?
- What were the nature and format of any past training or briefing events that included or were focused on top managers in the organization?
- What was the depth of past training or briefing events that included or was focused on top managers in the organization?
- What was the duration of past training or briefing events that included or was focused on top managers in the organization?

- Who conducted the past training or briefing events that included or were focused on top managers in the organization?
- How receptive were top managers to past briefing or training events in which they participated?

The goal is to garner the cooperation and support of top managers. If the security planners and trainers can answer any of the aforementioned questions, then they will have some insight into how to package the security message in a manner that top managers will be receptive to and support. With some knowledge about the top managers' receptivity and preferred methods of learning, the security team and trainers can now move forward with packaging the message. Informal discussions with trainers and human resource managers about training top managers revealed that

- Top managers value their time, so briefing or training sessions should be short in duration.
- Top managers pay more attention to people who have a professional demeanor and can demonstrate knowledge of their topic.
- Top managers expect their experience, knowledge, and opinions to be respected and heard.
- Top managers like to focus on solutions rather than overprocessing problems.
- Top managers like to get to the point and have little appreciation of superfluous information.

Following this advice, learning how top managers in an organization work and think, and preparing a briefing that focuses on what they really need to know will make delivering the message easier. When implementing new security measures or updating old security processes and procedures, it is important to not alienate the top managers because security efforts really need them to support the security team. A model briefing program for top-level managers is provided in Figure 4.2.

Just because top managers are in their position does not necessarily mean that they are the only people in an organization who can fill a leadership role in security. Security planners may very well find many middle managers or technical experts in an organization that other

Sample briefing outline for executive-level staff	
Area of security plan to be covered	**Desired outcomes for training**
The security planning process and what the planning team has accomplished	Understand the effort that has been put forth in developing the insider security plan.
Detailed table of contents	Understand the contents of the security plan and be able to use it as reference tool.
Disclaimer and instructions as to what to do when a situation arises that the plan does not address	Understand what employees should do when confronted with new situations.
Introduction	Understand and be able to make decisions based on the overall philosophy toward insider security.
Explanation of major laws that impact the security requirements of the organization	Understand laws and be able to make business plans that are consistent with legal requirements.
Overview of the types of assets for which the organization must maintain security	Understand the assets of the organization as well as the challenge and requirements of maintaining security against insiders.
Policies and expectations of suppliers, business partners and distributors	Understand expectations and be able to conduct business negotiations according to insider security requirements.
Appendix of definitions	Understand how to use the appendix as reference tool.

Figure 4.2 Insider security briefing for executive-level staff.

employees or managers consider leaders. Find out who these leaders are. Security planners can do so through observation as well as asking employees who it is that they go to for help when they are in a problem-solving situation. Regardless of how many leaders are found, once they are identified, they should be developed into security leaders and at least developed into security evangelists.

4.4 Achieving Vigilance to Enforce Strong Security

In the effort to build security to protect against insider threats, *security vigilance* is a valuable tool. Vigilance or observing and reporting incidents and potential problems are not the behaviors that security teams will be able to get out of every employee. Just as not all top executives are good leaders, not all mid-level managers or supervisors will be vigilant just because of their position. Vigilance is more like a personality trait than it is a skill. Some people will have vigilant traits and many will not have vigilant traits.[22]

Since all employees will not end up being vigilant, it is important to foster vigilance in the employees that demonstrate that they already have a vigilant personality. Doing this is easier said than done. First, identify who is vigilant and who is not. A reasonable goal is to evolve those who are vigilant into even more vigilant people. A second reasonable goal is to increase the level of vigilance that all employees exercise.

Teaching vigilance to those who are not vigilant is largely a process of planting the concept of vigilance with them and then watching to see if they do become more vigilant. Some people may naturally evolve, whereas others will show no movement whatsoever. These employees can be educated more about vigilance in general security training sessions until they demonstrate that their vigilant tendencies are evolving.

Returning to those that are already vigilant is a more important task and there are ways to leverage their vigilant tendencies. One way to know if an employee is really vigilant is to determine if they have actually participated in security efforts in the past. One indicator is whether the individual employee has reported any security violations and security problems to their supervisor or to appropriate security staff or other managers in the organization.

Once vigilant individuals are identified, it will not take a great deal of effort to further evolve the vigilant tendencies of these individuals. There are several training and development steps that can be taken to quietly encourage and grow these vigilant individuals:

- Conduct brief but detailed training sessions for those who have shown they will participate in security efforts and report security incidents.
- Establish a commendation system for these individuals and make sure that their employee record indicates that they made a contribution to security.

- Consider establishing a program of financial bonus compensation for those who have helped to prevent a security breach or have reported a security violation or security breach to encourage them to continue to make reports when necessary.
- Monitor the actions of the vigilant staff and coach them if they are overreacting to harmless situations.

The entire organization does not need to know what the vigilant individual contributes to security, and many people may not like extra public attention being paid to their efforts. Thus, some level of confidentiality regarding the role and contribution of the vigilant employee is probably prudent. The quiet recognition of their contribution coupled with an incentive program may get an organization much further along on the path to improved security.

4.5 Fostering Evangelism to Promote Strong Security

Evangelists can be powerful motivators for other employees to pay more attention to security and perhaps become more vigilant and active in their support of security programs. *Security evangelists* are not difficult to find because they generally stand out among other people. They may also be relatively easy to inspire by recognizing and perhaps even expanding their role in security efforts.[23]

There is no need to point out the evangelist because most people will recognize who they are with little difficulty. However, it is wise to leverage the evangelist for the impact they can have on the security program. There are a variety of things can be done to encourage the evangelist once they have been identified including the following:

- As with the vigilant employees, have brief but specialized briefing and training sessions to help foster more evangelism.
- A method of recognizing the contribution the evangelist makes to the security effort will be helpful in maintaining their commitment. This method does not need to be financial but should certainly be designed to stroke their egos and motivate them to continue supporting security efforts.
- Some of the evangelists may be able to make substantial contributions to the in-house training program. Once they have

been trained to train others, it is worthwhile giving them a trial run at training.

- In addition to conducting training, the evangelist may be of great help in designing new training materials as well as improving existing training materials.
- The evangelist may be able to contribute to other in-house efforts such as increasing awareness and publicizing security efforts internally.

4.6 Achieving High Levels of Performance Needed for Strong Security

The ultimate goal in increasing awareness, diligence, and vigilance is to make an organization more secure against all types of attacks, insider or outsider, or a combination of the two. To accomplish this, it is important that all employees perform their responsibilities through proper *security performance*. This is critical because even with well-planned security measures in place, it is the carelessness of an individual employee or the lax enforcement of security procedures in a single department that can lead to a security breach.

When people do not follow procedures or are unaware of specific procedures, they can make mistakes that the malicious insider can exploit.[24] Forgetting to lock file cabinets, leaving security doors unsecured, discussing confidential information in the break room, or allowing an unauthorized person into a secure area may be all it takes for the malicious insider to commit a breach.

Generalized training sessions can help employees better understand security policies and security procedures. But not all employees will remember everything that was covered in the classroom. In addition, some security procedures may be specific to a particular department or work area. This will require supervisors to have an active role in training their supervisees. This means that supervisors will need to know all of the security procedures that are relevant to their work areas or work processes.

Supervisors play a key role in the day-to-day operations of any organization. So, to achieve solid performance and maintain a necessary level of performance, all of those who work in supervisory roles will need to be thoroughly trained in security procedures relevant to their specific supervisory role. Then, in turn, they can be responsible for some of the training their supervisees need in an on-the-job training mode. It is common to find training sessions that are specifically geared to the supervisory level, and supervisors routinely go through a variety of trainings that include some that cover security.

Supervisors also have the responsibility of monitoring employee compliance with security procedures. So, in addition to training supervisors on security procedures, supervisors must also be trained to train their supervisees and also be trained to monitor performance and address performance issues of their supervisees.

The well-trained supervisor will play a critical role in improving security performance. To do so, supervisors need a wide breadth of communication and technical skills including security procedure knowledge. But they must also have a toolbox on which they can rely to help them train employees on security procedures and to evaluate employee performance. Supervisors need ongoing development in how to evaluate supervisee performance. They also need to be equipped with the appropriate evaluation tools including evaluation forms and guidelines that include security topics.[25] A sample training outline for supervisors and midlevel managers is shown in Figure 4.3.

4.7 Infusing Awareness Needed for Strong Security

Awareness of the importance of security and the role of security in organization sustainability on the part of all employees, contractors, business partners, and customers is helpful in maintaining security performance. *Security awareness* is not difficult to achieve and it is a good starting place for all employees.

Awareness establishes a foundation on which to build better security performance. When employees are aware that security is an issue, they will not be surprised when they are required to participate in training sessions or when they have security performance as part of their annual performance evaluation.

Increasing security awareness need not be a major production or communications campaign. When an organization has visible security, such as security guards, surveillance cameras, or security audits, employees will start to recognize that security is in place. Small efforts such as a mention of security in a company newsletter or the occasional motivational poster can help to reinforce security awareness. As

Training for middle managers and supervisors	
Area of security plan to be covered	**Desired outcomes for training**
The security planning process and what the task force has accomplished	Understand the effort that has been put forth in developing the security plan.
Detailed table of contents	Understand the contents of the security plan and be able to use it as reference tool.
Disclaimer and instructions as to what to do when a situation arises that the insider security plan does not address	Understand what supervisors and line employees should do when confronted with new situations.
Introduction	Understand and be able to make decisions based on the overall philosophy toward insider security.
Guidelines for how employees should explain the insider security policies of the organization to customers, clients, or suppliers.	Understand the guidelines and be able to implement proper procedures for dealing with inquiries that come to their department.
Explanation of major laws that impact the insider security requirements of the organization	Understand laws and be able to make business plans that are consistent with legal requirements.
Detailed explanation of the specific assets for which the organization must maintain insider security	Understand the assets for which security must be maintained and be able to meet the requirements of maintaining privacy.
Explanations of the roles each department plays in maintaining protection from insider security threats.	Understand the role of each department and be able to work with other departments to maintain security.
Policies and expectations of suppliers, business partners and distributors	Understand expectations and be able to conduct business negotiations according to security plan requirements.
Procedures for the proper disposal of data and information in all formats, including print, computer-based, and magnetic storage.	Understand the procedures and be able to meet the requirements of maintaining insider security during the disposal process.
Appendix of definitions	Understand how to use the appendix as reference tool.

Figure 4.3   Training for middle managers and supervisors.

supervisors work with groups of employees or with individual employees on performance of security procedures, they are also increasing awareness.[26]

Selecting an appropriate approach to heighten security awareness in an organization is more a question of style than it is trying to utilize an off-the-shelf approach to enhancing security awareness. Security

Training outline for general insider security training	
Area of insider security to be covered	**Desired outcomes for training**
The security planning process and what the task force has accomplished.	Understand the effort that has been put forth in developing the security plan.
Introduction	Understand the overall philosophy toward security against insider threats.
How to identify potential insider security problems and what they should do.	Understand what employees should do when confronted with security related situations.
Explanations of the roles each department plays in maintaining security against insider threats.	Understand the role of each department.

Figure 4.4　Training outline for general insider security.

planning teams can deploy a loud campaign with fireworks, movie stars, and picnics. They can also go to the other end of the continuum and make sure that some aspect of security is always noticeable and always present on a day-to-day basis.[27] Suggested training topics for general security awareness are shown in Figure 4.4.

4.8 Assuring Familiarity Needed for Strong Security

Achieving *security familiarity* is far less of a challenge than before September 11, 2001. At this point in history, security has been in the news to such an extent that it is almost impossible for people to not be familiar with security. The benefit of familiarity is that people are not alarmed when they see security in action. They may not be aware of why security is present in a particular location, but they will not be alarmed when they encounter security activity.

Familiarity is more important in situations where there is a constant flow of first-time people or infrequent visitors to a particular location. If there is such a location, then security staff should expect at least momentary confusion on the part of people who are not familiar with security. Given that, security staff at such locations will need to practice considerable patience.

One scenario that may illustrate the circumstance is when people have never been on an airplane. They can be seen at the airport walking around dazed and confused. If an organization needs to deal with the dazed and confused, then that will present a unique set of circumstances and challenges.

Communicating with those who are not familiar with facilities need not be complicated. Way-finding signs are helpful for directing people down the proper path so they can be checked through security. Instructional or information boards in transit or waiting areas can be an effective way of making people more familiar with the security process and procedure.

4.9 Training Employees on Data Security and Privacy Expectations

Over the last 20 years, there have been many laws passed around the world addressing the privacy of individual data and information. Much of the early efforts to legislate privacy protection have now become customs that most people in the business world are in agreement with. Much of what we now see as customary started with the European Union's (EU's) privacy legislation called the Directive on Data Protection, which became effective in 1998. After several years, the United States and the EU agreed on what is now called *safe harbor standards*.[28] The principles of safe harbor are relatively easy to understand and are as follows:

- An organization must inform individuals as to why information about them is collected, how to contact the organization with inquiries or complaints, what types of third parties the information will be disclosed to, and the options and means the organization provides individuals to limit its use and disclosure of information.
- Notice must be provided to individuals in clear language at the point when individuals are first asked to provide personal information or as soon thereafter as is practicable. In all circumstances, the organization must inform individuals before it uses information for any purpose other than that for which it was originally collected or before it discloses information to a third party.
- An organization must provide individuals with an opportunity to choose (opt out) if and how personal information

that they provide is used or disclosed to third parties if such use is not compatible with the original purpose for which the information was collected. Individuals must be provided with clear, readily available, and affordable mechanisms to exercise this option.

- With sensitive information such as medical and health information, racial or ethnic origin, political opinions, religious or philosophical beliefs, trade union membership, or information concerning the sex life of the individual, the individual must be given the opportunity to specifically affirm (opt in) that the information can be used.

- An organization is allowed to disclose personal and proprietary information to third parties in manners that are consistent with the original principles of notice and choice. When an organization is sharing information that another organization has approved, the use of it must first determine that the receiving party subscribes to the safe harbor principles.

- As an alternative to meeting general safe harbor requirements, the receiving party must enter into a written agreement with the organization providing the information, ensuring that the receiver will provide at least the same level of protection as is required by relevant safe harbor principles.

- Organizations that create, maintain, use, or disseminate personal information must take reasonable measures to ensure that it is reliable for the intended use. In addition, organizations must take reasonable precautions to protect their information from loss, misuse, unauthorized access, disclosure, alteration, and destruction.

- An organization may only process personal information for the purposes for which the information was originally collected. In doing so, an organization is responsible for ensuring that data is accurate, complete, and current.

- Individuals who provide information must have reasonable access to personal information about them that an organization holds and be able to correct or amend that information where it is inaccurate.

In addition to safe harbor principles, there are several fundamental concepts that are the basis of understanding data protection and privacy in the United States. The basic starting place is that there shall not be unreasonable intrusion on an individual's privacy. Second, it is not appropriate to make private facts public, including such things as income tax data, sexual relations, and medical treatment records.

There are numerous laws, rules, and regulations at various levels of government to protect personal information in specific situations. These include medical records, bank statements, academic records, court records of minors, and telephone conversations.

Employees do not need to be trained in every data protection and security law in the world. However, if they are provided with the basic principles and guidelines outlined earlier, they will have a better understanding of how they should handle sensitive data and personal information.

4.10 Promoting Security as a Positive Thing

There are various philosophies about the appearance or presence of security. Some organizations want to instill fear in people, and security is promoted as and appears as something rather ominous. On the other end of the continuum, some organizations want security to be viewed as a positive and friendly. Consider the differences between the *visual appearance of security* and the message sent by that visualization at a prison compared to security at an amusement park.

How security is presented and the extent to which it is made visible will be largely dependent on the purpose or location of a facility. The visual and psychological impact of security on employees or everyday visitors to a facility can make a big difference in how security is perceived and the extent to which security is embraced. High-profile security makes some people feel more secure and safer, whereas it makes others feel paranoid and oppressed.

As an organization develops and evolves security, keep in mind that the appearance of security, and the mentality from which it is implemented, is a reflection on the organization. Managers and security planners need to be aware of the image they are portraying. Does management want to put people on edge or do they want them to feel comfortable and welcomed?

Also bear in mind that beating people over the head every day with security can also have a negative impact. One way to take the edge off security for people is to disguise it as something other than security. For example, a big push to improve security may alienate as many people as it inspires. In the case of opening a new facility, numerous security features blended into the design will attract less attention than razor wire fences and moats. In such a case, the human reactions can be tamed or even neutralized.

The same applies to how security personnel treat people. Are they gestapo-like creatures that deliberately instill fear in all of the people around them or are they the plainclothes amusement park host that is an intricate part of the security plan at an amusement park? Managers get to decide what they want to be and how they want people to perceive security efforts. But everybody should choose carefully.

Think for a minute about the public perception of police in America. In some communities, police are viewed as violent adversaries who use excessive force on any occasion they can; and if they do not like you, they will shoot your dog or even your kittens. In other communities, police are viewed as an integral part of the community and local society. The police are trusted and respected by the community members because they are polite and helpful except when they must be otherwise. Again, management gets to decide what it wants the company to be and how it wants people to perceive the security efforts.

4.11 Summary

This chapter explained the various personalities in an organization that can contribute and participate in improving and maintaining security. It also examined ways that those various personalities can be exploited for the sake of security and how their talents and personalities can be fostered and leveraged to improve security and support the security culture. Key areas covered include the following:

- Issues with the effectiveness and cost of past organizational change models and efforts
- Different ways employees can contribute to security by leading, evangelizing, being vigilant, or properly performing their security-related duties and monitoring how other people perform their security-related duties

- Various tactics that can be used to improve employee participation in security efforts at a level that they feel comfortable and at a level that they can constructively contribute
- How the personal tendencies of different types of employees can be reinforced and further developed to improve security efforts
- How managers should consciously decide what type of image they want security in their organization to portray
- Safe harbor principles for data protection

COURSE CASE STUDY   THE JAMES MARTIN MANUFACTURING COMPANY (CONTINUED)

Tonya Martin recently became CEO of the James Martin Manufacturing Company, a privately owned company that had been in her family for over 80 years. After reviewing several years of records, Tonya discovered that the late Harold Smith had been embezzling and stealing equipment and supplies from the company for the last decade before his death.

To assess and work to improve security, Tonya has been working with Ronald Thomas, the new director of security (DOS), and Samuel Davis, a new hire with experience in a similar company. One decision they had to make was just how far and how fast they would move to improve security including having a security plan that covered all of the security needs of James Martin Manufacturing.

After much discussion, they decided that they would work toward a comprehensive security plan, but for the time being they were going to focus on the areas that needed the most protection and work to develop solid security measures for those high priority areas. Once better security was in place for the most important areas or assets, they would move forward one step at a time toward the comprehensive security plan.

DOS Ronald Thomas had started to review and update existing security policies and procedures that focused on the financial management of the company. Samuel Davis, the new hire with experience in a similar company, was focusing on examining security for physical assets.

Things were moving along fine until another security incident occurred. Just a week ago, Ronald Thomas found a car backed up to the loading dock at the rear of the building. The back door of the building was propped open and there were two wheeled carts sitting on the dock. They were full of boxes. Thomas caught Larry Jacobs, a long-time employee, stealing large amounts of tools and materials. He was arrested and the police later found that his garage was full of items stolen from James Martin Manufacturing.

Tonya, Ronald Thomas, and Samuel Davis decided they needed to start getting other people involved in promoting and improving security. They understood that because there had been such a lack of security over the last few years, suddenly cracking down on security could be a shock to the employees of the company. They also believed that there was knowledge and talent among the employees that could be leveraged to help promote security and monitor compliance with security procedures.

Tonya wanted to add people to the security leadership team. She did not have the resources to hire a dozen security guards, but she felt that she needed to find a few people that could help keep an eye on James Martin Manufacturing facilities. This would be important to maintain an increased level of vigilance in protecting company assets. Ronald Thomas suggested that they needed some people to help ensure that other employees were complying with security procedures. Samuel Davis suggested that having more people to help train employees on security policies and procedures would hasten the process of improving security.

Tonya also believed that she wanted a friendly security atmosphere and did not want employees to feel that James Martin Manufacturing had become militarized. She also wanted to encourage cooperation with and good feelings about the upcoming changes in security practices at the company.

COURSE DISCUSSION QUESTIONS

1. Discuss the pros and cons of bringing other employees into the security planning and the security improvement process at this time. Is it a good idea? Is it a bad idea? Is there another way Tonya could go about this?

2. What do you think about the talent mix that the security team wants to bring into the security planning and security improvement process: leadership, vigilance, evangelism, and compliance? Is it a good idea? Is it a bad idea? Is there another way to go about this?

3. Discuss how the security team should go about recruiting the talent they think they need to help improve security. Is there another way to go about this?

4. At this point in the process, do you think Tonya should hire an outside consultant? Why do you think that?

COURSE PROJECTS

1. Outline the content of a security training course for supervisors in James Martin Manufacturing. Compare your outline to those of others in the class.

2. Describe how you think a security evangelist could help in improving security in James Martin Manufacturing and give examples of specific things they could do. Compare your examples to those of others in the class.

3. Design a form that could be used by supervisors in James Martin Manufacturing to report to the director of security that there is a continued lack of compliance with security procedures by an employee that they supervise. Compare your form design to that of others in the class.

4. Draft a memo to company employees announcing upcoming efforts to improve security. Compare your draft to the draft of others in the class.

COURSE TEST QUESTIONS

1. An organization culture in which security pervades every aspect of daily life as well as all efforts to change, evolve, or realign the organization is known as _____.
2. The manners in which an individual or classes of individuals prefer to learn new material, ideas, concepts, and technical skills are known as _____.
3. Safe harbor standards were jointly developed by the _____.
4. A basic level of understanding of security and recognition of the importance of security by employees or groups of employees in an organization is known as _____.
5. Individuals in an organization who speak of the benefits of good security whenever they have the opportunity to express their support and encourage others to support security efforts are known as _____.
6. Knowing that security exists and is necessary in certain situations but involves little knowledge or understanding of security processes and procedures is known as _____.
7. A high-ranking and/or respected person in an organization that supports security efforts on a day-to-day basis as well as in organizational activities such as budgeting, planning, and managing, and speaks on behalf of security efforts when appropriate is known as a _____.
8. The constant attention given to security during day-to-day operations and contributes to security by encouraging the reporting of security violations and makes suggestions on how to improve security when weaknesses are observed is known as _____.
9. The manner in which security presence and security operations are visible or are displayed in a particular environment is known as the _____.
10. The people in an organization that have the day-to-day responsibility of monitoring employee compliance with security procedures are called _____.

Key Terms

Culture of security: is an organization culture in which security pervades every aspect of daily life as well as all efforts to change, evolve, or realign the organization.

Learning styles: are the manners in which an individual or classes of individuals prefer to learn new material, ideas, concepts, and technical skills.

Safe harbor standards: are the joint European Union–United States developed standards for handling data and personal information, which have become the de facto standards around the world.

Security awareness: is the basic level of understanding of security and recognition of the importance of security by employees or groups of employees in an organization.

Security evangelists: are individuals in an organization who, although they are not necessarily directly responsible for security, speak of the benefits of good security whenever they have the opportunity to express their support and encourage others to support security efforts.

Security familiarity: is knowing that security exists and is necessary in certain situations but involves little knowledge or understanding of security processes and procedures.

Security leader: is a high-ranking and/or respected person in an organization that supports security efforts on a day-to-day basis as well as in organizational activities such as budgeting, planning, and managing, and speaks on behalf of security efforts when appropriate.

Security performance: is the proper implementation of security procedures and adherence to security policies.

Security vigilance: is the constant attention given to security during day-to-day operations and contributes to security by encouraging the reporting of security violations and makes suggestions on how to improve security when weaknesses are observed.

Visual appearance of security: is the manner in which security presence and security operations are visible or are displayed in a particular environment.

5

DEVELOPING SOCIAL MEDIA POLICIES AND TRAINING EMPLOYEES

This chapter explains how to develop *social media policies* and procedures to protect an organization from insiders either maliciously or carelessly damaging social media activity or compromising sensitive information via social media. It also covers how to establish a practical training process and how to integrate security topics in other training programs as well as how to embed training into nontraining activities. Training is an expensive process, and the training team will want to ensure that training efforts are effective.

Public image is an asset that needs to be protected just as physical assets are protected. Protecting the public image asset from insider sabotage or irresponsible actions is part of that challenge. The public image must also be protected from carelessness as well as embarrassing non-work-related acts of employees. Years ago, the impact of employee misbehavior was mostly localized. However, the emergence of social media has created an environment where local acts came become globally known overnight and sometimes in minutes.

Protecting an organization's image from negative social media is a twofold process. First, protect the organization's own social media tools and accounts on the various Internet platforms. Second, it is prudent to protect the public image from harm that can be caused by employees using their own social media accounts.

5.1 Protecting Social Media Accounts and Content

Social media applications can become available and into widespread use at a far faster pace than the skill to use them and the common sense on how to use them evolves. As a result, people tend to go rather wild and use social media applications in a very reckless manner. Eventually common sense will catch up with this recklessness, but only after several disasters along the way, and the consequences come far faster than does the evolution of common sense.

Social media is viewed by many people as a fun way to communicate and network, and it has also become a widely used tool by numerous types of organizations. As an organization begins to use social media and establishes social media accounts and a *social media presence*, it will be able to utilize a variety of pages, portals, discussion groups, news feeds, or one of the many other social media applications. Managers may find this all very helpful in promoting services or products. However, with the use of social media also comes the necessary responsibility of monitoring and controlling what happens with those tools.

These new responsibilities come with a price tag. It is relatively inexpensive to establish a minimum social media presence. Although social media, as we now know it, can be relatively easy to become involved with, it brings with it a long-term overhead. First, employees cannot be allowed to use social media tools without controlling how the tools are used and who gets to use the tools on behalf of an organization. Second, employees cannot just begin using a social media tool and then release it into the wild without monitoring what happens.

To secure social media tools from abuse or misuse by employees and nonemployees, one of the first steps you need to take is to understand how each social media tool can be protected with its built-in control and security features. Before starting to use a specific tool, social media staff needs to evaluate how much control the built features provide and decide if that is sufficient to protect the organization from damage. Staff can evaluate social media tools by questioning what types of controls and security are available for the tool and what resources are required to safely use the tool by asking and answering a series of self-assessment questions:

- Who in the organization will be responsible for managing the use of the social media tool?
- Who in the organization will establish policies and procedures necessary for governing the use of the social media tool?

- How secure can the tool be made from hacking and keep it from being hijacked?
- How much control will management have over how the tool is used?
- How can control of the account be regained if it is misappropriated?
- How will staff be able to tell if something malicious has happened to the account?
- How will management know if the tool is being improperly used?
- How will staff know who has misused the account and its related functionality?
- Who will be able to post to the social media account and how can that be controlled?
- Who in the organization will be responsible for the day-to-day monitoring of the account including postings or comments?
- Who in the organization will be responsible for training employees on the appropriate use of the social media tool?
- When should management evaluate the results gained from using the social media tool and how will that been accomplished?
- Where will the expense for using and managing the social media tool be covered in the organization's budget?

As a logical first step, a person or persons in an organization should be designated to have responsibility for the use and control of the use of social media. But before they go too far into the realm of social media, management should develop policies regarding the use of social media tools that are officially used by and represent the organization. In addition, before jumping in too far, management should establish some basic policies that are designed to protect the organization from inappropriate use of the tools by insiders.

How to assign responsibility for social media in an organization is dependent upon how existing communication functions are organized. This responsibility could end up in the public relations department just as easily as it could end up in the marketing department, and that is all up to management. Regardless of where responsibility is placed for social media, the process of developing policies is very important in protecting against insider threats. Experience has shown that social media staff can get rather carried away if policies are not set and if their activity is not preapproved or monitored. Social media policies should address how and who uses social media and what constitutes appropriate use, including the following:

- The social media tools that are authorized for use in the organization
- The types of content and examples of services to which the policies apply

---

Guiding principles for social media use in a non-official/personal capacity use posted by the United States Department of Interior

The following principles should be employed when using social media services in a non-official/personal capacity within DOI:

- Be aware of your DOI association in online social networks. If you identify yourself as a DOI employee or have a public facing position for which your DOI association is known to the general public, ensure your profile and related content (even if it is of a personal and not an official nature) is consistent with how you wish to present yourself as a DOI professional, appropriate with the public trust associated with your position, and conform to existing standards, such as Standards of Ethical Conduct for Employees of the Executive Branch. Employees should have no expectation of privacy when using social media tools.

- When in doubt, stop. Don't post until you're free of doubt. Be certain that the post would be considered protected speech for First Amendment purposes. Also, add a disclaimer to your social networking profile, personal blog, or other online presences that clearly states that the opinions or views expressed are yours alone and do not represent the views of the Department of the Interior or your bureau.

- In a publicly accessible forum, do not discuss any agency- or bureau-related information that is not already considered public information. The discussion of sensitive, proprietary, or classified information is strictly prohibited. This rule applies even in circumstances where password or other privacy controls are implemented. Failure to comply may result in fines and/or disciplinary action.

Figure 5.1 Sample guiding principles for social media use. (From United States Department of the Interior, Social Media Policy, September 2015, retrieved June 9, 2016, from https://www.doi.gov/notices/Social-Media-Policy.)

- When and why it is appropriate to use social media tools
- When and why it is not appropriate to use social media tools
- Nonofficial/personal use of social media and social networking by employees[29]

It may be difficult to cover every potential use or abuse of social media by employees. This may be especially true when it comes to the nonofficial and personal use of social media by employees. Establishing guiding principles for nonofficial and personal use of social media use can be helpful in covering unforeseen circumstances. The guiding principles used by the U.S. Department of the Interior provide a good example and are shown in Figure 5.1.

Most organizations that get involved with social media have rather strict policies about how social media will be used and who is allowed to use social media platforms on behalf of the organization. After reviewing several social media use policies, it was found that there is considerable consistency between organizations. The major theme among public agencies and other organizations that want to use social media but avoid irritating the general public is to stay safe and avoid potential areas of conflict. A consensus policy on social media posts is shown in Figure 5.2.

Sample policy on the content of social media posts

All published (organization name) social media content is subject to monitoring. This content may take the form of digital text for Twitter and Facebook, and photography images for Flickr.

Typical policies state that user-generated posts will be rejected or removed if possible when the content of a post:

- Is off-subject or out of context
- Contains obscenity or material that appeals to the prurient interest
- Contains personal identifying information or sensitive personal information
- Contains offensive terms that target protected classes
- Is threatening, harassing, or discriminatory
- Incites or promotes violence or illegal activities
- Contains information that reasonably could compromise public safety
- Advertises or promotes a commercial product or service, or any entity or individual (other than the account owner)
- Promotes or endorses political campaigns or candidates

Figure 5.2   Sample policy on the content of social media posts.

The laws that apply to an organization's product promotion, marketing, and advertising off-line equally apply to those activities when using online tools including social media. For example, an organization is required to comply with truth in advertising laws and regulations. The U.S. Federal Trade Commission (FTC) reiterates this several times and provides several guides to help ensure that employees do not violate these laws when using social media.[30] These laws also apply to the social media post that are done for an organization by part-time insiders including contractors, marketing firms, and freelancers.

5.2 Legal Issues Encountered with Social Media Policies

Establishing policies for the social media sites and tools that have been selected and deployed in the name of an organization can be a relatively straightforward process. Those pages belong to the organization and the organization can determine how they are used as long as it is in compliance with the policies and rules and regulations of the service provider. Social media staff need to make sure that they control, monitor, and police social media tools by utilizing the settings the website provides. If they encounter issues with use of the accounts, then they need to address those with the service provider.

On the other hand, establishing and enforcing nonprofessional and personal use of social media by employees on the wild world web is a bit more of a challenge. As well intended as policies might be and as reasonable as guidelines may sound to policy makers, there are numerous laws that govern the extent to which an organization can control its employees' personal use of social media. Management can act if employees post the organization's proprietary information and can gain the cooperation of social media service providers to have proprietary information removed.

The U.S. National Labor Relations Board (NLRB) has reviewed numerous cases where conflict has arisen between an employer and an employee regarding polices covering guidelines and policies set by employers to govern personal use of social media by employees as it may relate to a specific organization.[31] A review of findings in the "Report of the Acting General Counsel Concerning Social Media Cases" released in January 2012 shows that controlling employee actions in social media can be complicated. Summary statements of cases reviewed by the NLRB include the following:

- Discharge for Facebook comments and for violation of non-disparagement rule was unlawful.
- Discharge for Facebook comments was lawful, but social media policy and no-solicitation rule were overly broad.
- Work rules were overbroad, but discharge under rules was lawful because employee's Facebook posts were not protected.
- Employer's social media policy was overbroad, but employee's Facebook posts were not protected.
- Portions of employer's communications systems policy were overbroad.
- Employer's initial social media policy was overbroad, but amended version was lawful.
- Provisions in drugstore operator's social media policy withstand scrutiny.
- Employee was unlawfully discharged for her Facebook complaint about reprimand.
- Employees' Facebook postings about supervisor and promotion selection were protected concerted activity.
- Employee's Facebook postings about manager's attitude and style were protected concerted activity.
- Employee's critical online postings were protected concerted activity that did not lose act's protection.
- Employee's Facebook postings about irritating coworker and workplace incident were not protected.
- Truck driver was not engaged in concerted activity and was not constructively discharged.
- Employee's Facebook criticism of supervisor was venting and was not concerted.

After reviewing numerous cases, the NLRB came to two major conclusions. First, "employer policies should not be so sweeping that they prohibit the kinds of activity protected by federal labor law, such as the discussion of wages or working conditions among employees." Second, "an employee's comments on social media are generally not protected if they are mere gripes not made in relation to group activity among employees."[32] Also note that the NLRB does not provide legal advice and urges employers to consult with their own attorneys to discuss the legality of their policies on non-work-related social media activities of their employees.

The bottom line management faces when establishing a policy to protect the organization from damage done by non-work-related and personal social media posts by employees is that in many cases employees are protected by labor laws covered by the National Labor Relations Act. Management should seek legal counsel if it feels that its related policies may be in violation of the labor laws. It is probably best to consult counsel before implementing social media policies.

5.3 State Laws on Social Media Use by an Employee

In efforts to mitigate damage caused by an employee using social media, organizations will also need to pay attention to state laws that dictate how and when they can control and employee's social media use. Management should check the state laws for any state in which they have employees. Corporate social media policies may not be applicable for use in all states. Do not make any assumptions about this and have the corporate attorney double check the policy and compliance with appropriate state laws. As of spring 2016 over 20 states had enacted laws that cover employer's access to employee's social media accounts.[33]

The State of California passed Assembly Bill No. 1844 Chapter 618 in 2012 that added language to existing laws covering employer–employee relations involving social media. The addition states that an employer shall not require or request an employee or applicant for employment to

- Disclose a username or password for the purpose of accessing personal social media
- Access personal social media in the presence of the employer
- Divulge any personal social media activity[34]

However, nothing in the law prohibits a private company or any employer from requesting that an employee "divulge personal social media reasonably believed to be relevant to an investigation of allegations of employee misconduct or employee violation of applicable laws and regulations, provided that the social media is used solely for purposes of that investigation or a related proceeding."[34]

The State of Washington has a very similar law to that of California. It protects an employee's privacy in their use of social media. However, an employer may request or require social media content to make a factual determination in the course of conducting an investigation to "ensure compliance with applicable laws, regulatory requirements, or prohibitions against work-related employee misconduct; or investigate an allegation of unauthorized transfer of an employer's proprietary information, confidential information, or financial data to the employee's personal social networking account."[35]

The State of Texas provides considerable detail regarding an employee's use of an employer's computer systems and quotes the NLRB regarding employees' social media use. Texas is very strict regarding employees use of an employer's computer systems and expressly forbids any non-business use of an employer's electronic systems. In addition, if an employee violates the policies, they could be subject to disciplinary action, up to and including dismissal.[36]

The State of Illinois is very conservative when it comes to protecting an employee's right to privacy, including what an employee does on social media. An employer cannot require an employee to reveal their private social media activity. However, employers can, through legal means such as Internet searches or allowed searches within a social media platform, discover what employees or potential applicants for employment do on social media.[37]

5.4 Monitoring Employee Use of Social Media

Certainly it is reasonable to be concerned about how employees use social media or any Internet website, functionality, or social application because of the virtual unlimited exposure that the Internet provides. In addition, we have come to learn that people tend to do really stupid things on the Internet. Using the Internet seems to make people very careless in many instances. But people often start out using the Internet with the best of intentions, not knowing or thinking about potential negative consequences.

Yes, the Internet empowers, it entertains, it makes life more convenient, and it provides opportunity for those who know how to exploit that opportunity. One of the most popular ways to use the Internet is to network with other people that may have the same economic interest and want to advance their career. Many people also use the Internet to search for new jobs or to make themselves available to recruiters seeking talent for their organization or for their clients.

There are many popular networking sites. A survey of one of the largest websites and social networking applications where people can post their skills and background information shows just what a presence people looking for new opportunities can create. A simple survey of the website shows how many employees from nine very large anonymous companies have made their information available. They may also be making information about their employer available. The number of current or past employees of the nine high-profile companies that have made their profile and background information available on the popular networking site is shown in Figure 5.3.

Employees of large companies posting their profile online		
Type of company	**Information of current employees**	**Information of past employees**
Major agriculture	17,000	29,000
Big box store	150,000	190,000
Large brewery	1,700	190
Major auto manufacturer	73,000	15,000
Clothing retailer	15,000	50,000
Major telecom company	180,000	32,000
Large beverage company	45,000	9,000
Large software company	1,800	5,000
Large computer company	390,000	90,000

Figure 5.3   Employees of large companies posting their profile online.

By posting their professional information and work experience online, employees are working to better themselves in their careers and in their lives. They are also exposing themselves to a world that may well want to take advantage of them as an information source. Like it or not, in the past some companies would interview an employee of a competitor just to see what information they could find out about the person's present employer.

Many companies have been known to hire from their competitors when they believed that the new employee would bring a treasure trove of proprietary information with them to their new jobs. The new social media networking websites and applications have taken much of the work out of finding potential employees and finding ones that may sail that treasure ship right to the loading dock.

However, one of the advantages a company gains from these types of *social and professional networking websites* is that it gets to see which employees are making themselves available and see what skills or knowledge they claim to be able to bring with them to the new job. As it turns out, management and security staff are able to use networking sites to track employees as much as employees can use the networking sites to seek new opportunity.

Management and security staff can also track which employees have posted their resume on job websites when they are specifically looking for work and not just participating in some friendly professional networking. A survey of a very large job website for use by employees of the same anonymous nine companies surveyed on the professional networking site is shown in Figure 5.4.

Management and security staff can also view an employee's resumes on the job sites. Note that there are often monthly fees to search resumes on many of these job sites. However, depending on what management and security staff suspect or what is being investigated, the fees may be worthwhile for the information gained back in return. There are, of course, people and special interest groups who will probably criticize management and security staff for monitoring the online job-seeking efforts of employees, but there does not appear to be any legal restrictions on using the job websites for such purposes.

A test of several other social media websites searching for users claiming to be from one of the same nine anonymous companies used in the other surveys did not yield as strong of results. It is still possible

Employees posting resumes on job website (People that were employed by the company)	
Type of company	Popular internet job site resumes
Major agriculture	2,000
Big box store	21,000
Large brewery	350
Major auto manufacturer	45,000
Clothing retailer	40,000
Major telecom company	4,000
Large beverage company	6,000
Large software company	100,000
Large computer company	100,000

Figure 5.4   Employees posting resumes on job website.

to find out if employees are using those social media websites, but the search usually requires using a specific person's name or moniker in order to find information about them or the pages they have created on the social media website. If management and security staff decide to put the time into it, they may find how much information employees have posted, and this might be a reasonable approach when investigating insiders who have committed malicious or careless acts against the organization.

5.5 Monitoring Websites for Posts about Your Organization

The World Wide Web gets bigger everyday, and tracking website posts, newsgroup posts, photos, blogs, and other places that reflect on your organization in some way has become a gargantuan task. Management and security staff might as well conclude that it has become virtually impossible. To illustrate just how big of a task tracking everything on the Internet about an organization can be, a search of the name of the companies used in Figures 5.3 and 5.4 was conducted using popular search engines. The volume of results from the search using three different search engines was consistently staggering. The resulting entries came back in the millions and up to 100 million. A smaller to midsize company will likely have fewer. But what can management and security staff do when they are facing such a huge volume of possible places that their company could be mentioned and places that an insider could have revealed proprietary information? Figure 5.5 shows the results of searching the company name for the nine anonymous companies in the test.

Chances are management and the security staff are never going to be able to monitor the entire Internet for information or posts about their company. However, they can still learn something about

Number of search results for large companies			
Type of company	Results from search engine #1	Results from search engine #2	Results from search engine #3
Major agriculture	26,000,000	9,600,000	4,800,000
Big box store	100,000,000	40,000,000	43,000,000
Large brewery	4,500,000	1,800,000	1,700,000
Major auto manufacturer	950,000,000	14,000,000	14,000,000
Clothing retailer	88,000,000	13,000,000	13,000,000
Major telecom company	100,000,000	6,200,000,000	45,000,000
Large beverage company	13,000,000	9,500,000	17,000,000
Large software company	140,000,000	19,500,000	15,000,000
Large computer company	180,000,000	16,000,000	15,000,000

Figure 5.5 Number of search results for large companies.

potential negative posts that have been made or proprietary informa-tion that may have been posted. One method is to ask that employees report anything they may come across. This can be done by providing a web page on which they can report the posts or an e-mail address to which they can send a link to the offending post or page.

Another way to reduce the volume of entries in the search results is to add key words like "hate" or a term that people use describing an organization. Management and security staff can also keep narrowing the search as much as possible by adding other key terms. Figure 5.6 shows the results of searching for the company name plus the word "hate" for the nine anonymous companies in the test. The results are considerable fewer but still daunting.

Management and security staff are not going to be able to spend the time searching through the World Wide Web every week to see who

Number of hate-focused search results for large companies			
Type of company	Results from search engine #1	Results from search engine #2	Results from search engine #3
Major agriculture	500,000	650,000	670,000
Big box store	9,900,000	5,500,000	6,300,000
Large brewery	75,000	55,000	59,000
Major auto manufacturer	900,000	39,000,000	1,000,000
Clothing retailer	33,000,000	49,000,000	4,000,000
Major telecom company	590,000	11,000,000	4,500,000
Large beverage company	550,000	27,000,000	1,300,000
Large software company	700,000	1,900,000	2,000,000
Large computer company	550,000	1,800,000	1,800,000

Figure 5.6   Number of hate-focused search results for large companies.

is posting bad things about the organization and following up to see if there are insider offenders. However, they can keep an ongoing list of websites, social media accounts, and user names in discussion groups to follow up on occasion. This type of monitoring is easier to accomplish and the list can be helpful during investigation of security incidents at corporate facilities or with social media or other online accounts.

5.6 Developing Internet Etiquette and Ethics for Employees

Developing and training employees can be a long and expensive process, and nothing may be more challenging than teaching them etiquette and ethics. Let's face it, some people have proper etiquette and good ethics, and some people will never have either.

If everybody had good manners and strong humanistic ethics, the world would be a better place and companies would not need to train employees on how to behave when using Internet functions such as e-mail, discussion groups, or social media. Such is not the case. The concept of starting with the basics and building a strong foundation in order for people to have a better understanding of why policies exist and the goal of the policies is a good beginning. After that, a more detailed venture into policies or procedures will probably be easier.

That just leaves one major question: How do you instill good manners, personal and professional responsibilities, and ethical behavior in people who, if otherwise were left alone, would, perhaps inadvertently, make sure the world stayed relatively uncivilized?

There are a few proprietary websites that provide helpful information. One very popular website is Netiquette (www.networketiquette.com), which provides rules of good behavior online. Another helpful website is Education World (www.educationworld.com), which provides 10 commandments of computer ethics. Both may be helpful in providing ideas for training materials. Both sites are protected by copyright and permission is needed for reuse of material in most circumstances.

Interesting enough, the National Oceanic and Atmospheric Administration (NOAA) has great etiquette and ethics training material through the NOAA Workforce Management Office, Workplace Resources and Enhancement Division (www.wfm.noaa.gov/workplace/). There are several *A WorkLife4You Guide* publications available that have been time tested to help train employees on workplace etiquette and ethics from a variety of perspectives. It is public domain material, and organizations should not encounter any issues adapting the material for their workplaces.

The National Cyber Security Alliance (NCSA) has provided leadership in online security education since the early 2000s. The basic training that NCSA suggests is helpful for businesses as well as individuals. The website StaySafeOnline.org provides excellent guidance in training employees on a range of Internet safety and ethics.

Kids.gov (kids.usa.gov) is a federal-government-sponsored website that provides material that is most often used to teach younger people about Internet safety and Internet use issues. There are several helpful items for training depending on training goals and much of it can be adapted for use with adults.

There are also for-profit training organizations that provide employee training on variety of topics. Then, of course, there are always a wide selection of books and videos that cover almost every training topic imaginable. Many are relatively inexpensive, but a word of caution: Make sure that the material covers the topics that inside trainers consider the most important and that the material is appropriate for an employee audience.

5.7 Training Employees on Social Media Policies

Once an organization has developed social media policies, the training department or staff will need to spend some time training employees on the policies. This training can be delivered in tiers to different types of employees and delivered in ways that are appropriate for an employee's involvement in social media or in non-work-related social media. Several different modules or delivery mechanisms can be helpful including the following:

- General social media usage directed to a broad audience that address etiquette and ethics issues as well as safety issues. It should also specifically address the social media release of any proprietary information, images, graphics, and trademarks.
- Corporate social media use by those designated to manage and use proprietary social media activities.

- Social media use by executives and managers covering how to protect proprietary information as well as their privacy and security when they are identified as employees of an organization when using social media.
- Social media use by technical specialists on how to not only protect proprietary information but to be sure that to not inadvertently provide hints or insights into their work on new products or processes.

Focusing training efforts toward the different categories of employees and delivering appropriate information to each group can save time and money, and can result in more effective training outcomes. Using the material provided by the resources mentioned in Section 5.6, combined with policies and procedures covering a range of workplace activities trainers, can create easy-to-use and easy-to-learn-from modules and supporting media including handouts, posters, and tip sheets.

5.8 Summary

This chapter explained some of the many challenges an organization will face in controlling the use of social media and how to train employees on appropriate social media use. It also examined issues with employees using social media for nonwork activities that may impact an organization's reputation or its security. Key areas covered include the following:

- The importance of protecting an organization's social media image
- The importance of controlling and monitoring the social media tools an organization has selected for use
- The importance of monitoring negative social media posts about an organization or social media posts that result in an unauthorized discloser of proprietary information by Internet users
- Legal issues in creating and enforcing corporate policies and procedures for the use of social media on behalf of an organization and the nonwork use of social media by employees
- Designing general or specialized training for the various groups of employees in an organization

COURSE CASE STUDY   THE JAMES MARTIN MANUFACTURING COMPANY (CONTINUED)

Tonya Martin recently became CEO of the James Martin Manufacturing Company, a privately owned company that had been in her family for over 80 years. Tonya's biggest challenge right now is to address security issues that have surfaced since she took over the management of her father's company.

Tonya has been working with Ronald Thomas, the new director of security (DOS), and Samuel Davis, a new hire with experience in a similar company. They have had several meetings and they are starting to gain momentum in their work. Once better security was in place for the most important areas or assets they would move forward one step at a time toward the comprehensive security plan.

Tonya believes that she would best serve the company by having a friendly security atmosphere and did not want employees to feel that James Martin Manufacturing had become militarized. She also wanted to encourage cooperation with and good feelings about the upcoming changes in security practices at the company.

James Martin Manufacturing was a latecomer to social media, but Tonya had already discovered some unfriendly social media posts made by some former employees as well as a few current employees. The little social media work that has been done on the behalf of the company seems fragmented and lacks focus.

Tonya feels that social media is a good tool to help promote the company's products as well as its involvement in the local community. James Martin Manufacturing does not have a designated person responsible for social media and does not have a social media policy. She wants to pursue social media but feels that the company is not prepared to move ahead at this point. She is also concerned about employees misusing social media. She is considering hiring a social media consultant.

COURSE DISCUSSION QUESTIONS

1. Should Tonya hire a social media consultant or appoint an employee to be responsible for social media including developing social media policy? Discuss the pros and cons of the two alternatives for moving ahead in social media at James Martin Manufacturing.
2. How should Tonya go about establishing social media policies for James Martin Manufacturing?
3. How should Tonya determine what type of training employees should have on social media use including etiquette and ethics of social media?
4. How should Tonya go about monitoring social media posts that refer to James Martin Manufacturing?

COURSE PROJECTS

1. Draft a social media policy for James Martin Manufacturing. Compare your draft to that of others in the class and discuss the differences in your policies and the content of your policies.
2. Design a process that can help Tonya monitor social media posts that refer to the James Martin Manufacturing Company. Compare your process to that of others in the class and discuss the differences in your processes.
3. Tonya may decide to appoint an employee in James Martin Manufacturing to be responsible for social media. Draft a job description of the responsibilities of the position and describe what qualifications are necessary for an individual to fill the position of social media manager. Compare your job description to that of others in the class and discuss the differences in your job descriptions.

COURSE TEST QUESTIONS

1. The purpose of social media policies is to specify _____.
2. An organization's use of social media accounts and applications to communicate to individuals or groups as well as the mention, comments, discussions, and display of any material

on any social media application that relates to or depicts an organization is known as _____.

3. Before you start using a specific tools you need to evaluate how much control the built features provide and decide _____.

4. How you assign responsibility for social media in your organization is dependent upon _____.

5. When it comes to a company requesting that an employee divulge personal social media activity state laws generally do not prohibit a private company or any employer from requesting that information if _____.

6. By posting their professional information and work experience online employees are working to better themselves in their careers and in their lives, but they are also _____.

7. A company's public image is an asset that needs to be protected just like _____.

8. Social media, as we now know it, can be relatively easy to become involved with, but it also brings with it _____.

9. A company's social media policies should address how and who uses social media on behalf of the company and what constitutes _____.

10. To help avoid unintended consequences of employee personal use of social media, a company should _____.

Key Terms

Social and professional networking websites: are websites that are specially geared for like individuals to communicate with each other as individuals or groups in order to better communicate, facilitate professional connections, seek employment, or hire new staff.

Social media applications: are any existing or future networked computer program that facilitates communication between individuals or individuals and groups.

Social media policies: specify who in an organization is responsible for social media operations; specify when, why, where, and how social media can be used on behalf of an organization;

and provide guidance on the inappropriate use of social media by corporate media staff and employees.

Social media presence: is an organization's use of social media accounts and applications to communicate to individuals or groups, as well as the mention, comments, discussions, and display of any material on any social media application that relates to or depicts an organization.

6

EVALUATING SECURITY
SERVICES AND SECURITY
PRODUCTS

It is likely that all organizations will need to acquire security technologies and perhaps even contracts for security services. This chapter covers methods for evaluating and selecting security products and services, including how to develop a critical review process and who should be included in the review process. Recognize that many security products are brought to market with less than adequate testing of their reliability and effectiveness, which requires buyers to conduct a strong product review during the selection and acquisition process.[38]

Keep in mind that some security products and services can be used effectively to deal with insider threats as well as outsider threats. In those cases, an organization can gain an economy from both types of protection. There are products and services that may be more helpful for dealing with outsider threats more so than they are for dealing with insider threats. The reverse is also true; some products may be more effective in mitigating insider threats than they will be in addressing outsider threats.

6.1 Types of Technology to Protect against Insider Threats

Several types of technology can help maintain the security of corporate information and physical assets. Although the security planning team will not necessarily be responsible for selecting security technology, it will likely set policies and procedures that help establish security requirements and thus determine the selection of various protection technologies. Security planning team members should be aware of what technology can and cannot do to maintain corporate security. The key role of technology is to control access and allow only authorized individuals to view, manipulate, or use information or gain physical access to facilities or assets. Technology that can be used to help maintain security of corporate information and physical assets can be classified into six basic categories:

1. Technology to protect computer-based information
2. Technology to protect data communications
3. Technology to protect voice communications
4. Technology to protect physical copies of information
5. Technology to protect physical assets
6. Technology to protect employees and visitors

It has become obvious over the last several years that computer systems are highly vulnerable to hacking attacks, break-ins, and virus attacks designed to either cripple the systems or to steal information. There have been numerous examples of large quantities of credit card numbers, customer names and addresses, and confidential financial information being stolen by insiders as well as outsider criminals. Once the security of a computer system is breached, the data can be readily compromised.

Each type of computer system has its own strengths and weaknesses, but all are vulnerable to break-ins or data theft, and this makes them potential points of failure in an organization's efforts to protect against insider threats. Because it is not likely that an enterprise can operate without computers and because computers are so vulnerable, the security plan needs to address not only the security of data but also rules and procedures on how computer-based data is stored and used. A security plan needs to address the protection of information in several types of computer technology including the following:

- Enterprise (large) systems most often found in centralized data centers
- Desktop computer systems found throughout an enterprise
- Laptop systems used by employees to access data from remote locations
- Web-based systems including supply chain and extranet applications and websites
- Mobile computing devices and smart phones
- Computer and telecommunications networks
- Data storage and archival systems

There are two primary methods of protecting the security of computer-based information. The first method is to control access to computer-based information, which is a fundamental requirement to ensure that information security is maintained. *Access control for computer systems* is achieved through a variety of means, including rights assigned to individuals and groups of computer users in an organization, password protection of information assets, and a user authentication system used to verify that users are who they claim to be when they are using computer systems. The second method to ensuring the security of computer-based information is to control what individual and groups of users can do with the information to which they have access. Usage is controlled through several means including restricting who can modify, delete, add, move, or manipulate computer-based information.

One of the biggest challenges to effective access management is ensuring that the software products are properly installed, configured, and managed. It is important that the proper training on the software products is provided to information technology staff or other people in the organization that may have some degree of administrative or supervisory responsibility for the network management and access control.

Professional staff installing and managing the software products should be trained and certified as to their skill level. The security planning team or a subcommittee thereof should review the skills and certifications of all staff responsible for network management and access control software products in the organization and make recommendations for additional training if necessary.

A second area of weakness in the use of network management and access control software products is that too many users in the organizations are allowed access to possible sensitive data and information. In the 1990s, the growth in the use of desktop computers (personal computers) in client–server computing environments became more popular and at this time is almost universal. One of the major selling points vendors relied on when marketing the new client–server and desktop solutions was that they provided greater access and usability of data and information. For the last decade we have been going through the same scenario, except this time it has been mobile devices such as tablets, smart phones, and a variety of digital assistants.

The new marketing philosophy was and remains that the more employees could do with data and information, the more productive they could be and the more successful the organization would be in meeting goals and expanding market share. These assertions may be true to some degree, but with greater access and usability of information come greater security threats from insiders.

The increased vulnerability of information stored on computer systems is only one of the weaknesses in technology that organizations now face. The vulnerability and potential compromise of information that is electronically transmitted from one corporate site to another, information transmitted from an organization to a client or customer, and information that is transmitted to and from suppliers or service organizations has also increased. The use of the Internet to move information between organizations and their constituents is very dangerous and increases the potential of compromising security. The use of *virtual private networks* (VPNs) to move data is a safer approach, but it is still not completely secure and presents problems as well.

As the growth of the Internet increased in the 1990s, more organizations as well as individuals started to move data and information between organizations and other people using the Internet. This was done largely without organizations or individuals understanding the process of data transmission or how the Internet differed from private networks. The transmission of sensitive and private information over the Internet in raw text form or in attached word documents or spreadsheets has become commonplace because few people realize how dangerous it can be and how readily information can be compromised.

Unfortunately, most organizations do not have strong policies about how to use the Internet and most employees are not trained on the vulnerabilities of using the Internet for data transmission purposes. The first challenge is determining who is transmitting what types of data, documents, or information. The second challenge is to determine how to change habits and implement new rules or procedures.

Although more people are becoming aware of the security issues surrounding data communications and computer-based information, the security of voice communications is most often taken for granted. People have become so accustomed to using the telephone that they do not think about the need for security or how privacy can be compromised using the telephone. There are numerous dangers lurking in the realm of voice communications. Now, with smart phones and internal wireless telecommunications networks, there is even more vulnerability. Illegal wiretapping, monitoring the use of wireless phone systems, or using scanners to listen in on cellphone calls is very easy to accomplish. A trip to the local electronics store or a visit to a few websites can equip even amateurs with all the technology they need to easily drop in on voice communications.

Securing voice communications between organization locations can be more easily accomplished because both ends of the call are under the control of the organization and voice encryption technology is fairly easy to implement. On top of all of the technical difficulties involved in voice communications security, the biggest challenge is convincing management that voice communications is even worthy of protection. In addition, many companies are now delivering web content and services to users of wireless Internet devices, which is creating an entirely new set of technology challenges.

There are several areas about physical security methods that need to be addressed, including how they protect information and data from unauthorized insider access. The security planning team should focus some energy on reviewing

- Building and facility security procedures and technology
- Security for the long-term storage of physical copies
- The disposal of physical copies
- The disposal of used and obsolete computer equipment
- The disposal of used magnet media such as disks and tapes

Without rigorous security protection, it is very easy to gain access to physical premises and equally as easy to walk away with printed reports and files from almost any office complex. Second, because there is a high volume of paper, it could be weeks and perhaps even months before it is discovered that documents are missing in the case of a security breach. Finally, old records and files, as well as those that are not frequently accessed, are often put in some form of ancillary or off-site storage that may not be as well protected or may have no security at all. This potential combination of circumstances may make customer records and other material very vulnerable to compromise.

As with the management of physical document storage, the disposal of physical records at most organizations is currently very haphazard and is a major point of vulnerability in efforts to protect data and information. Most organizations fill trash containers full of old records assuming that they will be safely hauled to the trash dump and that no one would have an interest in the contents. This is a grievous error. Corporate spies and competitive intelligence analysts know very well that one of the best ways to find out anything about anyone or any company is to go through their trash. This situation is intensifying because identity theft has become a crime that even amateurs can perpetrate using the Internet. The security planning team needs to evaluate record disposal at all organization sites and establish procedures for the proper disposal of paper records.

The disposal of used and *obsolete computer equipment* is also another major weakness in security efforts to prevent insider violations. Old computer equipment is often not operable when it is disposed of and it is often cleared out of corporate premises in bulk and sometimes even given to employees. What often remain intact on old computer equipment are the hard disk drives. Problems arising from the bulk disposition of obsolete equipment are compounded because there is usually not an adequate budget for cleaning disk drives. The disposal of magnetic media is equally as hazardous as the disposal of old computer equipment. The only way to ensure that data and information that is or was on magnetic media are not accessible is to physically destroy the disk or tape.

6.2 Basic Product and Service Selection Wisdom

There are several dynamics that can make product and service acquisition a challenging situation and far too often make it end up a disastrous costly experience. These dynamics between producer or provider and potential customers can be riddled with false promises and unwarranted expectations. When products and service fail to meet the expectation of the buyers, they most often blame the producer or provider, who in many cases should shoulder much of the blame. But there is plenty of blame to go around.

The product manufacturer and service provider are in very competitive fields often facing slim margins and tough sales situations.

Marketing and advertising for products and services is incredibly expensive. Consumers constantly compare companies to one another and strive to pay the least possible during acquisition. It is like a Darwinist jungle where there will be few survivors.

These dynamics push product and service providers to constantly expound on how great they are and how much they can help a company. In the security field, they are claiming that they can keep you safe and that they can keep a company safer than their competitors. So they create very colorful marketing material, brochures, websites, social media applications, and webinars. These materials are designed to make buyers feel good about the product or service. The goal of the marketer is to make buyers feel that they will be safer if they purchase that particular company's product. The marketing material may tell buyers almost nothing about how the product actually works or how well it works.

Once the product or service company has gone through the time and expense of creating its arsenal of marketing material, it is under even more pressure to make sales. The company sends out a team of people to tell buyers about its offerings and to make buyers feel good about purchasing its product. The sales team members are trying to convince buyers that their product will make them safer. They want buyers to feel good about purchasing. Bear in mind that many of these sales folks are trained closers who care about one thing and that is making the sale and earning more money.

The buyer is looking for a product or service to help meet some of their security needs. In many cases, the buyer will have little if any experience with security products. The buyer has a job to do and in this case it may be just to acquire a product or contract for a service. The buying agent for the consumer organization may end up having no responsibility for actually deploying the product or managing the service and will conduct minimal evaluations of the providing company or the security product or service. The sales representatives can sniff out the buying agent's attitude and intentions in a matter of minutes and use that assessment to help them close the sale.

Somewhere in the consumer organization there is pressure to improve security. Without a professional security staff in place to help evaluate products or service providers, the decision makers are often just floundering in the acquisition process. Decision makers are looking for a solution and far too often want an easy way out of a situation they would rather not be involved in. They are looking for a silver bullet, a product offering that promises to solve all of the problems they really do not want to deal with any longer. Decision makers in the acquiring company may also end up having little to do with the deployment of a security product or managing a contract with a service provider.

So the deal is done. It is now up to somebody in the buying organization to deploy a new security product or to integrate a new security service provider into corporate operations. A midlevel management person will probably be assigned to the project. Hopefully, they have experience in service contract management. Regardless, the implementer then has the responsibility to make a success out of the product or service.

As the implementer starts down the road to implementation, they find out that it will take longer and cost more to get the product or service in place and functioning. They may or may not report this to upper management. If they do not report that the lack of resources is impacting deployment, then the projects may just flounder. If they do report that they need more resources than originally allocated based on vendor promises, then they are on the spot. The decision makers in the acquisition do not want to be embarrassed by having made a less than great acquisition.

These dynamics are a dangerous and expensive trap that can have a negative impact on an organization's ability to mitigate security risks for years to come. Do not fall into this trap. It is not necessary. But the only way to avoid the trap is to spend time and resources doing a proper product evaluation and a realistic assessment to determine if the product or service is a good fit for an organization. The assessment should include staffing requirements and other overhead costs to make the product work properly. It should also include a life-cycle plan for the product or service. If a company is really lucky, it may also end up with a realistic return on investment analysis for the product or service.

6.3 Public Sources of Product and Service Evaluation Information

Evaluating security products and services can be an expensive and lengthy process depending on the depth and the scope of an evaluation.

However, before starting a product evaluation division, it is prudent to look at existing sources of product and service evaluations. Taking advantage of evaluations that have already been completed can save a considerable amount of time and money as well as the frustration of having to go through an evaluation.

One of the keys to capitalizing on product or service evaluations conducted by other organizations is to find out who has evaluated what type of technology. There are many government entities that must have security technology and services, and routinely apply relatively thorough evaluation methods before acquiring any products including security products.

Buyers can certainly use a search engine to try to find which government entity is evaluating which technology, but that can be a lengthy process. There is a web portal that specializes in providing search of government entities online material that can save considerable time and money when trying to locate technology product evaluations. The website USA.gov is an interagency product that provides information on government services.

USA.gov is legislatively mandated through Section 204 of the E-Government Act of 2002. Everybody can use the USA.gov search engine to search information from the federal government or all governments that provide searchable information including state and local entities. The service is provided without a fee and has been available since 2001–2002.[39] The search engine lets researchers search numerous relevant sites at one time.

A search of USA.gov yielded several government entities that have evaluation methodology available on their websites, as well as the results of security technology evaluations they have performed in the past. For example, on the federal level, the National Institute of Standards and Technology (NIST) (www.nist.gov) has a Public Safety Portal with a lot of information about security processes. The NIST also provides a Computer Security Resource Center (CSRC) (www.csrc.nist.gov) with helpful information about computer security.

Another federal agency buyers will find helpful is the General Services Administration (GSA), which provides central contract negotiation services for the federal government (www.gsa.gov). The GSA website shows contract and pricing information for thousands of products that may be helpful in product evaluations and the procurement process.

At the state government level, New York's Office of General Services provides procurement and contract negotiation support for public entities in New York state (www.ogs.ny.gov/BU/PC/) and makes copies of contracts and state pricing information available to the public. Several states have similar information available on the Internet, but there is little consistency between states on the extent of data posted and the format the information is packaged. On the local level, King County (Seattle), Washington (www.kingcounty.gov), also provides information on the results of its product evaluations. These are just a few examples of the types of organizations evaluators can find through USA.gov.

There is an economic advantage to taking into consideration the product evaluations that government entities have performed as well as the general evaluation approach recommended in many NIST publications. That economic advantage comes down to cost savings and added evaluation reliability because the governments use structured consistent methods of evaluation.[40] In the past, there have been some private-sector folks who have been rather critical of the government's evaluation approach and general security management abilities. That has subsided because a constant stream of private-sector security breaches clearly demonstrates that the private sector does not do a better job than the public sector when it comes to security.[41]

6.4 Customer Comments and Testimonials about Products and Services

Many people talk or write about their experiences with products or services, and comments abound on social media that may be helpful in some circumstances. This is certainly a good avenue for people to make comments, but the objectivity of these comments is often questionable. Customer comments are becoming an integral aspect of product marketing and evaluation. When considering the comments of product users it is important to recognize that some of those comments may have been posted via surrogates by the manufacturers or sellers of the products. So there can be some question about authenticity.

Second, if customer comments about a product or service are overwhelmingly positive or negative, then the overall comments may not be very helpful. If there are specific details provided in the customer comments, those tidbits may be helpful. The best customer comments are balanced and consider the strengths and weaknesses of a product or of a service provider.

Modern marketers are very skilled at packaging bits and pieces of customer comments with their own testimonials to paint a positive picture of their product or service. Consumers and evaluators should not get distracted by this marketing approach or the marketing material. Marketers have also shown a tendency to present longer videotaped or otherwise documented customer testimonials. Realize that many of these are staged and edited, and should be viewed with at least a bit of skepticism.

It is also important to bear in mind that some customers who may have had a less than good experience with a product or working with a service provider may be critical just because they did a poor job and perhaps underfunded their own efforts in deploying a product. Their criticism can be a way of passing off blame for what was, at least in part, their own failure.

On the other end of the continuum are the really happy customers who have nothing bad to say about a product or anything in life. It is pleasant to be around happy people, but when it comes to taking their input into consideration when making product selections, buyers may find little if any value in that input. Again, the best customer comment is one that is balanced and discusses positive aspects of a product's performance as well as points out weaknesses or problems encountered using the product.

Another source of customer comments and testimonials is the Better Business Bureau (www.bbb.org), which accredits businesses of all types. It may be helpful if there have been complaints a company an organization is considering contracting with for services.

Finally, customer comments and testimonials do not always address the key question being asked when evaluating a product or service: Is the product or service *the right fit* for the organization?

6.5 Input from Application Managers and Users in an Organization

Staff input can be very helpful when evaluating a product or service. Individual staff members may have had experience with a product or its manufacturer. They may have also had experience with a specific service provider or its competitors. Potential purchasers should capitalize on experiences of employees when making a selection.

There is also some built-in bias in staff member's perspectives. Security staff should recognize this and take their biases into consideration. Some staff members want to try new things, whereas others do not want to try new things. Also realize that staff members can reach a point in their careers when they do not want to learn new things. In some cases, staff like to rebel against the mainstream and select products from smaller companies or from start-up companies just to fight back against industry dominance of large players.

One thing that is very important to consider when working with in-house staff is their skill base and competencies. Consider conducting a self-assessment of staff skills and determine if additional training will be required to integrate a new product into ongoing security efforts. Some training will probably be necessary, but ground-up training in a product area can be very expensive.

It is also wise to consider future staffing needs. Will the organization be able to readily recruit staff to manage and maintain the product being considered? The next big issue is whether the product under consideration requires staff that is more expensive than another product. If so, is that cost acceptable to the organization?

6.6 Using a Product or Service Evaluation Company

Potential buyers can hire a consultant to do just about anything, and product and service evaluations are among them. A *product or services evaluation company* specializes in determining if a prospective product or service will perform as necessary in the target environment and meet the objectives for which they are designed. Consultants can bring a wide range of experiences to in-house technology evaluation efforts. Bear in mind, these consultants can have just as many built-in biases as anybody and some will have a conflict of interest because of their financial relationship with companies that produce the technology that is being considered for purchase and deployment to improve security.

The range of services potential buyers can get from consultants is probably unlimited, but if they are hiring a consultant they are likely trying to address a problem for which they do not have in-house expertise. For example, testing the capability of the technology that has been put in place to protect information most often involves intrusion testing. Most organizations contract out for intrusion testing to a reputable computer security company. This testing can be fairly expensive with prices ranging from $5,000 to $500,000 depending on what types of systems are involved. In addition, or if budgets do not allow for intrusion testing, the security planning team should review the security logs for the last 12 months to determine any trends and identify potential weaknesses in technology that is already in place.

The ideal situation with a consulting firm would be that it has staff with experience with a range of security products and it can readily provide product comparisons and information about the experience its clients have had with a product or service. If potential buyers can find a consultant they are comfortable working with, this could help save the organization both time and money.

Consulting firms may also be able to help test for weaknesses in corporate security policies and procedures and do so more objectively than an in-house staffer who has been involved in security efforts. Testing of security weaknesses needs to be done in several major areas. The first area is to test the strength of the information security unit by presenting it with questions from an end user to determine both how good the support is that it provides as well as if the questions reveal information about security that they should not. The second area of testing is end-user compliance with procedures and end-user security habits. A third area of testing covers actual conditions and the capability of the technology in place to protect information.

Potential buyers can benefit from having consultants help them with security planning and product selection, but they must keep control of the relationship. Keep in mind that consultants make more money the more hours they can bill an organization for, and they will try to increase that number of hours as much as possible. Be sure that managers know what they want from a consultant before they end up overspending on services that are not directly related to their security goals.

6.7 Evaluation of a Security Product to Protect against Insider Threats

Product evaluations are an important part of all security efforts designed to prevent insider attacks. Product evaluations can be as complicated as potential buyers want them to be, but they can also be rather straightforward depending on an organization's security requirements.

If an organization does face legal or contractual security requirements, it will save time if it adopts products that are a standard for an industrial sector. The basic question is what the de facto standards in the industry are, and that is not difficult to ascertain. Just look at what other organizations facing the same requirement have deployed. If potential buyers do not face rigid security requirements, then the range of products they may select from will probably be wider and the products more competitive.

In keeping with the spirit of practicality, just start out slowly and be as thorough as possible. The first step is to gather what information there is available from relevant standards organizations, agencies, or associations that have already conducted evaluations; in-house staff; and their professional network.

Once potential buyers have the basic information in front of them, and staff has been assigned to review what has been collected, then it is time to see if a quick but good decision can be made about the products under consideration. As a self-assessment step, answer the following questions:

- Is there a clear *industry leader* among the products under consideration?
- Are the alternatives to the leader just as capable of protecting an organization from insider attacks?
- Is the acquisition price something the organization finds acceptable?
- Is the ongoing usage and maintenance cost acceptable?
- Does the organization have the capability of deploying the product in-house?

If the leading product has a good reputation, the costs are acceptable, and buyers can readily deploy the product with in-house staff or with minimum consulting or installation fees, then select the leading product and move forward. Now bear in mind that numerous people will not agree with this conclusion. Some people just overprocess; it is part of their nature. Other people just like to make projects larger than they need to be and will spend endless time and money if they are allowed.

If there is not a clear leader or if the price of the leading product is not acceptable, then potential buyers have more work to do before they make a decision. At this point they need to conduct a side-by-side comparison of functionality. It is important to stay focused on what the deployment of the product is meant to accomplish and not get distracted by bells and whistles that do not contribute to accomplishing the main goal. Also keep in mind that many software-driven products eventually incorporate functionalities they do not have today in their future releases of the product. If possible, acquire a road map that shows future product direction from the product manufacturer.

The key questions at this point are, does one product stand out over the other, and is the acquisition price acceptable? If there is a standout product, then select it and move on to another project. If there is not a clear standout, consider asking the manufacturers for a free trial. The trial process can help staff learn more about the product and how well it is actually suited for the environment. The trial process does take time and will have costs associated with the trial for installation, staff training if necessary, and deinstallation if an organization decides not to deploy the product.

If staff is running a trial on the product, it should get input from the users and from the application or product manager that are involved in the trial. This input, though not necessarily definitive, can help to make a decision on product selection.

The key advice here is to be thorough to the point that everybody reaches a comfort level with the product. However, if the team members get hung up on the selection decision for a long period of time, they are probably overprocessing and should consider having fresh eyes look at the situation and help with the decision. Avoid pain if possible and by all means do not waste time and money. A sample checklist for product selection derived from a model established by the U.S. Combating Terrorism Technical Support Office (CTTSO)[42] is shown in Figure 6.1.

Sample security product selection checklist		
Selection criteria	**Yes**	**No**
Product meets the stated requirements.	Yes	No
Product has multiple users (U.S. government or commercial).	Yes	No
Cost has been analyzed and is acceptable.	Yes	No
Performance has been successful in similar environments.	Yes	No
Producer has demonstrated ability to deliver products within budget and on schedule.	Yes	No
Product approach is feasible, achievable, and complete.	Yes	No
In-house technical team has expertise and experience to manage product.	Yes	No
Deliverables and products are clearly defined and will meet the requirement.	Yes	No
Technical risks and mitigation are defined and reasonable.	Yes	No

Figure 6.1   Sample security product selection checklist.

6.8 Evaluation of a Security Service to Protect against Insider Threats

Many of the same questions and criteria used to evaluate security products to guard against insider threats will apply to evaluating a security service. These services could include surveillance systems and support, alarm services, security guards, and even security evaluation services. The main difference consumer organizations face when evaluating services is that they need to pay special attention to the quality of the service provider and its employees.

In most cases, it is very important to be sure that a potential service provider has an excellent reputation and that its employees hold the proper certifications and licenses required by the state. A sample checklist for security service selection derived from a model established by the CTTSO[43] is shown in Figure 6.2.

It is important to note that security guards are licensed in many states and there are minimum requirements set for security guard training. New York, for example, has several requirements in place. For unarmed security guards, the state requires an eight-hour preassignment training course, which is a general introductory course. In addition,

Sample security service selection checklist		
Selection criteria	**Yes**	**No**
Service meets the stated requirements.	Yes	No
Service has multiple users (U.S. government or commercial).	Yes	No
Cost has been analyzed and is acceptable.	Yes	No
Service delivery has been successful in similar environments.	Yes	No
Provider has demonstrated ability to deliver services within budget and on schedule.	Yes	No
Service approach is feasible, achievable, and complete.	Yes	No
In-house technical team has expertise and experience to manage services when necessary.	Yes	No
Services are clearly defined and will meet the requirement.	Yes	No
Services risks and mitigation are defined and reasonable.	Yes	No
Service provider conducts background checks on employees.	Yes	No
Service provider properly supervises its employees.	Yes	No
Service provider ensures licenses and certifications are current.	Yes	No
Service provider has acceptable response time to incidents if necessary.	Yes	No

Figure 6.2   Sample security service selection checklist.

the state requires 16 hours of on-the-job training (OJT) that is relevant to the duties of guards, requirements of the work site, and the needs of the employer. The state of New York also requires eight hours of annual in-service training.

For armed security guards, the state of New York requires an eighthour preassignment training course, which is a general introductory course, and 16 hours of OJT that is relevant to the duties of guards, requirements of the work site, and the needs of the employer. For armed security guards, the state also requires 47 hours of firearms training and that the armed guard posses a valid New York State Pistol Permit and have security guard registration to enroll in the firearms course necessary to obtain the permit. The state of New York also requires eight hours of annual in-service training and eight hours of firearms training every year. Waivers are available to eligible retired police officers.[43] Several other states have similar requirements.

Note that some states post disciplinary actions taken against security companies for noncompliance with state regulations. This is a good thing to check on when considering hiring a security guard service. Reputable firms should not have any disciplinary actions against them, and those firms that have repeated disciplinary actions should be employed with greater caution.

In New York state, a security alarm company and individual alarm installer must be licensed to install, service, or maintain security or fire alarm systems to detect intrusion, break-in, movement, sound, or fire. Security alarm installers must be at least 18 years old, complete 81 hours of qualifying education, and pass an alarm installer examination. Individuals can be disqualified for certain criminal convictions.[44] Several other states have similar requirements.

6.9 Summary

This chapter examined the process of evaluating security products and security services prior to acquisition. Background is provided on the type of security products or services an organization may be considering to protect against insider breaches. It also provided checklists that can be helpful in the evaluation process. Key areas covered include the following:

- The types of technology needed to secure an organization from insider violations
- The types of computer technologies that are vulnerable to insider breaches
- The need for securely disposing electronic media and sensitive paper documents
- The challenges of acquiring good security products and services
- Sources of information for evaluating security products and services
- Straightforward methods to evaluate security products and services

COURSE CASE STUDY   THE JAMES MARTIN
MANUFACTURING COMPANY (CONTINUED)

Tonya Martin recently become CEO of the James Martin Manufacturing Company, a privately owned company that had been in her family for over 80 years. When her father, James Martin Jr., developed health problems about 10 years earlier, he entrusted the company operations to long-time manager Harold Smith, who died a sudden death a few months earlier. Upon review, Tonya had discovered that Harold Smith had been embezzling and stealing equipment and supplies from the company for the last decade before his death.

To assess and work to improve security, Tonya has been working with Ronald Thomas, the new director of security (DOS), and Samuel Davis, a new hire with experience in a similar company. Tonya, Ronald Thomas, and Samuel Davis have decided they need to start getting other people involved in promoting and improving security. They understood that because there had been such a lack of security over the last few years that suddenly cracking down on security could be a shock to the employees of the company. They also believed that there was knowledge and talent among the employees that could be leveraged to help promote security and monitor compliance with security procedures. Tonya wanted to add people to the security team. She did not have the resources to hire a dozen security guards, but she felt that she needed to find a few people who could help keep an eye on James Martin Manufacturing facilities.

The three security team members agreed they should have more rigid access control for the computer network, the computers, and the data on the network. There was an access control program on the main server, but it had not been updated for several years. Tonya also wanted a new surveillance system, because the existing system was very outdated and did not cover as much of the facility that DOS Ronald Thomas thought should be covered.

COURSE DISCUSSION QUESTIONS

1. How should Tonya go about recruiting more people to help improve security and start training employees on the value of security toward the sustainability of James Martin Manufacturing?
2. What are the pros and cons of installing new access control software? Should James Martin Manufacturing staff first evaluate the overall condition and status of the computer systems and the network?
3. What are the pros and cons of installing a new surveillance system at James Martin Manufacturing? Should the system just be installed or should there be some employee orientation on the system?
4. At this point in the process, do you think that Tonya should hire an outside security consultant? Discuss the pros and cons of hiring outside advisers.

COURSE PROJECTS

1. Research the major functionality of access control systems for computer networks and computer systems. Create a 10-slide PowerPoint presentation for the class discussing your findings.
2. Research closed-circuit surveillance systems and develop an understanding of how they work. Create a 10-slide PowerPoint presentation for the class discussing your findings.
3. Create a one-page flyer that can be distributed to employees and covers some of the security issues at James Martin Manufacturing. Your focus should be on how much security can help the company, but do not reveal any details about Tonya's security work and her specific ideas to improve security.
4. Design a briefing for potential employees that may be recruited to improve security vigilance and security performance. Create a 10-slide PowerPoint presentation explaining the need for security at James Martin Manufacturing that can support an open discussion with select employees.

COURSE TEST QUESTIONS

1. A process that either allows or disallows individual users to have access to specific computer applications and computer data sets, including what the user is allowed to do on the systems with their level of access is known as _____.
2. A company or organization that performs better than its competitors bringing innovations to its field of endeavor and whose products or services become the industry standard to match or beat in open market competition is known as an _____.
3. Any computer equipment that can no longer provide any functionality in an organization's current computing environment because of the system's architecture or the inability to run current computer applications in an adequate manner is known as _____.
4. A term that refers to the compatibility of a product or service with its target organization and technology environment is a _____.
5. The key role of technology in security systems is to _____.
6. One of the biggest challenges to effective access management of computer systems is to _____.
7. The website USA.gov is an interagency product that _____.
8. When evaluating the comments of users about products, you are considering for acquisition it is important to _____.
9. When selecting products for your security efforts that are designed to prevent insider attacks, it is important that you conduct _____.
10. Part of the cost of using security products on a trial basis is that you _____.

Key Terms

Access control for computer systems: is a process that either allows or disallows individual users to have access to specific computer applications and computer data sets, including what the user is allowed to do on the systems with their level of access.

Industry leader: is a company or organization that performs better than its competitors, bringing innovations to its field of endeavor, and whose products or services become the industry standard to match or beat in open market competition.

Obsolete computer equipment: is any computer equipment that can no longer provide any functionality in an organization's current computing environment because of the system's architecture or the inability to run current computer applications in an adequate manner.

Product or service evaluation company: is a consulting firm that helps you evaluate products and determine if a specific product or service will perform in your environment to help meet the objectives for which they are designed.

The right fit: is a term that refers to the compatibility of a product or service with its target organization and technology environment.

Virtual private networks: are computer networks that control access of authorized users and keep unauthorized users from accessing the network or any computer system on the network.

7

ESTABLISHING AN IDENTIFICATION PROGRAM FOR EMPLOYEES, BUSINESS PARTNERS, CUSTOMERS, AND OTHER VISITORS

This chapter covers the basics on how to establish an identification system for all of the people working in a company's facilities and the people that may be entering those facilities as contractors or service personnel. It also examines how to determine who should be responsible for managing and operating the identification systems. An identity program and physical access management systems will help ensure that the right individual has access to the right resources when they need them.[45]

7.1 The Role of Identification Systems in Controlling Insider Access

Identification (ID) systems are developed for people, vehicles, machines, computing devices, boats, planes, trains, and about anything that exists. Many of these things need to be properly identified and tracked to ensure company facilities are appropriately secured. This chapter will focus on developing, implementing, and maintaining ID systems for people.

ID systems and *access control systems* are most effective in controlling insider activity when they are integrated. ID systems play an important role in managing and monitoring an insider's *authorized physical access* to an organization's property, buildings, and areas of buildings to which an employee has access to perform his or her job duties. The access is authorized by managers who assign an employee to various functional divisions or projects.

Generally speaking, an employee will be assigned to work in specific areas and access is authorized after appropriate background checks are conducted and security clearance levels are determined. Background checks are usually managed by the human resources department or the security office. A *physical access control system* is used to allow the employee to enter the designated physical areas, but prevents the employee from entering areas to which they have not been designated to have access.[46]

ID systems also have an important role in managing and monitoring an insider's *authorized logical access* to an organization's computer systems, computer applications, and communications functions that an employee has to access to perform their job duties. Again, this access is authorized by the employing organization and is determined by managers who assign an employee to various functional divisions or projects.

Generally speaking, an employee will be allowed access to the computer services they need to perform their duties but will not have access to other computer services. Even when authorized to access specific computer services, the employee's activities can still be limited by restricting user rights and limiting what they can do with computer services. The *logical access control system* will help manage the employee's access rights.[47]

To have an effective ID system for insiders, organizations must first authenticate the ID of the person for whom they are creating ID credentials for, such as photographic ID cards or other ID devices the person will use to pass through a physical access control system. In the United States, employers are required to only employ individuals who can legally work in the United States, including U.S. citizens and foreign citizens who have required authorization.[48]

The Citizenship and Immigration Services Division of the Department of Homeland Security (DHS) provides a free Internet-based service for properly verifying an individual's right to work in the United States. *E-Verify* allows businesses to determine the eligibility of their employees to work in the United States. The E-Verify system is relatively easy to use. An employee or potential employee completes Form I-9, Employment Eligibility Verification (https://www.uscis.gov/i-9) and the employer enters the individual's information into the E-Verify website (https://www.uscis.gov/e-verify/).[49]

Once the information has been entered, E-Verify makes a comparison of the information the employee provided to records available to DHS, which includes U.S. passport and visa information, immigration and naturalization records, state-issued driver's licenses and identity document information as well as U.S. Social Security Administration records. If there are no discrepancies, the E-Verify system provides an employment authorization. If the information cannot be matched, there is a tentative nonconfirmation result issued.[49]

Once an employee's identity has been verified and employment eligibility has been established, then an organization can process any necessary internal paperwork and issue an official corporate ID to the individual. The employee ID can then be used to allow access to physical facilities or, if applicable, logical systems. The IDs are usually issued by the human resources department, security office, or in cases where there are hundreds and even thousands of employees there may be a special office established to issue ID cards/badges.

7.2 Obtaining Equipment for Creating Photo ID Cards and Badges

There are many things to take into consideration when selecting ID cards and ID badges for use in company security systems. First and above all are what kinds of physical access control systems are now in place and what types of systems are being planned for implementation within the next few years. This decision should be made as an integral part of an insider security plan so that organizations can ensure that their ID system will support physical access control systems that are needed to achieve the desired level of security.

There are several components to a basic ID system including cameras, printers, scanners, and smart chips. However, the ID system selection need not be as complicated as it sounds. There are not many organizations that handcraft a do-it-yourself ID system anymore because it takes considerable time and expense to purchase and integrate the various components. Fortunately, the ID system business has been rather brisk since it has become an integral part of national security systems. In addition, many companies that are in the critical industry sectors are implementing a level of security in keeping with government programs and initiatives.

There are several ID system vendors that offer end-to-end ID systems that will integrate with physical access control system technology. These vendors can also provide support and maintenance services for ID systems as well future upgrades to keep the systems up-to-date and fully functional. There are also numerous equipment manufacturers that produce equipment to support ID systems as well as suppliers who specialize in ID systems products. Many of these companies are listed in Figure 7.1.

Manufactures and suppliers of ID system products		
3M Cogent	Fujitsu America	National Laminating
90meter	Fulcrum Biometrics	nCipher
ActivIdentity	Futronic Technology	Oberthur Technologies
Advanced Card Systems	Galaxy Control Systems	Observint Technologies
Alcor Micro Corp	Gallagher	Open Options LP
Algorithmic Research	Gemalto	Outpac Designs
American Greenwood	Genetec	Precise Biometrics
Ascertia Limited	Giesecke & Devrient	Quantum Secure
Athena Smartcard	Global Enterprise Technologies	Quintron Systems
Aware	Green Bit Americas	RS2 Technologies
Axway	Hewlett-Packard Company	RSA Security
BearingPoint	HID Global	Safenet
Belkin International	Hirsch	SecuEra Technologies
Bell ID	Honeywell	SecuGen Corporation
BIO-key International	IAM Technology	Secure Network Systems
Biometrika srl	ID Intelligence	SETECS
Brady People ID	Identity Stronghold	SMK-Link Electronics
BridgePoint Systems	Entrypoint	STARTEK Engineering
Brivo,	Identiv	Stenua Suprema
Bundesdruckerei GmbH	Identix	Symantec
CENTECH Group	ImageWare Systems	Technology Industries
Charismathics	Information Packaging	TecSec
Chase Corporation	Innometriks	Thales e-Security
ZF CHERRY	Integrated Biometrics	The Will-Burt Company
Cherry Electrical Products	Integrated Energy Limited	Thursby Software Systems
Chicony Electronics	IOGEAR	TRINITY TAPES PVT
Codebench	ITALDATA ingegneria dellidea	TrustBearer Labs
Cogent Systems	S.p.A.	Tumbleweed Communications
CoreStreet	Johnson Controls	Tyco Security Products
Creative Information	Key Ovation	Ultra Electronics Card System
Technology	Key Source International	Union Community
Cross Match Technologies	Laminex	UPEK
Cyber Armed Security	Lenovo	UTC Fire & Security
Daon	Liska Biometry	Utimaco Safeware AG
DAQ Electronics	Lockheed Martin	Veridt
Datacard Group	Logic First	VeriSign
DataStrip	Lumidigm	Viisage Technology
Dell	Matica Technologies	Viscount
DERMALOG Identification	MaxID	Viscount Systems
Systems GmbH	Monitor Dynamics	West TX Lighthouse
DigitalPersona	MorphoTrak	for the Blind
Edgeline Technologies	MorphoTrust USA	XTEC
EK Ekcessories	Motorola Solutions	XTec
Entrust Datacard	Muhlbauer	Zebra Technologies
Entrust		Zvetco Biometrics LLC

Figure 7.1   Manufacturers and suppliers of ID system products.

The basic components of an ID system will vary depending on how sophisticated the system needs to be to meet company security needs. For a simple system, organizations will need a digital camera, workstation with ID systems software for making ID card and badges, and a printer for producing the IDs. Companies like AlphaCard® (www.alphacard.com) and Entrust Datacard® (www.entrustdatacard.com) can provide individuals components as well as entire ID systems. These two suppliers have very useful information pamphlets that can help companies get started selecting and deploying an ID system for the first time or replacing an existing ID system.

More sophisticated systems can produce ID cards/badges with smart chips, bar codes, and one of the latest additions to ID systems, RFID tags, or other trackable technology. The systems are relatively easy to use because so much of the work is automated through the ID system software. Of course, the computer where the ID system software resides can be password protected to help prevent unauthorized use and the production of unauthorized ID cards/badges. It is still advisable for the production of ID cards/badges to be audited on occasion to ensure that unauthorized ID cards/badges were not produced.

7.3 Deploying an Appropriate ID Management System

The sophistication of installed physical access control systems varies widely, as does the sophistication of ID systems that help manage authorized access and prevent unauthorized access to facilities or systems. So unless a company already has state-of-the-art ID systems and physical access control systems in place, it needs to do serious long-term planning to keep its systems synchronized so that it can better provide security for company facilities.

A self-assessment process is helpful in determining what direction to go in and what level of security is needed to accomplish with an ID systems and physical access control systems. This is an important process because organizations can save money or at least make sure they are getting their money's worth out of the systems they have in place or they are planning. Keep in mind that there is very little utility gained when a company has a highly sophisticated ID system and cannot maximize the benefits it provides because its physical access control systems have not been updated since it was installed back in the dark ages. The reverse is true as well. Start a self-assessment by answering the following questions:

- Is the current ID system and physical access control systems integrated or interdependent?
- If the systems are integrated or interdependent, then assess both systems simultaneously and develop a road map for migration or upgrades. (Physical access control systems are covered in Chapter 8.)
- If the systems are not integrated or interdependent but the security plan calls for them to be in the future, then assess both systems simultaneously and develop a road map for migration or upgrades.
- If the systems are not integrated or interdependent and there is not a need for them to be in the future, then proceed in selecting an ID system.

What information does the security team want ID cards or badges to display or have bar coded or in chips? The security team needs to make sure that the ID system selected will meet all of the needs. Not all systems will do all things, but companies do not need to spend money on a system that has features they do not need to support their security efforts. Start a self-assessment by answering the following questions:

- Will the proposed system provide adequate photographic capabilities?
- Is the proposed system upgradable?
- Is the proposed system scalable?
- Does the proposed system have a clear migration path to future systems?

What is the anticipated routine volume for producing ID cards/badges as well as for any expected special events or unusual circumstances for which ID cards or badges will be needed? When selecting a system be sure to

- Take volume into consideration because if a system cannot meet routine demand, then there will end up being a bottleneck.
- Not buy a system that has a capacity that far exceeds needs because that means spending money unnecessarily.

Will the supplier or manufacturer provide an organization with the level of support and maintenance service that the proposed system will require over its life cycle? Start a self-assessment by answering the following questions:

- If the supplier or manufacturer of the proposed system does not provide maintenance and support, is there another vendor that can meet such needs?
- Is the cost of the maintenance and/or support package acceptable to the organization?
- Is the supplier or manufacturer able to provide the necessary supplies for continued use of the system?
- If the supplier or manufacturer is not able to provide the necessary supplies for continued use of the system, are there multiple other vendors who can provide the supplies?

Will the proposed system require training staff for its day-to-day care and operation? Start a self-assessment by answering the following questions:

- Does the supplier or manufacturer have a help line to call if staff encounters problems with the system?
- If training is required, can the supplier or manufacturer provide that training?
- If the supplier or manufacturer does not provide training, is there another readily available source of training?
- Is the cost of any required training acceptable to the organization?

Once the security team has worked through the assessment process and thinks it has selected an appropriate ID system for the organization, then it is prudent to have the proposal reviewed by the department managers in the organization who are in some way involved in managing identity verification and ID card/badge production and utilization. This step can be tricky in that people view the world very differently at times. Consider the following questions:

- Do the ID system administrators and users like or dislike the proposed system?
- If the ID system administrators and users like the proposed system, why do they like it?
- If the ID system administrators and users do not like the proposed system, why do they not like it?
- Does the proposed system present new challenges for ID system administrators and users? If yes, then are the ID system administrators and users embracing the new challenges? If no, what concerns ID system administrators and users about the proposed system?

The important thing about selecting an ID system is that it meets the immediate needs and can meet the anticipated needs through the life cycle of the system. Companies will get better results if all of the people that work with an ID system or are dependent on the ID management in some way are comfortable with the system. It is also helpful if the impacted people in the organization are supportive of the system and correctly follow documented procedures for the system's usage.

7.4 Developing ID Card/Badge Policies for Employees

If a company uses ID cards or badges, it should have policies that dictate how, when, where, and why they are to be used. A review of several policies across the United States showed that there is a great deal of consistency in ID card/badge policies. Written policies often start with an explanation of the purpose of the policy. A sample *ID card/badge policy purpose and scope statement* derived from the review of several public entity ID card/badge policies is shown in Figure 7.2.

It is important to be as specific as possible when setting policies for employees to wear their ID card/badges. A sample *ID card/badge*

Sample purpose and scope statement for ID card/badge policies

PURPOSE: The purpose of the identification badge policy is:

- To enhance the company's mission of providing high-quality public service
- To provide standards and requirements for the display of identification
- To provide a consistent method of identification
- To provide an additional means of establishing a safe work place for employees
- To provide a safe environment to conduct business

SCOPE: This policy applies to all employees (including full-time, permanent part-time, part-time and temporary) and contracted service providers while on company property, and/or while conducting business on behalf of the company off of company property.

POLICY STATEMENT: It is the policy of the company that employees and the public be provided with the highest quality service in the safest possible environment while conducting business. To that end, all persons working or conducting business on company property and/or in the community will adhere to the identification standards.

Figure 7.2   Sample purpose and scope statement for ID card/badge policies.

display policy was derived from the review of several public entity ID card/badge display policy is shown in Figure 7.3. There does appear to be a consensus among organizations that issue ID cards/badges that the official policy is that employees will wear the card/badges at any time they are in a company facility.

7.5 Developing ID Management Policies for Frequent Visitors

An organization probably has some visitors to its facilities that visit frequently. These could include representatives and employees of contractors, representatives and employees of business partners or customers, the printer repair person, janitorial service employees, or HVAC repair contractors to name a few. It may be possible to cover all such visitors with one ID card/badge policy, or security planners may elect to have specific policies for different classes of visitors. The security planners and security team may also want policies for emergency medical teams or first responders of various types. However, they should coordinate those policies with local first responders and be

Sample ID card/badge display policy for employees
All company employees will display their photo ID card/badge at all times while on company property. Requests for exemption to this requirement shall be made to the Director of Security and the Vice President of Operations.
Display of the ID card/badge cannot be obscured by jackets or other outerwear.
If an employee changes their appearance such as hair color, dramatic change in hair style, or facial hair, they should request a new photo for their ID card/badge.
Employees may use judgment in deciding whether to wear their photo ID card/badge while conducting official business that is not on company property.
Badges will be provided by the company and will prominently show the employee's photo, the employees name, the company name, and logo.
If an employee has lost or misplaced their photo ID card/badge, they will report the incident to the director of security immediately during the work day and within 24 hours on a nonwork day.
Employees will not lend their ID card/badge to any person for any reason.
Employees should not bend, fold, insert holes, or modify or damage their ID card/badge.
Repeat violations of the ID card/badge display policies will result in disciplinary action.

Figure 7.3   Sample ID card/badge display policy for employees.

as accommodating as possible with those who come to help employees or protect facilities.

A generalized purpose and scope statement for ID cards/badges policies will probably suffice in most instances unless special circumstances dictate otherwise. However, visitors should be required to adhere to an organization's ID card/badge policy and violations should be taken seriously. If the visitor is employed by a contractor or service provider, then any violations should be reported to their employer. A sample ID card/badge display policy for frequent visitors derived from the review of several public entity visitor ID card/badge display policies is shown in Figure 7.4.

Many organizations that employee contractors on a regular and repeat basis have rather strict policies and procedures for contractor employees who work on company property. In some cases, all persons performing duties under service contracts are required to complete a

Sample ID card/badge display policy for frequent visitors
All visitors to company facilities are required to sign in at the front desk and will be provided with a visitor ID card/badge.
All visitors to company facilities are required to display their visitor ID card/badge at all times while on company property. Requests for exemption to this requirement shall be made to the Director of Security and the Vice President of Operations.
Display of the ID card/badge cannot be obscured by jackets or other outerwear.
Visitors in designated areas must have a company employee escort them at all times.
All visitors are required to stay in the areas in which they are performing work or meeting with company employees unless escorted by a company employee.
If a visitor loses or misplaces their ID card/badge, they will report the incident to their escort or to the front desk.
Repeat violations of the ID card/badge, display policies will result in the violating visitor not being allowed in company facilities or on company property.
Visitors employed by company contractors or service providers who violate ID card/badge policies will have all incidents reported to their employer.

Figure 7.4   Sample ID card/badge display policy for frequent visitors.

security screening by local law enforcement agencies at the expense of the contractor. They also must provide a social security card or passport as well as copies of their driver's license. Some companies will request information about where else the contractor's staff works and the security checks they have had to work in those facilities.

In some cases, the contractor's employees are issued photo ID cards/badges by the company at which they are performing a service. All ID card/badge policies and procedures in place at the host company often apply to contractors and their employees. The ID cards/badges remain the property of the issuing company and must be returned on demand to a designated person or office at the host company. In other cases, the host company can also reject a contractor's employee if they

- Have felony convictions
- Have convictions for crimes of moral turpitude
- Show a pattern of criminal behavior

- Demonstrate patterns of antisocial behavior
- Have convictions for illegal immigrant smuggling
- Have any unresolved warrants or are under investigation for suspected crimes
- Have other unresolved legal issues
- Have had restraining orders issued against them

7.6 Developing ID Management Policies for One-Time or Infrequent Visitors

The policies for issuing ID cards/badges to employees and how those ID devices are managed is often tied to levels or areas of access that an employee who has had appropriate background checks for and has been granted clearance to access. Frequent visitors such as contractors or their employees may have also been subject to some sort of background check and clearance process. In these situations, the ID cards/badges are expected to support an organization's business processes over a long period of time.

The one-time visitor or very infrequent visitor may not be subject to extensive background checks and is not expected to be on the premises for any extended period of time. Thus their ID card/badge will be issued only on a very temporary basis. The ID cards/badges issued to them should clearly reflect their status in relationship to the organization. This can be achieved by adding the word "visitor" or color-coding the ID cards/badges.

There should still be a procedure where the one-time visitor is checked in through reception or security, and their personal photo ID information recorded or copied. These visitors are generally under full-time escort while on the premises. A visitor policy is shown in Figure 7.5.

7.7 Developing ID Card/Badge Issuance Procedures for Employees and Frequent Visitors

All organizations should have written procedures covering the issuance of ID cards/badges to employees and frequent visitors. The procedures should cover every aspect of the issuance process and identify who in the organization is responsible for each step in the process. In

Sample visitor ID card/badge and admittance policy
Visitors may be admitted during normal business hours.
All visitors must sign in with the security officer at the desk upon arrival and be issued a visitor ID badge.
The visitor will return the visitor badge to the security desk when departing the building for the day.
The visitor must provide the security officer with valid photo identification and the name of the employee or department being visited. Valid identification may be a driver's license, employer identification, or other picture ID.
Family members may be admitted, but must be escorted at all times while on the premise so they do not disrupt business.
Visitor(s) will be issued a one-day visitor badge.
Escorts must sign the visitor log, provide their internal phone number, and verify the purpose of the visit.
Escorts must also record the destination within the building(s) where the visitor is allowed.
Escorts are required to remain with the visitor for the duration of the visit.
IMPORTANT: Visitors must wear their visitor badge on their outer garment, above the waist, at all times while in company facilities.

Figure 7.5 Sample visitor ID card/badge and admittance policy.

addition, all ID card/badge issuances should be recorded along with any supporting or relevant information.

A review of ID card/badge issuance procedures across organizations showed that the procedures were custom written for a specific organization with numerous references to offices or departments that have a role in the issuance process. There are, however, several commonalities in procedure content. So instead of drafting a procedure out of context, a checklist of what an ID card/badge issuance procedure should contain makes more sense. The following list breaks down actions and responsibilities by who is executing the various steps in the ID card/badge issuance procedure:

- Procedures should specify what an employee is responsible for when getting an ID card/badge from the organization, including any necessary personal identification items needed

by processors, all forms the employee should fill out, any signatures or permissions the employee should obtain, as well as
when and where an employee should go to process the request
for an ID card/badge.

- Procedures should specify what department or office is
  responsible for ID card/badge issuance along with its location
  and hours of operation.
- Procedures should also specify what kind of forms the issuance office requires and what type of records the issuance
  office should keep regarding the issuance of every ID card/
  badge.
- Procedures should specify what, if any, role the security
  department has in the issuance process, including all forms
  that should be reviewed, checked, or signed, and what information the security department should have on file regarding
  each ID card/badge.
- There should be detailed steps on what an employee does
  when and if they lose or misplace their company-issued ID
  card/badge.
- There should be detailed steps on what all departments or
  offices should do when an employee reports a lost or mis-
  placed company-issued ID card/badge.

When writing procedures covering processes like ID card/badge
issuance, it is best to leave nothing to chance. The procedure should
explain very strict structured steps to be taken during the process and
specify who in the organization is responsible for which step or action.

7.8 Photo ID Card/Badge Design

Each organization can, within the limits of its ID card/badge technology, determine what it wants the ID cards/badges to look like.
Everything from the color of the card to the location of the photo and
the specific information that a card will display or have bar coded or
embedded in a smart chip should be specified.

The design of the ID cards/badges should be uniform at least to
the facility level if not across the entire organization. A photo or dia-
gram of the authorized ID card/badge design should be kept at every

security checkpoint and functional offices to ensure that employees are familiar with the authorized design so that they can better spot a forged card.

An ID card/badge design is dependent on many factors. First, the design and the information contained on an ID card/badge must be adequate to support physical access control mechanisms. The more automated and complex the physical access control system, the more complex the ID card/badge. On the other hand, if there is a simple physical access control system, such as a security guard that checks IDs as people transit in and out of a facility, then a simple ID card/badge should suffice. There will be more discussion of ID card/badge requirements in Chapter 8, which covers access control systems. The basic components of ID card/badge design include the following:

- Single-sided or double-sided cards/badges
- Monotone or full-color printed features
- Embossed designs
- Holographic features for validation
- Magnetic stripe containing pertinent information
- Contact chip or contactless chip containing pertinent information

Depending on the design components of the ID card/badge and the functionality of a company's physical access control system, an ID card/badge workstation with appropriate printers and scanners and storage to manage direct-to-card transfer of photos and encoded information will be required. There is also the option of capturing information in a database for future use or for verification in physical access control systems, including an employee's photo, signature, biometric data, and personal data. ID management staff may also want to laminate the ID cards/badges to make them longer lasting.

It is convenient to utilize a photo ID card/badge color scheme to help immediately differentiate key characteristics of the ID card/badge holder. The National Aeronautics and Space Administration (NASA) has an interesting color scheme that reflects the international character of the organization's work.[50] An organization may have several types of visitors that security would like to immediately make recognizable by adding a color scheme to the ID card/badge design. The basic NASA ID card/badge color scheme includes the following:

- Gold NASA photo ID—Issued to civil service personnel and is accepted for access to all NASA centers, as appropriate.
- Gold NASA photo ID with flag—Issued only to active members of the NASA Astronaut Corps. Astronauts are issued badges according to their citizenship. Foreign national members of the Astronaut Corps have a representation of their national flag superimposed on the badge.
- Blue NASA photo ID—Issued to NASA grantees, research associates, vendors, construction workers, and consultants.
- Blue NASA with "IP A" photo ID—Issued upon approval to foreign nationals under the Intergovernmental Personnel Management Act.
- Blue NASA with "NAC" photo ID—Issued only by NASA headquarters as authorized by the administrator to individuals serving on the administrator's NASA Advisory Council.
- Blue NASA with "ASAP" photo ID—Issued only by NASA headquarters as authorized by the administrator to individuals serving on the administrator's NASA Aerospace Safety Advisory Panel.
- Green NASA photo ID—Issued to U.S. military and federal government agency personnel detailed to NASA.
- Violet NASA photo ID—Issued to any intern/student (U.S. citizen) who requires access to a NASA center to perform their duties. Accepted at center of issuance only.
- Orange NASA photo ID—Issued to any foreign national contractor personnel from nondesignated countries that require access to a NASA center or NASA-controlled facility to perform their work. Accepted at center of issuance only.
- Orange with "LPR" NASA photo ID—Issued to any foreign national contractor personnel from nondesignated countries that are U.S. lawful permanent residents and require access to a NASA center or NASA-controlled facility to perform their work. Accepted at center of issuance only.
- Red NASA photo ID—Issued to any foreign national contractor personnel from designated countries that require

access to NASA information systems or have a need to work a NASA-controlled facility to perform their work. Accepted at center of issuance only.

- Red NASA with "LPR" photo ID—Issued to any foreign national contractor personnel from designated countries who are U.S. lawful permanent residents and require access to a NASA center or access to NASA IT systems or have a need to work at a NASA-controlled facility to perform their work. Accepted at center of issuance only.
- Brown NASA photo ID—Issued to any accredited member of the media (United States only) who may require access to "public" areas only of a NASA center. Accepted at all centers as appropriate.
- Silver NASA photo ID—Issued to employees of the Jet Propulsion Laboratory (JPL). Acceptance at NASA centers is at the center discretion.
- Black and white NASA photo ID with red letters "Cill" denoting "Center Director Issued"— May be issued to retired NASA personnel under specific conditions.[51]

7.9 Summary

This chapter explained many basic concepts of identification management programs along with how to develop ID management policies and procedures. Background is provided on the type of products or services an organization may be considering to support an ID management system. It also provided self-assessment questions that can be helpful in selecting ID system products. Key areas covered include the following:

- How identification systems can help control insider access to organization property and secure areas of organization facilities
- The relationship between ID management systems and physical access control systems
- The available features of ID cards/badges and how they can help secure facilities
- How to evaluate and select ID card/badge technology
- Developing policies for ID card/badge usage and display at corporate facilities

COURSE CASE STUDY   THE JAMES MARTIN MANUFACTURING COMPANY (CONTINUED)

Earlier this year, Tonya Martin become CEO of the James Martin Manufacturing Company, a privately owned company that had been in her family for over 80 years. Tonya discovered that the late Harold Smith, a long-time manager whom her father had entrusted the company operations to, had been embezzling and stealing equipment and supplies from the company for the last decade before his death.

Tonya has been working with Ronald Thomas, the new director of security (DOS), and Samuel Davis, a new hire with experience in a similar company, to assess security measures and to improve security. After much discussion, they decided that they would work toward a comprehensive security plan but for the time being they were going to focus on the areas that needed the most protection and work to develop solid security measures for those high priority areas.

Once better security was in place for the most important areas or assets, they would move forward one step at a time toward the comprehensive security plan. Tonya, Ronald Thomas, and Samuel Davis understood that because there had been such a lack of security over the last few years, suddenly cracking down on security could be a shock to the employees of the company. They also believed that there was knowledge and talent among the employees that could be leveraged to help promote security and monitor compliance with security procedures. Tonya wanted to add people to the security team and was in the process of starting a security training program for managers and supervisors.

The top three security team members agreed they should have more rigid access control for the computer network, the computers, and the data on the network. There was an access control program on the main server, but it had not been updated for several years. Tonya also wanted a new surveillance system because the existing system was very outdated and did not cover as much of the facility that DOS Ronald Thomas thought should be covered. In addition, Tonya wanted to add a new ID management system. The existing ID management system was antiquated, and many employees had lost their ID badges and they had not been replaced since the old security guard died a few years ago.

COURSE DISCUSSION QUESTIONS

1. Tonya has been delaying hiring a security consultant partially because of cost and partially because she wants to learn more about the state of security at the company. Is it time for Tonya to hire a security consultant? Discuss the pros and cons of hiring an outside consultant at this point.
2. Should Tonya implement a new ID management system at this point or should she wait until they are further along in their efforts to improve security? Discuss the pros and cons of implementing a new ID management system at this point.
3. Should Tonya hire an outside firm to implement a new ID management system or should she proceed with the staff she has in place? Discuss the pros and cons of hiring an outside ID management firm to implement a new system.
4. When Tonya implements a new ID management system, what minimum administrative support functions should be put into place before launching a new system?
5. How do you think James Martin Manufacturing could benefit from a color-coded ID badge system? Discuss the pros and con of a color-coded ID badge scheme for Martin Manufacturing.

COURSE PROJECTS

1. Design a minimum ID management system for James Martin Manufacturing that can support the approximately 250 permanent employees and anywhere from 100 to 200 seasonal or peak capacity employees the company may need in the future. Compare your design to that of your classmates and discuss the differences in your systems.

2. Design a color-coded ID badge scheme that you think would best serve James Martin Manufacturing. Compare your design to that of your classmates and discuss the differences in your schemes.
3. Draft an ID card/badge policy for James Martin Manufacturing. Compare your draft policy to that of your classmates and discuss the differences in your draft policies.

COURSE TEST QUESTIONS

1. The automated and human functions that allow a properly identified person or logical entity to access to an organization's facilities or computer systems are known as _____.
2. Authorized logical access is _____.
3. The access that an insider is allowed to have to an organization's property, buildings, and areas of buildings that an employee may need to perform their job duties is known as _____.
4. The free Internet-based service of the Citizenship and Immigration Services Division of the U.S. Department of Homeland Security (DHS) used to verify an employee's identity and authorization to work in the United States is called _____.
5. An organization's policy that informs employees and visitors as to the organization's requirement for ID card/badge display when on the organization's property is known as the _____.
6. The system that is used to identify a person for the purposes of allowing access to an organization's facilities is known as a(n) _____.
7. Systems that manage each individual's access rights allowing access to the computer services they need to perform their duties but prevent their access to other computer services as well as what they can do with computer services to which they do have access is known as _____.
8. Systems that are designed specifically to allow an individual to enter specific areas of a facility and block their access to areas

of the facility to which they have not been granted access are known as _____.

9. Generally speaking, an employee will be assigned to work in specific areas of a facility and access is authorized after _____.

10. To have an effective ID system for insiders, first your must _____.

Key Terms

Access control systems: are those automated and human functions that allow a properly identified person or logical entity access to an organization's facilities or computer systems.

Authorized logical access: is the access that an insider is allowed to have to an organization's computer and communications systems that an employee may need to perform their job duties.

Authorized physical access: is the access that an insider is allowed to have to an organization's property, buildings, and areas of buildings that an employee may need to perform their job duties.

E-Verify: is a free Internet-based service of the Citizenship and Immigration Services Division of the U.S. Department of Homeland Security (DHS) used to verify an employee's identity and authorization to work in the United States.

ID card/badge display policy: is the organization's policy that informs employees and visitors as to the organization's requirement for ID card/badge display when on the organization's property and it can also cover employees on official business not on company property.

ID card/badge policy purpose and scope statement: communicates an organization's purpose for having an ID card/badge policy and should apply to all people on an organization's property.

Identification (ID) systems: are those automated and human functions that are used to identify a person or logical entity for the purposes of allowing access to an organization's facilities or computer systems.

Logical access control systems: manage each individual's access rights by allowing access to the computer services they need to perform their duties but preventing their access to other computer services as well as what they can do with computer services to which they do have access.

Physical access control systems: are designed specifically to allow an individual to enter specific areas of a facility and block their access to areas of the facility to which they have not been granted access.

8

IMPLEMENTING STRONG PHYSICAL ACCESS CONTROLS

Managing and controlling physical access to facilities and buildings is a critical aspect of a good security program. This chapter discusses how to design, implement, and manage a physical access control system. Technology is a key part of physical access control systems, and this chapter reviews various types of technology and the process of selecting that technology. Chapter 8 also discusses how to control knowledge of the systems and how to keep access systems secure. This chapter continues the spirit of practicality and examines the continuum of physical access control systems and some of the pitfalls involved in deploying such systems.

Access to facilities and access to security information about buildings can be protected from outsiders through a variety of *physical access control systems*. However, as effective as strong physical access controls can be to keep the dangerous outsider from committing damaging acts, they may not be as effective in mitigating the threat from potential insider exploitation of building vulnerabilities or misappropriation of building security information that can be exploited by outsiders.[51]

Thus, when thinking about protecting buildings, be aware that they need protection from both outsiders as well as insiders. Insiders may often have more access than they need and access controls must be strong enough and appropriately applied to keep insiders from obtaining detail information on an organization's security controls and systems.[52]

8.1 Physical Access Control System Models

Over the last 15 years there has been a much heightened awareness of the need to have strong physical access control systems in place because of the threat of terrorist attacks. The threat of terrorist attacks is widely known but not very widely understood. Aside from the federal government, there are many facilities owned or operated by organizations in one of the critical industries designated by the Department of Homeland Security (DHS) that have implemented strong physical access control systems. Security and access-controlled facilities have now become rather commonplace in the age of terrorism.

The need for strong physical access control systems put a lot of people into a state of shock, much of which has subsided at this point. Bear in mind there have been hundreds if not thousands of very high security facilities in the United States and around the world, and for many people a day-to-day life surrounded by strong security is not new. Military organizations and various agencies of governments have long had strong physical access control systems in place. This type of facility proliferated in World War II and throughout the Cold War decades spanning from the end of World War II through the late 1980s.

With the terrorists' threat-driven need for strong physical access control systems have come a vast array of security improvement efforts and security education on the part of governments and military organizations. A lengthy tour of federal government websites yields encyclopedias full of information designed for agency staff as well as interested nongovernment organizations to learn more about security in general and specifically about strong physical access control systems. The volume of information can take weeks if not months to sift through.

In the spirit of practicality, the volumes of information about strong physical access control systems are reduced to basic models that can be implemented in their entirety or pieces can be selected as necessary to meet the immediate needs of many different types of organizations. All of these models can provide strong physical access control against outsiders, and properly equipped strong ID management systems and surveillance systems can be effective in controlling insiders as well.

- *Secure communities*—There have been many secure communities in the past and the model is reminiscent of the towns that the U.S. government established to support nuclear research efforts during World War II and the Cold War. A contemporary extension of the model is a military base or research campus. This model has perimeter security that can be strengthened on demand, has some public areas without secured access within the perimeter, secure facilities within the outer perimeter, secured buildings, and buildings with secured areas.
- *Secure facilities*—Secure facilities have also been around for many years. Smaller than a military base or research campus, a secure facility can be comprised of numerous special purpose secured buildings with strong perimeter security surrounding the entire group of buildings. There are generally no unsecured public areas; buildings have secured access levels based on need; and areas of buildings have higher levels of security based on need.
- *Secure buildings*—Secure buildings may stand alone without a secure perimeter but have strong physical access control systems that only allow in people who have authorized access and appropriate security clearances. Secure buildings may also have stronger security for designated floors and areas of the building.
- *Secure areas of buildings*—Buildings without secure perimeters and without secured and controlled access to the building can have secured areas of the building with strong physical access controls in place.
- *Secure storage devices*—Vaults, safes, cabinets, or other storage devices that can be secured with only authorized personnel having access are elements of many insider security programs. Secure storage devices can be helpful in any of the physical access control models to provide extra levels of security for documents of other valuable items.

Any of the physical access control models will provide better security when they are integrated with a strong ID management system. The physical access control models and how they can protect against insider security violations are examined in the following sections.

8.2 Secure Communities

The secure communities model is reminiscent of the towns that the U.S. government established to support nuclear research efforts during World War II and the Cold War. The idea behind the concept was to create an environment that provided public access areas necessary for normal commerce and family life where the people that lived there were the ones working at nearby secure facilities. This application of a secure community model was very similar to a company town where, for the most part, only people somehow associated with the owning company would live and work.

The model was relatively successful, but bear in mind that this all occurred before contemporary technologies like wireless communications and spy drones were even thought of, let alone posed a threat. The key to security in such communities is that outsiders seldom came and they were never welcome.

A contemporary extension of the model is a military base or research campus. This model has perimeter security that can be strengthened on demand, has some public areas without secured access within the perimeter, has secure facilities within the perimeter, has secured buildings, and has buildings with secured areas. This version of secured communities works rather well with the exception that during the normal course of day-to-day business, the ease-of-use perimeter lets too many people in and that is when there can be and have been incidents. When the threat levels are raised, the outer parameter can be locked down and restricted access can be enforced. A mockup of a secured community or campus is shown in Figure 8.1.

The security incidents that have occurred, at least the ones publicly discussed, were very messy but did not involve the more secure areas of the base or campus and did not jeopardize the secure buildings. When alert levels are elevated and perimeter security is tightened,

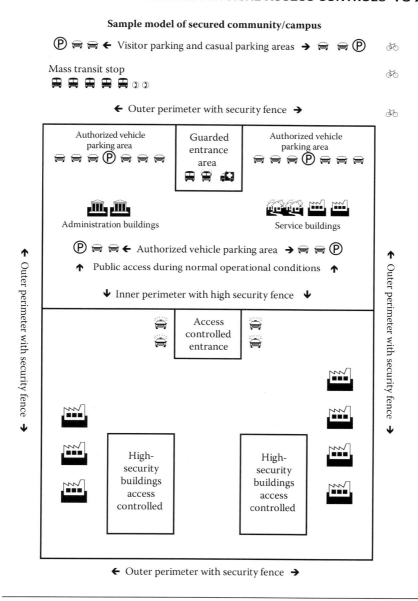

Figure 8.1 Sample model of secured community/campus.

the secure communities work relatively well. Most recent incidents involved single attackers that had some animosity against a person working in the secured community.

The upside of the modern implementation of the secured community model is that security can be very effective when perimeter security is tightened because of threat levels. The main downside of the model is that it can be very expensive to maintain given current economic conditions. A second problem is that the community in its totality is difficult to protect from insider threats. The secure buildings and secured areas of buildings are easier to protect from insiders because the people that do have access to them are a relatively small percentage of the people that have access to the larger secure community.

Modern technology makes it more difficult to protect the secured community. Satellite imaging is a threat in that it is easier now than ever to determine the layout of the secured community. Drones and other unmanned aerial vehicles that can fly low to the ground when necessary are at present difficult to detect and difficult to stop. They can also collect extensive information about the physical layout of a secured community.

We will reach the point where localized radar and advance detection systems will become more commonplace to help protect the secured community. The combat will eventfully reach the level of the friendly drone fighting the intruding drone. It is safe to assume that such systems are either being tested or are already in place. The movies and the spy thriller novels will soon proliferate.

So what it all comes down to is that if an organization needs a secure community and does not have one yet, then it is facing an incredible expense. It is also important to note that this discussion of secured communities does not have any relationship with the secure communities model that was an immigration enforcement program administered by U.S. Immigration and Customs Enforcement (ICE) from 2008 to 2014.[53]

8.3 Secure Facilities

A secure facility can be comprised of numerous special purpose secured buildings with strong perimeter security surrounding the entire group of buildings. Unlike the secure community model, in a secure facility there are generally no unsecured public areas in the facility and everybody who enters the facility does so with authorization. Within the secure facility, buildings have physical access control systems and some areas of buildings have higher levels of security based on need.

In reality, facility security exists on a continuum depending on what level the owners or occupiers deem necessary. The Department of Defense (DOD) has set standards for secure facilities under its jurisdiction and for defense contractors working on products or projects for which DOD requires strong security. The Defense Security Service (DSS) is responsible for certifying facility security.[54]

Meeting DOD requirements for a secure facility is a lengthy and very detailed process. If an organization has been impacted by the National Industrial Security Program, then security staff already know about the process and the requirements. If an organization is not directly impacted by defense security requirements, it can still benefit greatly from material provided by the DSS. The Center for Development of Security Excellence (CDSE) provides courses that are intended for use by the DOD and other federal government personnel and contractors within the National Industrial Security Program.[55]

There are many organizations impacted by federal government standards for security, and, as mentioned, those organizations most likely know who they are. Then there is the rest of the world. When deciding to secure a facility or build a new secure facility, federal government standards for security can be very helpful.[56] The CDSE provides several online courses and also provides numerous downloadable manuals and reference guides for security.

One manual in particular would be very helpful when working to improve physical security for a facility. The "Unified Facilities Criteria (UFC): DOD Security Engineering Facilities Planning Manual" has more useful information than can be found in most places.[57] One key point made in the manual is that it is essential to the effectiveness of the design that an interdisciplinary team be involved in the planning process. The manual provides a typical 10-step process for designing facility security plans and is as follows:

Step 1—Convene the planning team
Step 2—Identify assets
Step 3—Determine asset value
Step 4—Identify aggressor likelihoods

Step 5—Identify tactics and threat severity levels
Step 6—Consolidate into initial design basic threat information
Step 7—Determine initial level of protection
Step 8—Determine planning risk levels
Step 9—Assess acceptability of risk levels
Step 10—Identify user constraints

One of the steps that is rather unique to this planning process is step 10, identify user constraints. This step really hits reality head on because in most situations there are numerous *user constraints* to take into consideration that are specific to an asset, facility, site, entire installation, or city, including the following:

- Physical characteristics of the facility, the surrounding land, and surrounding assets
- Operational considerations that may require deliveries, frequent visitors, and production requirements
- Political climate such as consequences from local or regional governments
- Adjacent landowners or other tenant organizations' perceptions and reactions
- Appearance and the public perception of the appearance and any related local ordinances on appearance
- Public access that may be required or that can be restrained
- Financial considerations including overall costs and availability of funding
- Occupancy requirements and building ordinances
- Local infrastructure such as nearby public parking lots, roads, easements, and right-of-ways
- Fences and lighting that will be necessary for facility security
- Electronic security systems that will be required for facility security

The major point about the design considerations listed here is that a security planning team will not be able to design a secure facility in a vacuum. This is especially true in urban areas where there is an abundance of opinions and perspectives on new construction and renovation of existing facilities. A sample of a secure facility is shown in Figure 8.2.

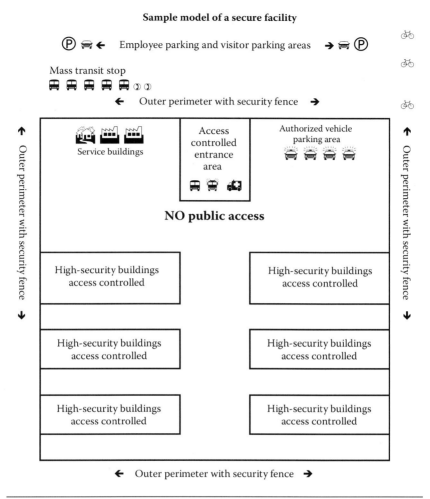

Figure 8.2 Sample model of a secure facility.

8.4 Secure Buildings

Securing an individual building is far less complicated than attempting to secure a campus or large facility. There are numerous resources available to help an organization construct a new building or retrofit an existing building that will help improve security. As mentioned in Chapter 1, the National Institute of Building Sciences, which supports the Whole Building Design Guide (WBDG), is a very helpful resource. The WBDG focuses, in part, on how to design and create integrated security into new building construction and in the remodeling of existing buildings.[5] The Building Security Council's (BSC)

Building Rating System (BRS) and certification for professionals has also been established with the goal of integrating security into the design and construction of buildings.[6] The BSC also provides a certification for building design professionals.

The major challenge in securing a building is to maintain a level of functionality that is necessary for continued smooth operations. The everyday comings and goings of delivery trucks, maintenance staff, and visitors with official business are often just a necessity of doing business. There are several ways to minimize the impact of security on everyday operations but like many things, those methods require changes in perceptions and behaviors and of course cost money.

Organizations can maintain strong physical access control by minimizing the need for access by the long list of people who help the organization. Instead of having deliveries to the secure building, there can be another building that functions as a service center for the secure building. The service center can handle shipping and receiving, mail, package delivery, and receipt of equipment and supplies. Once received and processed, such items can be moved to the secure building by company employees who have had background checks and are monitored on a constant basis. Another simple step is to have meetings off-site at a service facility or another building that can provide meeting space such as a local hotel or civic club.

Organizations can also decide to have security for specific areas of a building and to also utilize secure storage devices for important documents or data throughout the building. This can reduce the cost of building totally ironclad security and can be very effective in securing assets from insiders. Secure areas of buildings and secure storage devices are covered in the following sections.

Designing security for an individual building still involves many of the same steps required for designing security for a facility. The main differences are scale and costs. A single building is easier to secure and is less expensive to secure against most threats. As with all security efforts, there are key physical and mechanical security methods planners will finding necessary to secure a building including strong physical access control systems, ID management systems, and surveillance systems, as discussed in other chapters of this book.

Secure buildings need to be strengthened in a variety of ways including doors, windows, underground access ways, and rooftop equipment and facilities. In addition, each floor should have location-specific access control and strengthened security appropriate to the value of assets and personnel located on that floor. Floor-appropriate security measures are shown in Figure 8.3. Bear in mind that these are generalized characteristics and security measures, and each individual building should have customized security for each floor based on a security and threat analysis.

Secured building architectural and security characteristics		
Entire building	ID card security elevator access	ID card security door access	Surveillance systems
	Roaming security guards		
Roof top	ID card access doors	Motion detectors	Alarm systems
Executive floors	ID card controlled elevator exit	Authorized access only office spaces	Panic rooms
Office floors	Authorized access only office spaces	Fire suppression systems	Emergency equipment and supplies
Mezzanine	ID card security elevator access	No public access to facilities	Security monitors
Ground floor	Lobby with ID card access	ID card elevator access	No public access to facilities
	Access controlled entrances	Security guards and surveillance systems	Bullet proof glass
Lower levels	Sealed passage ways	Security doors	Targeted surveillance systems

Figure 8.3 Secured building architectural and security characteristics.

8.5 Secure Areas of Buildings

One of the methods to contain security costs and avoid the need for strong physical access control systems for an entire building is to designate and design secure areas of the building. Areas can be secured on a zoning basis or as necessary based on security needs for a specific location. However, there may be areas of a building that cannot be made completely secure, especially if there is a walk-in customer service component to day-to-day business operations.

Open access areas of a building can pose security risks from outsiders, insiders, and former insiders. There has been a rash of former-insider attacks on buildings and facilities across the United States. Many of these crimes have taken place in offices that have little security in place. Open-access offices can be easy targets for theft, unlawful entry, forcible occupation, violent acts by former insiders, and even sabotage. There are several physical security steps that can help reduce risks in the open-access offices of a building including the following:

- Have security guards at the main building entrance with those officers visible at all times.
- Install a metal detector at public entrances to the building.
- Upgrade perimeter security systems with intercoms and closed-circuit surveillance systems.
- Develop crisis communication among key open office personnel and the security office involving intercoms, telephones, duress alarms, or other concealed communications.
- Have a secondary communication system, such as a two-way radio system, in case of phone sabotage or electrical failure.
- Install concealed emergency alarm buttons in several places in the open office areas.
- Arrange lobby and open office space so visitors can be easily seen and monitored.
- Install service counter with security windows between employees and customers.
- Create natural barriers such as countertops and service windows that keep people from trying to leave the open office areas and entering secure areas of the building.

- Keep all doors leading to other areas of the building or service closets and rooms locked to prevent access from the open office space.
- Follow strict physical access control procedures that prevent people from passing from open office spaces to secure areas.
- Open offices should be clean and orderly to make identifying strange objects or unauthorized people easier.
- Minimize the number of trash receptacles and frequently empty the ones in use.
- Keep publicly accessible restroom doors locked and set up a key control system.
- Train employees on steps to take if a life-threatening or violent incident occurs.
- Develop code words to alert coworkers and supervisors that immediate help is needed.
- Designate and equip an area in the office for employees and/or customers to escape to if they are confronted with violent or threatening people.
- Train employees on the location of emergency supplies such as first-aid equipment, fire extinguishers, and large flashlights and batteries.[58]

If there is open office areas with limited controls on public access, it is important to prevent people from transiting from the open areas to secure areas of a building. Insiders or former insiders have an advantage with this office configuration because they may be familiar with the various ways to get from an open access area into a secure area. There are several physical security steps that can help reduce risks of people transiting from open access offices of a building into a secure area including the following:

- Install access-control combination locks or key-card access systems at entrances to secure areas.
- Install closed-circuit television cameras for monitoring controlled-access doors leading into secure areas.
- Use access control badges, with recent photographs, for all employees and authorized contractors entering secured areas.
- Follow strict access control procedures for entering secured areas.

- Within secure building areas install multiple levels of access doors all requiring access cards or codes.
- Install closed-circuit television cameras for monitoring interior spaces in secure areas.
- Keep security guards briefed on former employees that have been involuntarily discharged or had a tumultuous severance of some sort.
- Block or remove windows that provide views into secured areas.[58]

Secure rooms are often used when larger storage needs exceed the capacity of secure cabinets or safes. These secure environments can be designed and built to enhanced commercial construction standards but still may not provide the extra security that is intrinsic to large vaults. There are design and construction standards that cover floors, walls, ceilings and roofs, windows, and other openings.[59]

8.6 Secure Storage Devices

There is a wide variety of secure storage equipment available on the open market, including large high-security vaults, lockable and fireproof filing cabinets, and lockable storage cabinets. When deciding if a specific container or storage device is adequate for storing classified material or other valuable items, keep in mind that the more sensitive the material being stored, the stronger the storage devices should be and the more strict protection methods and procedures.

If dealing with U.S. military or government material, organizations need to follow Department of Defense or General Services Administration guidelines for handling and storing material. These guidelines and requirements cover the range of security levels from official use only to top secret. Additional handling requirements cover highly sensitive classified information that requires the highest possible levels of protection such as sensitive compartmented information (SCI). The required protection measures dictate the types of storage containers or facilities used for storage along with other controls including guards, alarms, and electronic surveillance systems.[59]

Security filing cabinets are available in a variety of sizes including one-, two-, four-, or five-drawer legal and letter size models and can have a variety of locking systems including a single lock controlling all drawers or separate locks on individual drawers. Locks come in a range of strengths and related costs. These filing cabinets are designed and manufactured to specifications such as Federal Specification AA-F-358J. There are also securable cabinets for storing confidential maps, plans, and oversized documents as well as film, photos, and other sensitive or proprietary material.[59]

Organizations can also install vaults that can be used for open storage of large volumes of documents and other materials. Vaults are generally designed and built to meet high forcible entry standards and they provide more security than secure rooms. They can also be equipped with concrete walls, ceilings, and floors along with hardened steel doors. Large vaults are generally constructed in place but can also be of modular design and be prefabricated and delivered to the site of use and assembled there.[59]

There are several manufacturers of safes for business uses, and they produce a very wide variety of safes to protect against burglary and fire loss. Information on several of these manufacturers and the products they offer can be found at Dean Safe (www.deansafe.com), which is one of the largest safe sellers online and off-line.

Most organizations are aware of the need to protect sensitive and proprietary documents that are current and provide some sort of present-day utility. Unfortunately, many organizations do not extend these levels of protection to retired or obsolete documents and move those documents into off-site bulk storage that often does not provide the same levels of protection available in on-site storage systems. To ensure that sensitive and proprietary documents are adequately protected through their life cycle, a comprehensive records management systems is necessary.

Many organizations apply a series of categories for sensitive and proprietary documents that help in determining how they should be handled, stored, and disposed of properly. Some classifications commonly used include archived documents, closed records, permanent records, regulated records, and legal documents.[60] The Association of Records Managers and Administrators (ARMA) (www.arma .org) provides training as well as many guidance publications on how to establish and maintain a *comprehensive records management system*.[61]

8.7 Focusing on Mitigating Insider Damage

Insiders have been damaging U.S. national interests since the American Revolution with Benedict Arnold. However, the ability of insiders to misappropriate data and information and to compromise trade secrets has increased dramatically. As industry expands and the military grows, to counter new threats there is an increased need for personnel and many of those personnel will require access to sensitive information to perform their job responsibilities. New personal technology devices have made moving and transmitting information incredibly easy, and there is an increased demand to designate information as sensitive and proprietary around the world.[62]

One of the most important things to do to mitigate the insider threat is to limit access to and knowledge of proprietary information as much as possible. This chapter discusses some of the physical access control systems that are critical to controlling the movement of insiders within an organization's facilities and offices. However, organizations cannot merely take all of the methods of controlling access and install them and walk away thinking that proprietary information is safe. Although it will be safer, it will not be totally secured just by using access control methods and ID management systems.

An organization must learn how to use all of the features that access control technology, ID management systems, and surveillance systems can provide in order to mitigate insider threats. It is a widespread habit among organizations to install security systems and think that all will be well. To maintain high levels of security, the mitigation measures put into place need to be maintained and periodically reviewed to ensure that they are working properly. Security staff also needs to monitor and examine the behavior of individual employees.

To effectively penetrate an organization's defenses, insiders must constantly work to expand their access. When employees seek higher clearances or expanded access outside their job scope, engage in classified conversations without a need to know, work hours inconsistent with their job assignment or they insist on working in private, and possibly have repeated security violations such as trying to enter areas to which they are not authorized access, then there may be a problem.[62] Such occurrences should be reported and recorded to determine if patterns of behavior exists. This is all part of *security vigilance.*

Security systems can provide a variety of data to help maintain security. This is where security vigilance becomes of upmost importance. Record all of the data from the physical access control systems and from the ID management systems. A record of occurrences of the aforementioned behavioral characteristics is useful to maintain and then used to triangulate with data from security systems. But systems can provide actual data on insider behavior that observation may not capture and that can be useful to security efforts including the following:

- Data from the physical access control systems that shows employees that try to use their access cards to enter areas that they are not authorized to enter
- ID management systems for computer access that can show attempts to access applications or data that users are not authorized to access
- Surveillance video that can be time matched to insider attempts to access controlled areas to which they do not have authorized access
- Surveillance video that shows an employee wandering the halls of areas they do not work in and those areas have doors to access-controlled rooms

Security system data can be combined with observations of behaviors that may indicate that an employee is attempting to infiltrate and breach an organization's security procedures and protocols. Once observations are combined with actual data, security staff may find evidence that there is an unfavorable pattern of behavior. Then a decision must be made on what to do with the employee in question. The security department should at least continue to monitor the suspicious employee. The security department or staff should also decide if immediate intervention is necessary and if there should be a face-to-face meeting with the employee to discuss these behaviors. One thing to can count on is that security vigilance is a never-ending process.

8.8 Summary

This chapter explained many basic concepts and designs of physical access control systems and how they can interact with ID management systems. Secure facilities and buildings were described and their major characteristics were discussed. Background was provided on the type of products or services organizations may be considering to support physical access control systems. It also explained specific steps to take when implementing and management physical access control systems. Key areas covered include the following:

- Physical access control models, including secure campuses, secure facilities, and secure buildings
- The process of designing facilities and buildings for better security
- Many of the issues that need to be taken into consideration when designing facilities and buildings for better security
- How to control secured areas of buildings
- The importance and use of secure storage devices
- Collecting security systems data that shows insider activity that may be inappropriate

COURSE CASE STUDY   THE JAMES MARTIN MANUFACTURING COMPANY (CONTINUED)

Tonya Martin recently became CEO of the James Martin Manufacturing Company, a privately owned company that had been in her family for over 80 years. To improve security, Tonya has been working with Ronald Thomas, the new director of security (DOS), and Samuel Davis, a new hire with experience in a similar company.

So far Tonya, Ronald Thomas, and Samuel Davis have taken several piecemeal steps to improve security, including reviewing and modifying existing policies and procedures, developing security awareness, getting people involved in promoting and improving security, improving computer security, and selecting an ID management approach.

Tonya also believed that she wanted a friendly security atmosphere and did not want employees to feel that James Martin Manufacturing had become militarized. She also wanted to encourage cooperation with and good feelings about the upcoming changes in security practices at the company.

The three security team members agreed they should start focusing on improving physical access controls for the facility as well as specific areas in the buildings located within the James Martin Manufacturing facility.

COURSE DISCUSSION QUESTIONS

1. Discuss what options James Martin Manufacturing has to improve physical access control.
2. Discuss ways that James Martin Manufacturing could integrate an ID management system with a physical access control system.
3. Discuss which model of secure facilities or secure buildings and secure areas of buildings would best serve a company the size of James Martin Manufacturing.
4. Discuss which approaches James Martin Manufacturing could take to utilize data from an ID management system and a physical access control system to monitor potential insider threats.

COURSE PROJECTS

1. Design a physical access control system for James Martin Manufacturing. Compare your design to those of your classmates and discuss the difference in the designs.
2. Design a process to correlate data from a physical access control system at James Martin Manufacturing with observations made through its security vigilance process. Compare your design to those of your classmates and discuss the difference in the designs.
3. James Martin Manufacturing has three functional areas that need to secure sensitive and proprietary documents. Select three secure storage devices that can be used to store an unknown but relatively small volume of documents but still be capable of handling future growth in documents that need

to be secured. Compare your selection to those of your classmates and discuss the difference in the designs.

4. Design a general document and records retention and destruction system for James Martin Manufacturing. Compare your
design to those of your classmates and discuss the difference
in the designs.

COURSE TEST QUESTIONS

1. A comprehensive records management system is designed to
_____.

2. Secure areas of buildings have several characteristics including _____.

3. Secure buildings have several characteristics including _____.

4. Secure communities have several characteristics including
_____.

5. Secure facilities have several characteristics including _____.

6. Secure storage devices are designed to _____.

7. When designing buildings for security, user constraints that
need to be addressed include _____.

8. An insider becomes suspicious when _____.

9. One of the most important things to do to mitigate an insider
threat is to _____.

10. When deciding if a specific container or storage device is
adequate for storing classified material or other valuable items
you should keep in mind that _____.

Key Terms

A comprehensive records management system: dictates how all
documents and records an organization has will be handled,
moved, used, stored, and destroyed during their life cycle.

Physical access control systems: are systems designed to specifically
allow an individual to enter specific areas of a facility and
block their access to areas of the facility to which they have
not been granted access.

Secure areas of buildings: are spaces that have strong physical access
controls and strong security features even though the building

with which they are contained may not be secured and have general public access areas.

Secure buildings: have strong physical access control systems that only allow people to enter that have authorized access and appropriate security clearances. Secure buildings may also have stronger security for designated floors and areas of the building.

Secure communities: are relatively self-contained special purpose communities, such as a military base or research campus. Secure communities generally have perimeter security that can be strengthened on demand, have some public areas without secured access within the perimeter, secure facilities within the outer perimeter, secured buildings, and buildings with secured areas.

Secure facilities: are generally comprised of one to several special purpose secured buildings with strong perimeter security surrounding the entire group of buildings. There are generally no unsecured public areas, buildings have secured access levels based on need, and areas of buildings have higher levels of security based on need.

Secure storage devices: are designed to limit access to their contents with strong locking mechanisms and/or durable construction that cannot be easily dismantled or neutralized.

Security vigilance: is a constant attention given to security during day-to-day operations and contributes to security by encouraging the reporting of security violations and makes suggestions on how to improve security when weaknesses are observed.

User constraints: are constraints on designing and implementing security mitigation methods that arise from local concerns about building appearance, local building codes, and local political dynamics.

9

MANAGING RELATIONSHIPS WITH VENDORS, BUSINESS PARTNERS, AND CUSTOMERS

Working with vendors, business partners, and customers is a part of everyday life for most organizations. It is an essential part of the business process. For the sake of security, it is important to stay in control of those relationships and to ensure that facilities and buildings are protected from potential threats. Because of the increasing reliance on a wide array of service providers, organizations should establish and maintain effective vendor and third-party security management programs. This is especially true when it comes to financial services. It is critical to understand the complex nature of arrangements with outside parties and ensure adequate due diligence for interaction with related outside organizations and the ongoing monitoring of those relationships.[63]

The employees of related organizations often become part-time insiders when they visit facilities, especially those who visit often. Over time, these frequent visitors develop relationships with employees and these relationships need to be regulated and monitored. This chapter goes beyond managing access by part-time insiders and covers methods that will help an organization maintain control over those relationships as well as the people or groups that employees may need to have interactions.

9.1 Inventory of Relationships

The major security goal in dealing with vendors, business partners, and customers is keeping them from harming an organization. The first step in this effort is to gain and keep control of the relationships including how and when representatives from those related organizations visit facilities or otherwise interact with employees. An organizations needs to keep both the outsiders and the insiders in these relationships from compromising security. This includes all forms of interactions including voice and e-mail.

Companies should set strict policies that govern how relationships are managed. Managers need to know with whom the organization's employees interact. A *relationship inventory* is helpful, and the data recorded about the organizations in-house staff interacts with needs to be continuously updated. The inventory, or list, should be used by employees that do interact on behalf of an organization to determine if and what type of interaction is permissible. Security staff should profile of each authorized organization and should include at least the following information:

- The legal or trade name of the organization with which the company conducts some sort of business
- The official address, phone number, website, and e-mail address of the organization
- The name of authorized representatives of that organization who are allowed to conduct business, along with their contact information
- The purpose of the relationship
- References to any ongoing contracts or agreements
- Any background information that was collected about the organization
- Any background checks or security clearance information about the employees of the outside organization
- Notes on any potential conflicts of interest that company employees may have when dealing with the outside organizations

This inventory serves many purposes. One of the most important of those purposes is to inform employees with whom the company has established an authorized relationship. It also provides employees with enough information by which to confirm the legitimacy of an interaction and that the proper people in a related organization are involved in the interaction.

Security staff can add organizations to the authorized list as management deems appropriate and can also delete entities from the list and revoke authorization. The updated list is a tool for everybody in an organization, including security staff, accounting, purchasing, shipping and receiving, and customer service.

Knowing and recording what security staff knows about related organizations is helpful in investigating security breaches, controlling insider-outsider relationships, and monitoring transactions to detect for fraud or embezzlement.

9.2 Developing General Policies for Interaction

An organization may need specific policies to help control interactions with each type of related organization such as vendors, business partners, and customers because of the uniqueness of those relationships. Such policies can help to control what employees do in those relationships and help reduce the opportunity for insider exploitation. It can also be helpful to have a general policy that covers authorized interactions and how employees should conduct themselves during those interactions. A sample purpose and scope statement for policies that govern interaction with outside organizations is shown in Figure 9.1.

More detailed policies and procedures can be developed to meet the needs of an organization. Cold calling, for example, or calling prospective clients without an introduction should be restricted by an organization because it takes time and poses a security risk. Suggested policy statements or areas for more detail procedures for employees include the following:

- Employees may not participate in or receive an unannounced visit from an outside organization.
- All visits must be scheduled in advance and by appointment only.
- All visits must be formally documented through the use of a sign-in/sign-out log.
- Visitors shall be escorted by an employee during a visit throughout the facility.
- Employees who violate these policies may be subject to discipline.

**Sample purpose and scope statement for policies governing
interaction with outside organizations**

It is company policy that all employees who represent the company in interactions
with outside organizations will protect the best interest of the company when
dealing with all organizations who are interested in doing business with the
company.

The purpose of this policy is to establish a company-wide uniform policy that
guides interactions and visitation procedures for vendors, business partners, and
customers.

This policy is applicable to all employees within the company. Primary
responsibility lies with personnel having the need to meet with vendors, business
partners, and customers including, but not necessarily limited to employees with
purchasing authority, contract administration, or sales, marketing, or other
related duties.

This policy also applies to all representatives of our vendors, business partners,
and customers that conduct business or wish to conduct business with the
company. Employees and representatives of related organizations are required
to perform their daily activities in a professional and responsible manner to
maintain trust and integrity. Employees must avoid any appearance or perception
of impropriety.

Figure 9.1   Sample purpose and scope statement for policies governing interaction with outside
organizations.

- Employees shall not solicit or accept anything of value for
  personal use, either directly or indirectly, from anyone who has
  or is seeking to do business with the company.
- Employees shall not use or authorize the use of their position
  of employment to secure anything of value for personal use,
  or promise or offer to provide anything of value from anyone
  who has or is seeking to do business with the company.
- Employees shall not outwardly display in the workplace any
  promotional items provided by an organization that has done
  business with your organization or is seeking to do business
  with the company.
- Employees may not participate in business lunches, dinners,
  or trade events without permission of the company.[64]

More detailed policies and procedures that govern what representatives of outside organizations can do can be developed to meet

the needs of an organization. Such policies can help make it clear to both employees and outside representatives what they are authorized to do during their interactions. They can also provide a deterrent for *insider misconduct* and reduce the likelihood of insider-outsider threats. Suggested policy statements or areas to develop more detailed procedures for vendors, business partners, and customers include the following:

- All representatives of vendors, business partners, and customers who are actively doing business with or seeking to do business with the company are expected to perform their business activities in a professional manner and avoid any perceptions of impropriety.
- Vendors, business partners, and customers will be responsible for reviewing and becoming familiar with the policies of the company that govern interaction between the company and outside organizations.
- Any vendor, business partner, or customer that attempts to influence a company employee on the evaluation and/or award of a contract either directly or through an outside agent or representative will be disqualified and will not be able to participate in the business activity.
- Vendor, business partner, or customer representatives may not make an unannounced visit from an outside organization. All visits must be scheduled in advance and are by appointment only.
- Vendor, business partner, or customer representatives shall be escorted by an employee during their visit and throughout the facility.
- Vendor, business partner, or customer representatives who violate this policy may have their access to the company rescinded.
- Vendor, business partner, or customer representatives shall not solicit or offer anything of value for personal use, either directly or indirectly, to anyone working for the company.
- Vendor, business partner, or customer representatives shall not give or offer any promotional items provided by their organization that is or is seeking to do business with the company.

- Vendor, business partner, or customer representatives may not offer company employees business lunches, dinners, or trade events without permission of the company.[64]
- Vendors and business partners should have appropriate insurance coverage such as commercial crime policies.

Copies of policies should be made available to representatives of outside organizations so they know what is expected from them during the course of business interactions. An organization can even go as far as having the outside representative sign an agreement to follow the policies and procedures.

9.3 Developing Specific Policies for Service Providers

Service providers, whether they are on the premises for a one-time-only service call or whether they provide ongoing services under a contract or an on-call basis, can be very helpful in achieving an organization's mission. These service providers also pose a security risk because of the relationships that can develop between employees and the outside contractor that can result in an insider-outsider threat. There are many ways to reduce the potential *insider-outsider threat* that is born out of an employee–contractor relationship.

There are numerous state and local laws that address contractor licensing, competency requirements, and service contracts. There are very specific laws that govern contract security services, which are discussed in Chapter 6, along with policy considerations specific to such services. Many state laws are designed to protect the buyer of these services and those laws can be very beneficial to an organization. Thus it is prudent to keep current with laws in the company's state of business that govern contract services or contractors of any type.

Beyond state and local laws, an organization has the ability to set policies on how employees and service contracts interact and what they are authorized to do. The general policy areas are discussed in previous sections. An organization also has the right to set or at least negotiate contractual terms with service providers.

Companies need to address requirements in contracts for two major types of contractors. First are those service providers that work in company facilities and need access to appropriate areas to perform the job duties. Second are service providers that are not on site but may still have some electronic or networked connection with the organization's computer systems.

For *onsite contractors*, management can set policies to protect the organization, many of which are discussed in Chapter 7. These can include insurance requirements, licensing requirements, and background checks for individual employees of the contractor's company, and termination of contracts for nonperformance.

The nature of some contractual services including physical maintenance or repair work can place a contractor's employees side-by-side with in-house employees during the course of the contracted services being performed. This situation calls for policies and procedures designed to keep the insider from exposing unnecessary information to the outsider and to prevent the outsider from attempting to extract information from the insider.

The social dynamic between company employees and the employees of a contract service provider can quickly evolve into one of camaraderie and empathy unless the interaction is controlled. When the relationships between the insider employee and outsider employee reaches this point is when it is most likely for a security breach to occur. This may be unintentional on the part of both the insider employee and outsider employee but can just as easily be an intentional act on the part of the outsider employee to gain information from the insider employee.

So, in addition to the general policy areas discussed earlier, there are several areas where additional policies and specific procedures can help protect an organization including the following:

- Conversations and discussions between employees and the employees of contractors should be limited to the task at hand, and details about company operations or company business should not be discussed.
- Employees should report a contractor's employee who makes inquiries about the company that are not related to the task at hand.
- Employees should report a contractor's employee who attempts to wander unescorted into areas of the facility where they do

not need to perform any work or attempts to photograph or otherwise record any activity on the premise.

- A supervisory level employee in an organization should monitor the activities of the contractor's employee and the company employee that has been assigned to escort or work with the contractor's employee.
- A contractor's employee should be required to go through the same entry and exit procedures as an employee in the organization including bag and toolbox check.
- When available, a surveillance camera should monitor the contractor's employee while working on the premises even when under escort by company employees.
- Contractor employees should wear an ID badge that clearly indicates that they are a contractor employee so that company employees are aware of their presence and can behave and speak accordingly.
- The contractor employee should perform work based on the statement of work for which they have a written contract or work order for and any deviation to the standing work order should be approved by management.[65]

Service providers that are under contract to provide a service but do not provide that service on-site should be monitored in the same manner as the onsite contract work to the extent possible. Very often, off-site contracted services are performed electronically or through a networked connection of some type.

It is up to the information technology (IT) security staff to control the access of the contractor to proprietary systems and data. The IT staff should report violations of security or inappropriate behavior just as in-house employees do when there is a contractor's employee on-site at a facility. This should include efforts to access systems or applications for which they do not have authorization or making inquires that are not related to the task at hand.

9.4 Developing Specific Policies for Suppliers

Depending on the industry sector, an organization probably relies on a variety of suppliers to meet demand for raw material, parts, or supplies.

The same concerns and suggested policies for vendors, business part-ners, and customers apply to relationship with suppliers. There are, however, some additional concerns that should be addressed when controlling suppliers. Contemporary suppliers can provide several lev-els of service including just-in-time inventory, production advice, and logistical support. To accomplish many of the things that the modern *value-added suppliers* can do, they often develop close relationships with their customers and with the employees of their customers. This is where vulnerabilities and risks increase.

Suppliers who offer a wide range of robust services to help their customers achieve better performance and greater profitability usu-ally want and sometimes require in-depth knowledge and informa-tion about company processes, which can include trade secrets. They also tend to develop very close working relationships with in-house employees ranging from designers to production managers and even customer service personnel.

This is a challenging situation because companies may benefit from the types of assistance suppliers can provide and may need such help. In addition, staff from supplier companies often have high levels of expertise and can work hand-in-hand with staff to improve processes or production methods. Value-added suppliers foster team building and their employees can become as familiar with an organization as in-house employees have become.

It is difficult to create a policy that can cover every instance of interaction between company employees and the employees of a value-added supplier. Many organizations rely on policies that govern *professional relationships* versus *unprofessional relationships*. Professional relationships are those that contribute to effective organization func-tioning without compromising an organization's integrity, sustain-ability, competitiveness, and security. Unprofessional relationships are ones that detract from organizational goals and violate any specific policies covering employee behavior and interaction with employees of service contractors, suppliers, or customers that can quickly create the appearance of favoritism, misuse of office or position, or the aban-donment of organizational goals for personal interests.[66]

An additional step an organization can take with both its employ-ees and the employees of a contractor or value-added supplier is to require individuals and contractor companies to sign and adhere to a *nondisclosure agreement.* The agreement at minimum should restrict the use of the information to which individuals have authorized access. This should include disclosure to other parties in any form including oral disclosure.

By signing the agreement, the service provider, supplier, or business partner will agree to only share proprietary information with the employees, agents, and independent contractors who are required to have access to perform duties within the scope of work of their contract or business relationship.[67]

Further steps can be taken to protect disclosure of proprietary information by company employees and the employees of contractors or business partners by requiring disclosure of potential conflicts of interest. Such conflicts of interest could include moonlighting by employees in the same field or business sector in which an organization conducts business or performs work.

Such restrictions on conflicting activities could also include job hunting in the same field of endeavor and even volunteer work, serving on boards of directors, or owning physical or intellectual property that could hinder the organization's business efforts. Restrictions could also cover providing goods and/or services to a direct competitor.[68] It is advisable to check with a local attorney regarding state-level restrictions on agreements such as nondisclosure or having policies against potential conflict of interest.

9.5 Developing Specific Policies for Business Partners

Establishing policies for employees, service providers, contractors, and suppliers presents many challenges. The advantage an organization has in those relationships is that the proprietary information is owned by the company, and individuals in these relationships are being financially compensated for their work by the organization. Developing specific policies for business partners can be more challenging because the company may not be financially compensating the business partners on a work-for-hire basis and business partner contracts can be rather complicated.

The practice of establishing *business partnerships* has evolved greatly over the last century. Two major economic trends have influenced the latest direction in business partnerships: first, globalism, which has opened new and broader markets, combined with a worldwide tele-communications structure and the Internet that has decreased communications costs and the time it takes to coordinate business efforts on an international scale. The second is specialization with more companies focusing on core competencies to create products or deliver services.

The modern business partnership allows an organization to expand its markets without the necessity of having a physical presence in multiple countries. An organization in one country can collaborate with organizations in numerous different countries that can facilitate the promotion, sale, and delivery of finished products or delivery of services. An organization that has a narrow specialization can partner on a global scale to place its products in growing markets using local partners to handle in-country or regional business efforts.

Many advocates expound upon the great opportunities that the business partnership model offers. The advocates promote collaboration, openness, and trust in the partnership relationship. Although this approach to business partnerships has many advantages, there are also some pitfalls and one of the worse pitfalls is an increased security threat and the potential of compromising trade secrets and other proprietary information.

When protecting intellectual property in a business partnership, there are not ready-to-use off-the-shelf security products to solve the security problem. There are five important steps that will help protect an organization in a business partnership arrangement:

1. The first step to protecting intellectual property and sensitive information is to carefully vet potential partners including background checks on the organization and its top executives.
2. The second step is to develop and/or negotiate a detailed and explicit contract or business partnership agreement with a governance model that protects the company and does not compromise intellectual property.
3. The third step is to develop and implement strong policies and detailed procedures that govern the interaction between organizations and clearly explain to employees what can be done and what cannot be done when interacting with the business partner.

4. The fourth step is to foster strong security vigilance in company employees and require them to report potential security problems and any security issues that arise during interactions with business partners.

5. Finally, the interactions with business partners must be continuously monitored along with the actions taken by a business partner in the name of the partnership. It is also wise to monitor the business partner's other commercial activities to determine if they are consistent with corporate goals and business policies or if they pose a threat to the company's reputation of security.

In business partnerships, companies will rely very heavily on the security vigilance of their employees. Bear in mind that managers must tell employees what they can and cannot do when they interact with people from the partner organization. The need for training and monitoring cannot be overstated.

9.6 Developing Specific Policies for Customers

The old saying that the customer is always right may be true, that is until the customer steals proprietary information and compromises your trade secrets thus trashing a business. Great customer service is the hallmark of many organizations and it can certainly provide a competitive advantage in this age of slim staffing patterns and outsourced customer service efforts. An organization will certainly benefit from keeping customers satisfied, but managers need to set very rigid limits. These limits include who interacts with customers and what they are authorized to do for customers and what they are authorized to tell customers.

It is where, when, and who interacts with customers that need to be controlled, and it is during those interactions when the careless or greedy insider can cause problems. The first step in controlling insider interaction with customers is to determine who will interact with customers and for what reason the interactions will occur. The very nature of customer relationship management is the stuff of which security incidents are made. Security staff and company managers should step back from the organization and examine who interacts with customers and why.

Sales staff interact with customers to seal deals and sell goods or services ranging from one-time simple transactions to complex long-term relationships. Sales staff are frontline workers in competitive battles for customers and revenue. Many organizations cannot survive without them. Do not be fooled by the exuberance of salespeople, especially if they are commissioned or if their personal income is in any way dependent on closing sales. Salespeople have but one loyalty and that is to their own pocketbooks, and they will do and say just about anything to increase their income, including compromising trade secrets.

An organization can structure business units to keep salespeople from giving away the recipe for the secret sauce. Compartmentalizing knowledge in an organization helps to keep salespeople away from everything except what they need to close sales. That needed information should be determined by upper management, not the sales department.

Experience shows that salespeople will try to convince the production department or service department that they need to know everything in order to close that deal, and if they do not give the information and the recipe for the secret sauce, then they are handicapping sales people. Remember salespeople are not loyal to an organization and they will compromise anything to make more money for themselves.

Given that managers probably cannot trust salespeople, there is the need to train staff in other departments to protect the information and data they have and not provide anything to salespeople without first clearing that request through management channels. It comes back to security vigilance and protecting the proper dissemination of information. One key thing in training non-sales staff to not provide salespeople with sensitive or restricted information is to establish a system as to how such requests move from one department to another. This should be a very structured procedure. This will deter salespeople from running amuck and requesting and potentially disclosing information without proper authorization. This system can certainly be set out in policy, but the details need to be communicated in a step-by-step procedure. Employees must be trained in the procedure, and supervisors must monitor interactions between sales staff and other departments to ensure that the procedures are properly executed and that there is a very high level of security performance.

Customer service employees are also a risk because they interact with the customer company employees. Customer service staff is under pressure from the customer's company as well as in-house managers and supervisors to keep the customer happy when possible by fielding questions and providing status reports. This pressure makes it more important to control what customer service employees can do and say and what information they can have access to. Detailed procedures should be developed to keep the scope of customer service responses as narrow as possible. The same applies to accounting and billing staff.

Product designers and production planners and managers provide more of a security risk because they probably know more proprietary information and perhaps even trade secrets. They all must be trained to what extent they can share information with a customer and what information they can discuss. As representatives of the customer company interact more with key designers and production managers, they will likely try to learn more as the relationships evolves. The danger of insiders slipping up increases because of their familiarity with people working for the customer company and the peer-to-peer relationships that develop. Detailed procedures and ongoing training is the best defense in this type of situation.

High-level executives in an organization can also be a risk when they know details of trade secrets and they interact with customer company executives. Business lunches and golf outings with a relaxed atmosphere and perhaps a few martinis make for a bad circumstance and a potential for a security breach. High-level executives can also be difficult to train as previously discussed. The training, however, is a necessity, and security vigilance is essential to control high-level executive interactions.

Another viewpoint in controlling relationships with customers is to minimize customer penetration into an organization. As relationships between a company and a customer matures and familiarity sets in, it is important to stay vigilant about security breaches. Customer employees may have visited facilities, had lunch with high-level executives, and interacted with sales and customer service staff over the years to the point where people are on a first-name basis. That friendliness may help in customer relationships, but remember it can also relax employees into a less security-vigilant mentality.

9.7 ID Management and Access Control for Vendors, Business Partners, and Customers

One of the ID management methods discussed in Chapter 7 on ID management systems to help clearly and quickly identify a visitor's status is to color code and clearly label the ID badges issued to different classes of visitors. In the sample ID badge design in Figure 9.2, the color red could be used for suppliers, blue could be used for customers, and gold could be used for business partners.

Using bar codes or magnet strips on the ID badges to control or monitor where a visitor attempts to go can help keep track of a visitor who wanders off from his or her escort. Depending on the sophistication of a physical access control system, security staff would be able to generate very helpful data on potential security violations just as is done with employee ID badges.

The color codes will alert your employees as to what type of visitor is present and they can act according to policies and procedures pertaining

Visitor ID badge design for suppliers, customers, and business partners	
Design feature	**ID badge layout**
Company name slot	Your company name here
Color code	Color strip
Badge control number recordedon visitor log	**Badge 56789**
Authorized date and time	August 13, 2023
Escort name	Henry Davis
Color code	Color strip

Figure 9.2   Visitor ID badge design for suppliers, customers, and business partners.

to what they should do or not do when certain types of visitors are present. This quick identification technique should alert employees to not discuss restricted information in the presence of the visitor. The information on the ID badge can also be used by in-house employees to report any unauthorized behavior on the part of the visitor.

9.8 Summary

This chapter examined how to control relationships between an organization and its suppliers, customers, and business partners. Controlling these relationships will help to ensure that there is no leakage of proprietary or sensitive information or trade secrets from inside the organization to outside the organization. This is accomplished in part by controlling both insider and outsider behavior. Methods of control were discussed for each type of relationship. The chapter also explained specific steps to using an ID management system for controlling visitors that represent suppliers, customers, and business partners. Key areas covered include the following:

- How to use an inventory or database of suppliers, customers, and business partners to restrict and track interactions between outside organizations and in-house employees
- Developing policies for general interactions with outside organizations
- Developing policies for interactions specifically with different types of outside organizations including suppliers, customers, and business partners
- The need for training employees as to what is authorized and not authorized in their interactions with suppliers, customers, and business partners
- Using ID badge design to help track the movement and control the interactions with visiting representatives from suppliers, customers, and business partners

COURSE CASE STUDY THE JAMES MARTIN MANUFACTURING COMPANY (CONTINUED)

Tonya Martin is the new CEO of the James Martin Manufacturing Company, a privately owned company that had been in her family for over 80 years. Company operations had been entrusted to long-time manager Harold Smith, who died a sudden death a few months ago. Upon review, Tonya discovered that Harold Smith had been embezzling and stealing equipment and supplies from the company for the last decade before his death.

Tonya has been working with Ronald Thomas, the new director of security (DOS), and Samuel Davis, a new hire with experience in a similar company. They have had several meetings and they are starting to gain momentum in their work. So far, Tonya, Ronald Thomas, and Samuel Davis have taken several piecemeal steps to improve security, including reviewing and modifying existing policies and procedures, developing security awareness, getting people involved in promoting and improving security, improving computer security, and working toward selecting an ID management approach. Tonya has already planned on having more strict access control policies and an ID management system to help improve access control.

The three security team members agreed they should start focusing on improving physical access controls for the facility as well as specific areas in the buildings located within the James Martin Manufacturing facility. One issue they are aware of is the lack of security and formal protocols for interactions with their suppliers, business partners, and customers.

The security team recognizes that employees from their related organizations have pretty much come and gone as they pleased. One result of the familiarity in relationships between James Martin Manufacturing employees and those of related organizations is that there is an overabundance of some supplies as well as dozens of pieces of equipment that have never been unpacked and put into use in the production process.

Tonya is not sure what other damage or security breaches may have resulted from an absence of control over the relationships with suppliers, business partners, and customers. She did find that some customers had received excessive discounts on many of their orders from James Martin Manufacturing. She has also found that many offices are full of odds and ends with other companies' logos on them.

COURSE DISCUSSION QUESTIONS

1. How should Tonya approach implementing new security policies and procedures that govern the interaction between James Martin Manufacturing employees and the representatives of outside companies?
2. What research should Tonya do before she starts reducing the number of suppliers and business partners that James Martin Manufacturing has dealt with over the last decade?
3. Do you think that training James Martin Manufacturing employees on how to interact with outside companies will help meet new security goals?
4. How would you go about training James Martin Manufacturing employees on how to interact with representatives or outside companies?

COURSE PROJECTS

1. Outline a training program for James Martin Manufacturing employees on how to be vigilant about security when dealing with representatives from other companies. Compare your outline to those of your classmates and discuss the differences in the outlines.
2. Draft a policy that addresses the professional relationships between employees of James Martin Manufacturing and the employees of other companies. Compare your draft to those of your classmates and discuss the differences in the drafts.
3. Draft a policy letter that Tonya can send to the managers of James Martin Manufacturing's suppliers about professional

relationships and how she wants to set a new standard for those relationships. Compare your draft to those of your classmates and discuss the differences in the drafts.

4. Outline a strategy that Tonya can use to work with representatives from business partners to explain the policy changes she intends to make in how relationships between their organizations will be handled in the future.

COURSE TEST QUESTIONS

1. Business partnerships are _____.
2. Insider misconduct is _____.
3. An insider-outsider threat is _____.
4. Describe a nondisclosure agreement.
5. Describe what personal use means in the context of business relationships.
6. Describe the purpose of a relationship inventory.
7. A value-added supplier is _____.
8. How do color-coded ID badges aid in supporting a company's security effort?
9. What should an employee do if they find that a visitor under their escort tries to wander off on their own to tour a facility?
10. What should managers in an organization do if they find that a representative of a supplier is trying to bribe their employees to buy supplies from the representative's company?

Key Terms

Business partnerships: are relationships between two or more organizations designed to meet specific goals of one or more of the organizations.

Insider misconduct: is conduct by an employee that is against organization policies or procedures, or that otherwise can harm the employing organization.

Insider-outsider threat: is a threat that emerges as a result of a relationship between a company's employee and a person working for an outside organization or who is otherwise not related to the organization.

Nondisclosure agreement: is an agreement between two parties where one or both parties agree not to disclose information or data that has been communicated between the parties.

Onsite contractors: are those individuals or organizations a company hires for specific tasks or projects that perform their job duties within the company's facilities.

Personal use: means an item or service not used for the employing organization and is intended for use only by the recipient.

Professional relationships: are relationships between employees of organizations with which there is a business relationship that serves business interests and does not jeopardize or create risks for either side.

Relationship inventory: is a list or database of all of the outside organizations a company has a relationship with, and who is authorized to represent those organizations and who in the company is authorized to participate in interactions on behalf of the company.

Unprofessional relationships: are relationships between employees of organizations that do business transactions and those relationships do not serve business interests and can jeopardize or create risks for both sides.

Value-added supplier: is a supplier that does more than just provide a specific type of equipment or supply but helps an organization better leverage its product or processes in operations or manufacturing activities.

10

DEVELOPING METHODS TO MONITOR SECURITY THREATS AND NEEDS

Far too many organizations do not update their threat analysis and the steps they need to take to protect their organization from those threats. Monitoring security threats and modifying security processes and methods can be a time-consuming and costly process, but there are ways to accomplish this important task without excessive expenses. This chapter explains how to establish a process of monitoring threats and what sources of information or expertise should be utilized to develop a cost-effective monitoring process.

10.1 Watch, Listen, and Learn

Security threats are often driven by societal trends and security threats, and incidents in turn become societal trends. Somebody in every organization should pay attention to these trends and incidents, and compare what has happened in other places with the organization's ability to prevent similar incidents at facilities and in buildings. Do not be naive about whether the incidents seen on the evening news can happen to an organization in one way or the other. They can.

Do not discount the prudence of seeing things happen in the world around and then examining in-house security to determine if existing *mitigation efforts* can prevent such incidents. Far too often after an incident occurs, those impacted or those responding to the incident comment that they did not think to protect against such a breach. So the key is to learn from other's oversights or poor security planning, and change mitigation methods accordingly.

There are several types of threats that manifest themselves in repeated scenarios. These manifestations are often influenced by societal trends and by recently occurring incidents. Insiders and their collusion with outsiders can bring many unwanted experiences to corporate facilities. Ongoing threats that need to be monitored and observed come from many different threatening groups including the following:

- *Indigenous group* activity is socially motivated and is often provoked by recent events reported in the nightly news, including actions by groups opposed to animal research, genetically modified organisms, environmental issues, or social justice issues.
- *Domestic antisocial groups* are opposed to government control or intervention including land-use issues, urban problems, or radical philosophies.
- *International fanatics* are radical groups that cross borders or influence individuals or groups in other countries to kill, sabotage, or spread hate and fear.
- *Domestic fanatics* are radical groups that are residents or citizens of the countries in which they kill, sabotage, or spread hate and fear.
- *Criminal groups* focus on perpetrating theft to gain financial reward to support their criminal enterprises.
- *Disgruntled employees* are not happy with an organization and use their authorized access to commit crimes against assets or employees.
- Random incidents of vandalism and theft committed by rogue individuals that are not affiliated with any one group or cause but are provoked by social trends or recent incidents.[69]

Pay attention to these types of activities that are reported by the media or an industry association in which the organization has membership.

It is also wise to establish an enemies list or an inventory of groups that have something specifically against the organization or against its industry sector or business partners, and pose a threat based on their previous actions. It is also good to know if any current employees or their relatives are members of a group that does not like the company or the industry. An enemies list needs not be complicated but should include at minimum

- The name of the group or cause, and any information the security staff has related to their locations or centers of activity

- Known incidents that the group has participated in or shown support
- The names of individuals involved with the group, especially those in leadership positions
- The type of facilities or personnel the group has taken action against in the past
- Any changes that occur quickly in the leadership of the group or changes in the group's level or type of activity
- Any information the security staff has on any threats made by groups that specifically targeted their organization

Another area that security staff should keep current on is any news or announcements relevant to how well the mitigation efforts or security technologies that are in place are working or if they are failing. This type of news is far less dramatic then the highlights of a security incident, but bits and pieces come through in the details reported on an incident. This could include how access control systems were breached, how data was stolen, or how other crimes were perpetrated.

10.2 Deciding How to Identify Vulnerabilities

A *vulnerability assessment* can be a self-examination of a company's own facility to identify conditions that might be exploited or attacked by malicious attackers or insiders, or compromised by an unintentional act of one or more employees. Testing vulnerability against outside attackers requires trying to see a company's security faults as attackers would see them. Such an assessment is difficult for insiders to do effectively because they already have information about their facilities. To succeed, they need to set aside almost everything they already know about the staffing and operation of the facilities, and view the world the way an unfamiliar attacker would view the world.[70]

When evaluating vulnerabilities that can be exploited by insiders, security staff also should think like the insider who is trying to commit a crime. However, in this case security staff can also rely on supervisors and other staff to help identify weaknesses in procedures or in access control systems. Discussion sessions and brainstorming exercises can go a long way in helping to identify internal vulnerabilities. In very simple terms, a self-assessment of vulnerabilities requires people to find the weaknesses in facilities, buildings, office areas, and storage areas that security staff and supervisors may think are a secure environment but need improvements to security.[70]

Self-assessment should be an ongoing process, but security staff may not want to stop there. There are several methodologies and checklists that they can rely on to help them navigate through a self-assessment of vulnerabilities. One such evaluation aide is the U.S. Geological Survey "Physical Security Handbook (440-2-H)," which provides a structured approach to examining the physical characters of a facility to detect basic vulnerabilities.[71] This handbook is easy to use and communicates vulnerability terms and concepts in a very straightforward manner. There are numerous security and vulnerability self-assessment handbooks available on the Internet, but they tend to be redundant. However, security staff may find them useful and can find many of them through the search engine at www.usa.gov.

The next option that should be considered is hiring a security consultant who specializes in vulnerability evaluation. This can be rather expensive, but if in-house staff members have worked through the handbooks, they might find a consultant that can provide an independent eye and see things that they missed during the self-assessment. Keep in mind that the consultant will probably be looking at the same things the handbooks recommend but with a fresh perspective toward company facilities. Areas that are commonly examined when evaluating vulnerabilities include the following:

- The structure and staffing of the security department
- Awareness and training efforts
- Incident reporting and investigation
- Facility protection and design factors that either hinder or help facility security
- Perimeter security measures, physical barriers, fencing, gates, and protective lighting
- Entryways and exists including doors, windows, emergency exits, manholes, drains, and roof openings, and the types of locks used to secure the transit ways
- Mechanical areas including heating, ventilation, and air-conditioning (HVAC) systems

- Interior security controls, security vaults and security doors, intrusion detection systems, and surveillance systems
- ID management systems, physical access control systems, and computer access control systems

The question that is difficult to answer is just how much security and protection is really needed to guard against known threats or likely threats. The threat level is not always easy to determine, but the past history of incidents combined with the information on the enemies list is a good start. In addition, companies may be required to have certain levels of security because of contracts or when applicable government regulations dictate security requirements. A general rule has long been do not spend more money to protect an asset than the asset's financial value. This is a difficult rule to interpret when it comes to mitigation efforts to protect human lives.

10.3 Reevaluating Vulnerabilities When the Environment Changes

Just as threats change, so do communities, facilities, buildings, and the various offices or work areas that make up an organization's physical environment. Security staff needs to keep up on any changes that occur in the environment or any changes that are planned for the organization's environment. Changes can occur because of building expansions, remodeling, changes in landscape design, and construction projects in the near vicinity of company facilities. It is amazing how fast such changes can come about, so a periodic and at least an annual vulnerabilities check should be performed. At minimum, the vulnerabilities review should examine changes in

- The *exclusion area*, which is that area in which the organization has the authority to determine all activities including exclusion or removal of personnel and property from the area (outside the protected area)
- Activity areas, which are the spaces where business activities occur that are not required to be in secured areas (could be located outside or inside the protected area)

- The protected area within the exclusion area encompassed by physical barriers, such as one or more chain-link fences (generally surrounded by or adjacent to the exclusions area)
- Secured areas located within protected areas that have additional barriers and alarms to protect vital equipment and assets[72]

When changes are being made in the organization's environment, the *chaos factor* impacts security as construction projects are in progress, remodeling is being done, or there is considerable relocation of equipment, supplies, or work groups. During such activity, there can often be temporary changes in human traffic flow or changes in location of security guards or security barriers. These conditions provide an extra opportunity for an insider to gain unauthorized access to a secure area without being noticed or to remove items from the secured areas. So during such changes it is important to stay vigilant about security.

After changes are made in the organization's environment, confusion can still linger as construction projects are completed or remodeling is completed. After such activity is over, there can still be a period of time when people are getting accustomed to changes in human traffic flow or in entry and exit location or procedures. These conditions can also provide an extra opportunity for an insider to breach security and claim confusion as an excuse for ending up in the wrong place.

The best way to prevent security breaches during and after events that change the organization's environment is to conduct long-range planning and to ensure that security is appropriately maintained during the change events and postevent security is adequately designed to prevent incidents. The insider who is waiting for an opportunity to execute a deliberate security breach will be able to observe the weakness created during the change process and will likely also understand weakness that are left behind after the change event has been completed. Once an event is over that has required changes in mitigation efforts, the new security process and procedures should be reevaluated within a short period of time to ensure that they are addressing vulnerabilities and known threats.

It is also possible for an organization to face changes in its natural environment that can create new threats and increase vulnerabilities.

Climatic changes, whether they are short term like a five-year drought or long term like rising sea levels, can impact an organization's security capabilities. In addition to damage to facilities, a climatic event can be very disruptive to the normal operating routine of an organization. As with other disruptive events, climatic events contribute to the chaos factor that can lead to breakdowns in security and increased opportunity for the insider to cause or create security breaches.[73]

10.4 Reevaluating Vulnerabilities When an Organization Changes

Organizations go through all sorts of changes over time. There could be a transfer of ownership, a merger, downsizing, expansion, consolidation, or diversification. Projects come and go; staffing requirements change; contracts expire or new contracts are initiated; and work processes are modified, modernized, or automated. There can be layoffs, mass hiring, new business partners, budget cuts, or increased spending. All of these changes and other similar changes can contribute to the chaos factor.

As well intended as many organizational changes are, rapid and expansive change can provide an opportunity for the insider to spontaneously breach security or execute a plan they have worked on for a long time to steal or misappropriate assets. The chaos factor makes it easy for the insider because so many people are focused on the organizational changes that are occurring and they far too often become less vigilant about security.

When there are a large number of layoffs, there is often a lot of chaotic activity. If layoffs are to be announced sometime in the near future, the security department and the IT security staff are often provided notice so they can deactivate physical access control security cards and user IDs and passwords that enable employees to access computer systems and network capabilities. Without such notice, an organization can count on several days of chaos.[74]

Even if a mass layoff is well planned, there is usually some opportunity or perceived opportunity for the insider to commit security breaches. It is not uncommon for employees to delete or otherwise damage computer files they have worked on if their computer system access is not quickly rescinded. Layoffs and downsizing is also a time when theft of tools and supplies becomes commonplace. Often after the layoffs there are fewer people in a facility, many of whom may be focusing their attention on whether they will be the next to get a pink slip. Security can break down rather fast during these types of organizational changes and stay broken until the organization stabilizes. It is important to reevaluate vulnerabilities after an organization goes through such disruptive changes.[75]

Mergers, acquisitions, expansions, and diversification can also heavily contribute to the chaos factor. These organization changes often involved new personnel being added to a facility or work group and in some cases the movement of key personnel from the facility or the work group. When there is movement of personnel, especially at the supervisory and management levels, disorder and uncertainty can set in quickly and insiders can make their move to steal or damage assets. Once the personnel change has occurred, it is a good time to reevaluate vulnerabilities to determine if new people are properly following security policies and procedures.

Reorganizations of departments and work groups can also create security vulnerabilities. Many times, such reorganizations occur quickly and employees can be moved from department to department. In cases where these types of changes are done quickly, employees who have not previously had access to secure areas or to corporate data and sensitive information can suddenly end up with access. It is certainly best to preplan such changes to ensure that security is being maintained. When the changes are not preplanned, it is advisable to test if the changes have created new vulnerabilities and that employees have the proper clearance to work in their new assigned capacities.[76]

10.5 Reevaluating Vulnerabilities When Suppliers, Business Partners, and Customers Change

All of the security arrangements and agreements that have been made with suppliers, business partners, and customers can quickly erode when there are changes in their organizations. Just as with any organization, transfer of ownership, merger, downsizing, expansion, consolidation, or diversification in the organizations with which your company has developed relationships can contribute to the chaos factor within their organizations and that chaos can spill over into interactions and business transactions.

If managers receive advanced notice that such changes will occur in the organizations with which they are in relationships, they can prepare employees for changes and potential security issues. This preparation should include working with the outside organization undergoing the changes to ensure that they are complying with previous agreements and they are complying with security requirements. After the changes have occurred, it is advisable to evaluate any vulnerabilities that have been created as a result of the changes.

If there is not advanced notice of changes, then security staff should increase security vigilance immediately upon learning of the changes and until they can be sure there is compliance with security requirements. When suppliers, business partners, or customers go through such changes, employees may end up dealing with an entire set of new representatives from their organizations. This can go smoothly if action is taken quickly and employees practice security vigilance and security compliance in their interactions with the new representatives.

In some cases, new representatives will work with an organization and get to know the processes and procedures as well as the specific employees they are permitted to interact with during the course of business. However, cowboy mentalities can easily set in with the representatives, and they can become overly aggressive in their interactions and get pushy and even threatening if they do not get their way. This is a good time for an executive-to-executive interaction to smooth things out or to at least slow things down during the transition in dealing with new representatives or new policies in the changed organization. It is a time to practice great patience as well as increased security vigilance. After the change has settled in for a while, it is advisable to evaluate any new security vulnerabilities that have emerged out of the transition process.

10.6 Reevaluating Vulnerabilities When Contractors or Service Providers Change

Contractors and service providers that an organization employs are subject to the same types of organizational changes as any company over the course of time. Changes in these organizations differ in that the nature of the relationship with contractors and service providers likely requires their employees to have physical access to the hiring company's facilities. The chaos factor can easily set in during the transition to new contractor employees working in a facility and those new employees should be closely monitored.

If it is an emergency event or crisis situation that brings the new contractor employee to a facility for the first time, then security staff needs to make sure that the new contractor employee is under escort at all times and do so with absolutely no exceptions. If there is time to meet with the new contractor employee, it is advisable to brief them on in-house security procedures.

If the contractor or service provider has had a background check performed on it in the past, then it is advisable to have a new background check if there are new owners or new high-level executives working for the contractor. In addition, if policies required a background check on the past representatives of the contractor, then the new employees should also have background checks. If the contractor works for several organizations that maintain high security, then it will know that this is a requirement and there should be fewer problems.

It is also advisable to monitor the contractor's new employees' action when they are on the premises. All employees should report any difficulties or lack of security compliance that occurs during their interactions with new contractor representatives. A deliberate follow-up review of the interactions by the security staff should help to ensure that no new vulnerabilities have been introduced and that the contractor is complying with security procedures.

As companies may do with business partners and other relationships, they should take the time to monitor the new management and new employees of a contractor or service provider. They should also consider background checks for the new managers of those contractors that work in sensitive or restricted areas. This is time consuming and costly, but if security checks are not run and staff does not perform appropriate monitoring, then it will not be known if there is a new undetected vulnerability manifesting itself.

10.7 Reevaluating Vulnerabilities When Security Technology Changes

It would be great if every time a company upgraded an existing security technology or deployed a new security technology that everything went smoothly and things worked just as the advertisement claimed.

Well things are not always great. What it comes down to is that every time security staff deploys a new technology, the staff needs to thoroughly test the technology and monitor its performance over time to ensure that it is in fact working as expected and that any weaknesses in the technology has not introduced a new vulnerability into existing mitigation efforts.

One important step in the monitoring process is to get reports from security supervisors and staff about any problems they have encountered with the new technology and what the consequences were as a result of those problems. An organization can use this feedback loop to work with the technology seller or service provider to work out any problems.

However, it is also advisable to get such trouble reports on any security technology that has been deployed. In some cases, older security technology may not work well when staff tries to integrate the new security technology into an existing security infrastructure. The important thing is not to make assumptions that security technology is working correctly, including surveillance systems, physical access control systems, and ID management systems. Remember that an organization is very dependent on security technology performing as it is expected to perform.

10.8 Getting Security and Vulnerability Information to the Desktop

Security threats and vulnerabilities are constantly evolving, and with the constant threat of economic espionage and terrorism it is important to keep up on the threat and vulnerability trends as much as possible. There are several agencies and organizations that provide bulletins on the latest events and trends, and many of the bulletins will be sent to an e-mail box without fees. These fee-free bulletins include the following:

- U.S. Computer Emergency Readiness Team Bulletins provide weekly summaries of new vulnerabilities. Patch information is provided when available (https://www.us-cert.gov/ncas/bulletins).
- Information Technology Laboratory (ITL) Bulletins are published monthly by the National Institute of Standards

and Technology's Information Technology Laboratory, focusing on a single topic of significant interest to the computer security community (http://csrc.nist.gov/publications/PubsITLSB.html).

- Where possible and applicable, National Terrorism Advisory System (NTAS) advisories will include steps that individuals and communities can take to protect themselves from the threat as well as help detect or prevent an attack before it happens (https://www.dhs.gov/national-terrorism-advisory-system).

- The U.S. Department of Homeland Security Daily Open Source Infrastructure Report is collected each business day as a summary of open-source published information concerning significant critical infrastructure issues. Each daily report is divided by the critical infrastructure sectors and key assets defined in the National Infrastructure Protection Plan (https://www.dhs.gov/publication/daily-open-source-infrastructure-report).

- The U.S. Federal Bureau of Investigation Law Enforcement Bulletin delivers peer-reviewed articles submitted by a wide range of authorities, including subject matter experts, national security liaisons, officers and agents in the field, and legal instruction advisers (https://leb.fbi.gov/).

- SANS NewsBites is a semiweekly high-level executive summary of the most important news articles that have been published on computer crime and security during the last week. Each news item is very briefly summarized and includes a reference on the web for detailed information, when possible (https://www.sans.org/newsletters/). SANS also provides a number of white papers focused on security.

- IBM® Security Bulletins communicate security vulnerability information to customers when security vulnerabilities are discovered and disclosed in IBM offerings (http://www-03.ibm.com/security/secure-engineering/bulletins.html).

- U.S. Customs and Border Protection Alerts/Bulletins provide information on potential threats to, and security breaches within, international supply chains (https://www.cbp.gov/border-security/ports-entry/cargo-security/c-tpat

-customs-trade-partnership-against-terrorism/Alerts
/Bulletins).

- The Microsoft® Security Response Center releases security
bulletins on a monthly basis addressing security vulnerabilities in Microsoft software, describing their remediation, and
providing links to the applicable updates for affected software
(https://technet.microsoft.com/en-us/library/security/dn631937
.aspx).
- Android® Security Bulletins include information users can follow to ensure their Nexus® device has the latest security updates
(http://source.android.com/security/bulletin/index.html).
- Adobe® Security Bulletins and Advisories provide important information regarding security vulnerabilities that could
affect specific versions of Adobe products (https://helpx.adobe
.com/security.html).

10.9 Summary

This chapter examined practical steps that can be taken to monitor security threats and assess vulnerabilities on an ongoing basis.
Managers and practitioners are encouraged to continuously monitor threats and learn about new and evolving threats. Likewise, vulnerabilities will change as organizations change, including outside
contractors, suppliers, business partners, and customers. As those
organizations change, they can introduce new vulnerabilities just as
easily as they can reduce or eliminate old vulnerabilities. Key areas
covered include the following:

- Establishing and maintaining a list of individuals or organizations that may pose a threat to security and monitor their
activity
- The type of individuals or groups that can be threats to the
organization
- Straightforward methods of evaluating vulnerabilities
- Events in an organization and related organizations that make
it advisable to reexamine vulnerabilities that may be caused by
events that change organizations
- Sources of information on security threats and vulnerabilities

COURSE CASE STUDY   THE JAMES MARTIN MANUFACTURING COMPANY (CONTINUED)

Since Tonya Martin has assumed the CEO position of the James Martin Manufacturing Company, she has found numerous areas where security needs to be improved. The embezzlement and thefts that have occurred over the last decade have proven to her that better security is essential to the sustainability of the company.

So far Tonya, Director of Security Ronald Thomas, and Samuel Davis have taken several piecemeal steps to improve security, including reviewing and modifying existing policies and procedures, developing security awareness, getting people involved in promoting and improving security, improving computer security, and working toward selecting an ID management approach.

The three security team members also started to focus on improving physical access controls for the facilities and stronger security for specific areas in the buildings located within the James Martin Manufacturing facility. They have also started developing policies and procedures to control interactions between company employees and representatives of their suppliers, business partners, and customers.

The security team recognizes that employees from their related organizations have pretty much come and gone as they pleased in the past. One result of the familiarity in relationships between James Martin Manufacturing employees and those of related organizations is that there is an overabundance of some supplies as well as dozens of pieces of equipment that have never been unpacked and put into use in the production process. Tonya also found that some customers have received excessive discounts on many of their orders from James Martin Manufacturing.

As efforts to implement better security have stabilized, Tonya's team decided it was time to develop a list of threats to the organization and to make a more comprehensive assessment of vulnerabilities especially those that impact the physical security of James Martin Manufacturing facilities.

COURSE DISCUSSION QUESTIONS

1. Should Tonya move forward with a vulnerability assessment using the staff she now has or should she hire an outside security firm to conduct the assessment? Discuss the pros and cons of hiring an outside consultant.
2. What type of individuals or groups do you think could be threats to James Martin Manufacturing?
3. Based on your conclusions as to what types of groups could be a threat, what do you think would be the most expedient way to monitor the activities of those groups?
4. What type of bulletins or announcements should Tonya and the director of security have pushed to their desktops to help them keep up with trends and issues that may impact the security of James Martin Manufacturing?

COURSE PROJECTS

1. Draft a checklist of items that the security team at James Martin Manufacturing should make their first priorities when assessing vulnerabilities. Compare your checklist to others in the class and discuss the differences.
2. Draft a procedure that will help the security team at James Martin Manufacturing track changes in their suppliers, business partners, and customers that may impact the vulnerabilities that the company faces. Compare your draft procedure to others in the class and discuss the differences.
3. Create a list of ways that employees at James Martin Manufacturing can help to assess vulnerabilities in security. Compare your list to others in the class and discuss the differences.
4. Create a list of ways that employees at James Martin Manufacturing can help to identify any seriously disgruntled employees working at the company or who have left the company in the last few years. Compare your list to others in the class and discuss the differences.

COURSE TEST QUESTIONS

1. What is the chaos factor?
2. Explain what an exclusion area is.
3. Explain what security threats are.
4. What is a vulnerability assessment?
5. What should you keep in mind when you mix new security technology with older security technology?
6. Why should you be concerned about changes in the ownership of a contractor or service provider that your organization employs?
7. When there are a large number of layoffs in a company, what should the security department and the IT security staff do?
8. In addition to damage that a climatic event can cause to facilities, a climatic event can be _____.
9. The best way to prevent security breaches during and after events that change the organization's environment is _____.
10. When construction projects are in progress, remodeling is being done, or there is considerable relocation of equipment, supplies, or work groups what tends to happen?

Key Terms

Chaos factor: is a condition that occurs as a result of unsettled and disrupted routine operations of an organization or a facility, and an atmosphere of disorder and confusion prevails.

Criminal groups: are comprised of people who are organized for the purpose of committing criminal activity for economic gain or political clout or dominance in a specific geographical area.

Disgruntled employees: are individuals who are disenfranchised from an organization and often act out their frustrations or anger in violent or destructive manners.

Domestic antisocial groups: are groups of people or minisocieties that oppose the larger society in which they live and/or work.

Domestic fanatics: are radical groups that are residents or citizens of the countries in which they kill, sabotage, or spread hate and fear.

Exclusion areas: are those areas that are under the control of an organization in which activities are limited, construction is prohibited, and any type of occupation is usually curtailed that is maintained in order to establish a buffer of nonactivity around a facility or building as a security measure.

Indigenous group: is a group or class of people that live in their area of origin.

International fanatics: are individuals, groups of people, or minisocieties that are greatly differentiated from the world around them by a belief system that is totally disconnected from larger realities in which they live. They have a tendency to act out those differences in violent ways or politically or economically disruptive manners. They are members of radical groups that cross borders or influence individuals or groups in other countries to kill, sabotage, or spread hate and fear.

Mitigation efforts: are the processes, procedures, or technologies that an organization deploys to prevent security breaches.

Security threats: are conditions, people, or events that can jeopardize the security of an organization, a facility, or any asset belonging to an organization or the employees of the organization.

Vulnerability assessment: is a structured process by which to evaluate how secure facilities are based on the perception of threats and security needs.

11

INVESTIGATING AND RESPONDING TO SECURITY INCIDENTS

Determining if and when a security incident has occurred may be obvious in many cases, but in some cases it may not be as easy as it sounds because many security violations go undetected for months or years. Some security violations may never be discovered unless security staff members are vigilant, conduct appropriate audits, and monitor employee behavior. This chapter reviews straightforward reporting methods and useful steps to take when responding to an incident.

Computer security incidents involving insiders are generally handled by the information technology department with assistance from other departments as needed. Handling computer security incidents is a specialization that requires technical competence and experience. Other security incidents involving insiders are generally handled by the security department with assistance from the human resources department and other departments that can contribute to the investigation and employee discipline when deemed appropriate. Cyber issues and the insider are covered in Chapter 14.

11.1 Acting Quickly When Appropriate

When responding to or investigating security incidents, there are structured processes and several procedures that should be followed to effectively handle security incidents. There is one major exception to this principle. In an emergency or security incident that is life threatening or potentially life threatening, there is only one acceptable first step and that is to dial 911, or notify local law enforcement or other appropriate first responders by other means and do so immediately. Do not think about it, do not investigate, and do not try to be a hero, just call for help. There will be plenty of time to complete the paperwork later and there will likely be a pile of paperwork to contend with in the aftermath.

Historically, violent crimes in the workplace are not uncommon, and every year nearly one million individuals become victims of violent crime while working or on duty, which has accounted for as much as 15% of the acts of violence against people in the United States.[77]

Other security incidents that require immediate action are those such as an when an unauthorized truck backing up to the loading dock and two guys start loading it during the workday or after hours. Just call the police and, again, do so immediately. If employees arrive at work in the morning and find doors unlocked and standing open, this could mean that there is or has been an unauthorized person in a facility or building. Do not take chances in such situations; call the police and do so immediately.

11.2 Establishing a Process to Respond to Incidents

First thing, every organization needs established procedures to handle security incidents, and the procedures should clearly detail who is responsible for handling incidents in progress or incidents that have allegedly occurred. A *security violation* is a failure to comply with the policies and procedures established by an organization that could reasonably result in the loss or compromise of sensitive or proprietary information. In practical terms, a violation could also be an incident that endangers the workplace or results in the theft or misappropriation of assets, including equipment, supplies, or products. Lesser violations could include not complying with ID card/badge policies or unauthorized entry to secured areas.

Policies regarding the protection of the facility and assets as well as ID card/badge policies and authorized access have been discussed in previous chapters. Policies regarding civil behavior can be very general to very specific and include prohibiting physical altercations and belligerent behavior toward coworkers or supervisors. In the physical realm, any unprofessional behavior can be a violation of company policies and require intervention from a security team. Violations of computer access policies will be discussed further in Chapter 14.

All organizations need a formal documented procedure as to how to deal with the various types of security and workplace policy violations. When dealing with the security of government or military data and material, the policies and procedures will most likely be dictated by the contracting organization.

The most important cog in the procedure is to whom to report violations and how to report violations. This is not complicated if an organization has a security department of designated security personnel, which in most instances will be the most likely office to compile *preliminary security violation reports*. In the absence of a formal security unit, other administrative managers could be designated as the recipients of reports and be the first to react to the violation.

In the case of a continued disruption of the workplace that does not require law enforcement or other first-responder assistance, the first step should be to quell the disturbance. An initial report of a security violation or security incident should include the following information:

- The nature of the security violation, which is a description of the circumstances surrounding the violation and the relevant policies or procedures that were violated.
- The nature of the violation, such as unauthorized access, access control avoidance, and equipment stolen or damaged.
- The report should also specifically state who was involved, and when and where the violation occurred, including the type of personnel or visitors that were involved in the violation.
- A description of how the violation was discovered.
- The names of those who reported the security violation and when the report was completed.
- A description of any data, information, or assets that were impacted during the violation.[78]

The recipient of the first notice to management of a security violation should either conduct a preliminary inquiry or designate an appropriate person to conduct the preliminary inquiry. The purpose of the preliminary inquiry is to quickly gather all the facts, determine the status of compromised information or assets, and secure any compromised assets if possible.

11.3 Determining a Course of Action

Once the initial security violation inquiry is completed and any necessary immediate action has been taken, then the final report of the incident should be completed and the status of the security violation should be recorded. If the situation has been resolved, then the final report should indicate that along with the nature of the resolution. If more action needs to be taken as a result of the security violation, the report should state what actions should be taken or what damage has been done and could include the following:

- A recommendation that there should be a formal investigation initiated and reports sent to all impacted parties
- A recommendation that there should be a referral to law enforcement for criminal investigation and/or prosecution
- A recommendation that there should be disciplinary action taken with the violator or violators
- A description of any loss that involves sensitive, proprietary information, or physical assets, along with details of what loss has occurred
- A description of any compromise of sensitive or proprietary information, along with details of what has been compromised
- A description of any suspected but unconfirmed compromise, along with details of what may have been compromised
- A conclusion that there was not a loss, compromise, or suspected compromise

The final report should also include the essential facts surrounding the violation, the corrective actions taken to safeguard the sensitive or proprietary information, the disciplinary actions taken against the culpable individual(s) involved in the security violation, and any culpability notifications sent to impacted parties.

There should be a summary of *corrective actions* that includes a description of all actions taken/initiated by the organization to respond to the security violation. There should be details on what corrective actions were taken to improve security. In addition, there should be details on who took the corrective actions and when the actions were taken along with a determination of culpability, and a description that summarizes the procedures followed to investigate the individual(s) involved in the security violation. There should also be a recommendation for any additional necessary security training and explanations of the training, including the training schedule, title, description, and personnel receiving the training.[78]

In the event that disciplinary action was taken with the security violators, the final report should provide details as to what disciplinary actions were taken, which could include the following:

- Warnings issued to violators
- Reprimands given to violators
- Suspensions without pay for violators
- Forfeitures of pay for violators
- Removal of violators from facilities or work areas
- Loss or denial of access to sensitive of proprietary information for violators
- Termination of violator's employment
- Actions that will be taken under the applicable criminal laws and referrals to law enforcement[79]

11.4 Referrals to Law Enforcement Agencies

Depending on the nature of the security violation, a referral or report to law enforcement agencies may be necessary. If the violation involved theft or destruction of physical property or workplace violence, then that referral should be made to local law enforcement agencies. Although procedures may vary from jurisdiction to jurisdiction, police reports are relatively standard and should be completed by a representative of the victim organization upon referral. The representative should also be available after the report to assist law enforcement officers and prosecutors as needed by providing additional information, evidence, or testimony.

If the security incident involves the substantial theft, misappropriation, or *infringement of intellectual property* and that theft occurred in the United States, then it is likely that the company will need to report the incident to the Federal Bureau of Investigation (FBI). Intellectual property can be stolen, infringed upon, or misappropriated in several ways. These include copyrighted works, such as movies, music, books, business software, or games, being illegally reproduced or unauthorized copies being distributed. A trademark infringement can be the unauthorized sale of merchandise or packaging with a counterfeited trademark. In addition, a trade secret can be clandestinely misappropriated by a company insider or outsider on behalf of a competitor.[80] There are several significant laws that are designed to protect intellectual property including the following:

- The Trademark Counterfeiting Act, 18 U.S.C. § 2320(b)(1)(A), provides penalties of up to 10 years' imprisonment and a $2 million fine for a person who intentionally traffics in goods or services and knowingly uses a counterfeit mark.
- The counterfeit labeling provisions of 18 U.S.C. § 2318 prohibit trafficking in counterfeit labels. Violations are punishable by up to five years' imprisonment and a $250,000 fine.
- Copyright infringement is a felony punishable by up to three years' imprisonment and a $250,000 fine under 17 U.S.C. § 506(a) and 18 U.S.C. § 2319 if a person willfully reproduces or distributes at least 10 copies of one or more copyrighted works with a total retail value of more than $2,500 within a 180-day period.
- Pre-release piracy or willful infringement through distribution of a work being prepared for commercial distribution is a felony punishable by up to three years' imprisonment and a $250,000 fine under 17 U.S.C. § 506(a)(1)(C) and 18 U.S.C. § 2319(d).
- The theft of trade secrets is covered by the Economic Espionage Act that criminalizes the theft of trade secrets through 18 U.S.C. § 1831, which prohibits the theft of trade secrets for the benefit of a foreign government or agent of a foreign government and is punishable by up to 15 years' imprisonment and a $5,000,000 fine.
- The theft of trade secrets to benefit someone other than the owner is punishable by up to 10 years' imprisonment and a $250,000 fine. The penalties are higher for defendants who are companies and 18 U.S.C. § 1839(3) provides special protections to victims in trade secret cases to ensure that the confidentiality of trade secret information is preserved during the course of criminal proceedings.

- The Family Entertainment and Copyright Act criminalizes the use of camcorders and similar devices to record movies playing in public theaters and is a felony punishable by up to three years' imprisonment and a $250,000 fine under 18 U.S.C. §2319B(a).[80]

The U.S. Department of Justice warns victims that the *effective prosecution* of intellectual property crime will require a substantial amount of assistance from intellectual property owners who have been victimized. Once such crimes are reported, federal law enforcement authorities prefer to move very quickly to identify the details of the crime and conduct a swift investigation to successfully prosecute intellectual property violations.[79] The good news is that historically federal prosecution for intellectual property crimes has been successful, with a conviction rate of over 80%.[80] There are several ways to report an intellectual property crime to federal and local law enforcement agencies and security staff can contact one of many agencies, including the following:

- The National Intellectual Property Rights Coordination Center (IPR Center) is a joint effort of 20-plus U.S. government investigative and regulatory agencies and representatives from Canada and Mexico that work together to counter intellectual property crimes (http://www.IPRCenter.gov).
- The Federal Bureau of Investigation's Criminal Investigative Division has an Intellectual Property Rights (IPR) Unit that oversees a national intellectual property program. The IPR Unit encourages victims to report intellectual property crimes through the IPR Center or to any of the FBI's 56 field offices (http://www.fbi.gov/contact-us/field/field-offices).[81]
- Internet Crime Complaint Center (IC3) is a partnership of the FBI, the National White Collar Crime Center, and the Department of Justice's Bureau of Justice Assistance that receives, develops, and refers criminal complaints involving a range of cyber crimes, including online intellectual property crime (http://www.ic3.gov).
- U.S. Department of Justice Funded Intellectual Property Enforcement Task Forces are at the state and local levels (https://www.bja.gov/ProgramDetails.aspx?Program_ID=64).

- Intellectual Property Theft Enforcement Teams (IPTETs) created by the U.S. Immigration and Customs Enforcement work in 26 informal task forces to help coordinate intellectual property investigations (http://www.ice.gov/contact/inv/).
- InfraGard is a government and private sector alliance developed to promote the protection of critical information systems with 80 chapters in the United States (https://www.infragard.net/).
- Electronic Crimes Task Forces were created by the U.S. Secret Service and are located in 25 cities in the United States (http://www.secretservice.gov/ectf.shtml).
- Computer Hacking and Intellectual Property (CHIP) Coordinators embedded in each of the 93 U.S. Attorneys' Offices prosecute computer crime and intellectual property offenses (http://www.justice.gov/usao/about/offices.html).[82]

11.5 Information Needed When Reporting Intellectual Property Crimes

As security staff respond to and investigate security violations involving intellectual property crimes, they will need to compile and record as much relevant information as possible. This information will be useful if an organization is going to seek assistance from law enforcement, report an incident to an insurance company, take disciplinary action through human resources processes, update and make notes in personnel records, or plan to take civil or criminal legal action. The information will also be helpful when planning future training sessions and improving security plans and procedures. Details on the types of information that should be compiled are shown in Figure 11.1.

Some of the information needed for reporting will be part of an organization's records on intellectual property. It is also prudent to conduct interviews with various employees to compile information of which they may be aware. Interviewers should record those interviews when possible and keep on file very detailed notes on the interviews conducted. It is also advisable to seek information from people outside the organization if they have knowledge of the intellectual property crime, and record or keep notes on the results of those interviews.

Information to compile about security incidents(6)	
Categories of information	**Specific information needed**
Background information on the victim organization.	Name of company, primary address, nature of business, primary contact, phone numbers, e-mail, fax number, etc.
Description of the intellectual property.	Details about the copyrighted material or trademark/service mark/certification mark including any factors that make its infringement especially problematic.
Details on intellectual property registration.	Documentation on registered copyrights, patents, or trademarks including dates of registration and copies of documents, etc.
Description of the intellectual property crime.	How the theft was discovered, any evidence documenting the crime, photos of items, etc.
Description of the type of infringement.	This could include manufacture, reproduction, import, export, or distribution.
Description of the scope of infringement.	Quantity of illegal reproduction or distribution, etc. The time period that this occurred.
Location of the infringement.	Where intellectual property was reproduced or distributed.
Description of the economic value of the infringement.	Value of goods illegally reproduced or distributed, etc.
List of possible suspects and reason for suspicion.	All contact information available and reason to suspect each listed party.
Theory or knowledge of how crime was committed.	All known details as to how perpetrators accomplished the crime including use of the Internet.
Summary of actions taken to date.	Cease and desist notices sent, etc.
Details of any previous or pending legal actions.	Dates and status of any civil or criminal proceedings regarding the crime.

Figure 11.1   Information to compile about security incidents. (From United States Department of Justice, Computer Crime and Intellectual Property Section, "Checklist for Reporting an Intellectual Property Crime" in Reporting Intellectual Property Crime: A Guide for Victims of Copyright Infringement, Trademark Counterfeiting, and Trade Secret Theft, March 2013, retrieved July 13, 2016, from https://www.justice.gov/sites/default/files/criminal-ccips/legacy/2015/03/26/ip-victim-guide-and-checklist-march-2013.pdf#page=21.)

11.6 Disciplinary Actions and Terminations

Many organizations have adopted the concept of *progressive discipline* to deal with employee misconduct issues. Upon review, managers should consider the misconduct and evidence to determine what level of discipline is appropriate to correct the misconduct. The review and disciplinary process begins with an employee's first misconduct.

If the employee does not correct that misconduct, or engages in other types of misconduct, the *disciplinary action* will become progressively more severe until the employee corrects the misconduct or employment is terminated. If the misconduct is severe enough and there was significant compromise of proprietary or sensitive information or violations of federal, state, or local laws, then the appropriate disciplinary action can be taken without consideration of progressive disciplinary steps.[83]

There are several misconduct issues that can be handled administratively if it is not necessary to refer them to law enforcement. Organizations can set no-tolerance policies for incidents that management perceives as dangerous or disruptive or that compromises highly sensitive information. Other infractions that can be handled administratively through progressive discipline include the following:

- Disclosure of customer or business partner information
- Misuse of company credit cards or online accounts
- Failure to comply with company security policies or procedures
- Creating a disturbance or harassing other employees
- Discourtesy or unprofessional behaviors and actions
- Physical assaults or threats of assaults
- Failure to comply with supervisory or managerial directives
- Misuse of computer systems or networks
- Misuse or damage to company property or assets
- Misuse or damage to company vehicles[83]

The primary purpose of disciplinary action is to help prevent the recurrence of misconduct or violations of policies and procedures. Second, disciplinary action should be designed to improve an employee's attitude and behavior. Finally, disciplinary action should be taken in a manner that helps to maintain discipline and morale among other employees.[84]

All disciplinary actions should be thoroughly documented and kept with related incident reports. In addition, disciplinary actions should be taken as soon as possible after the incident occurred and the final reports on the incident have been completed. The timing of disciplinary action should take into consideration the level of disruption to an organization's operations and the impact of the violation on other employees.

Terminations for violations of security policies or procedures or for general misconduct should be very thoroughly documented and kept on file with any previous warnings and disciplinary action noted. The human resources department should advise management as to whether it is on firm legal ground when terminating an employee as a form of disciplinary action. State and federal laws do govern employee rights when employees are terminated, and an organization should be prepared to defend itself against wrongful termination lawsuits.

11.7 Training Gaps, Security Gaps, and Security Planning

When security violations occur or there are other compliance issues with employees regarding security procedures or workplace conduct, those violations and disciplinary actions taken with employees or contractors can be turned into a learning tool. The information derived from the incident reports can help an organization identify *training gaps* or *gaps in security* policies, procedures, or mitigate mechanisms. The same information can be useful when evaluating security plans and when planning improvements in security.

Examining the motivations driving incidents may help in gaining a better understanding of a local workforce. However, it is what can be learned from the incidents that can be used to improve training and security procedures that will be the most helpful in improving security. For example, if an employee or work group was following procedures and there was still a security violation, then the procedures should be evaluated to determine what weakness in the procedures allowed the security incident to occur. The weaknesses can be eradicated or at least decreased, and security can be made stronger. The process of using incidents as a feedback loop mechanism is an approach to the *lessons-learned process*,[85] which is illustrated in Figure 11.2.

If an incident occurs and it is determined that an employee or workgroup was not following procedures, then it is probably time for additional training focused on the procedures that were not being followed. The impact of the training should be followed up on through discussion sessions with employees, security monitoring, and workflow

The lessons-learned process				
Triggering events →	Security incidents ↓	Security training ↓	Major events or disasters ↓	Observations of day-to-day operations ↓
Step 1:	Collect information from incident reports, training result audits, event summaries, observations			
Step 2:	Aggregate and analyze information			
Step 3:	Validate applicability and relevance of lessons			
Step 4:	Store and archive lessons for future reference			
Step 5:	Disseminate and share lessons to organization's facilities, trainers, security staff, and security planners			
Step 6:	Decide whether to apply lessons learned and how to apply the lessons learned			
Step 7:	Develop training courses or modules for multiple deliver mechanisms			
Step 8:	Deliver training, and collect and analyze training evaluations from participants			
Step 9:	Observe, audit, or otherwise evaluate changes in behavior to verify effectiveness of training and that lessons were learned			
Step 10:	Evaluate and document the effectiveness of the lessons-learned process as applied to identified training objectives			
Step 11:	Use evaluation results to help guide future lessons-learned projects			

Figure 11.2   The lessons-learned process. (Adapted from United States General Accountability Office, Federal Real Property Security: Interagency Security Committee Should Implement a Lessons-Learned Process, September 2012, retrieved July 13, 2016, from www.gao.gov/products/GAO-12 -901. Steps 7, 8, and 11 were added by the author.)

audits to determine if the training was effective. If the training did not result in improved security compliance, then the training material should be reviewed and revised to improve employee comprehension and retention of the training material.

Improving security training and security procedures on the fly is prudent only if it works. Depending on the results of the retraining or the revision of security procedures, an organization may want to step back and review security incidents from the last year or so to determine if there are patterns in the violations that strongly indicate the need for more comprehensive and bottom-to-top training for areas of security that have been shown as weak because of similar repeated incidents. There are four types of training needs assessments:

1. *Organizational assessments* evaluate the level of organization-wide performance required to meet organizational goals and objectives. This type of assessment will help determine what skills, knowledge, and abilities an organization needs to alleviate weaknesses in security compliance with security requirements and procedures.
2. *Occupational assessments* examine specific occupational groups to identify which gaps exist in the skills, knowledge, and abilities required to perform their work duties that can potentially result in security violations.
3. *Task-based assessments* examine a wide range of types of employees to determine if there is a gap in the skills, knowledge, and abilities required to perform specific security procedures.
4. *Individual assessments* examine how well an individual employee is performing security-related tasks or properly executing security procedures, and if the employee has the skills, knowledge, and abilities required to perform the procedures.[86]

By using the feedback from security incidents and the evaluations of the effectiveness of training or modifying security procedures, an organization can decide which of type of training assessment may be necessary to reduce or eliminate security violations in general or specific types of security violations. It will be up to the training staff and security staff to determine if improving security and reducing security violations can be accomplished through training, or through revising security policies and procedures, or a combination of both.

11.8 Summary

This chapter examined ways to organize to respond to security incidents and the steps to go through when responding. This includes compiling preliminary and final reports about incidents, approaches to disciplinary actions, and contacting law enforcement agencies when necessary. The chapter also covered the type of information that should be included in incident reports as well as the type of information about the incident that will help law enforcement agencies respond to security incidents. It also covered methods that will help an organization learn lessons from security incidents and translate those lessons into improved training and more thorough security procedures as well as better mitigation techniques. Key areas covered include the following:

- How to respond when facing life-threatening incidents
- The need for formal documented procedures to respond to security incidents
- The importance of compiling thorough reports on security incidents
- The use of progressive discipline to change an employee's behavior
- Laws that govern intellectual property crimes
- Law enforcement agencies that handle intellectual property crimes and how to contact those agencies
- How to conduct lessons-learned analysis and take action based on those lessons learned

COURSE CASE STUDY THE JAMES MARTIN MANUFACTURING COMPANY (CONTINUED)

Tonya Martin recently became CEO of the James Martin Manufacturing Company, a privately owned company that had been in her family for over 80 years. When her father, James Martin Jr., developed health problems about 10 years ago, he entrusted the company operations to long-time manager Harold Smith, who died a sudden death a few months ago. Upon review, Tonya had discovered that Harold Smith had been embezzling and stealing equipment and supplies from the company for the last decade before his death.

To improve security, Tonya has been working with Ronald Thomas, the new director of security (DOS), and Samuel Davis, a newly hired supervisor with considerable experience in manufacturing. They had become the security planning team for the company. The team has made considerable progress in getting other people involved in promoting and improving security.

Tonya wanted to maintain a friendly but strict security atmosphere at the company and did not want employees to feel that James Martin Manufacturing had become militarized. She was successful in encouraging cooperation and good feelings about the changes in security practices at the company.

The three security team members agreed they needed a more structured approach in dealing with security violations and incidents because they were implementing several new security methods, procedures, and systems, and wanted to be able to handle violations uniformly and fairly. They suspected that some security violations occurred because employees had not been well trained on security procedures and could have ended up making unintentional blunders in handling sensitive data.

One of their next projects will be to establish a system for reporting security violations, investigating the violations, and responding appropriately. Tonya has been very concerned about being able to protect the intellectual property of the company because long-term sustainability for the company is essential. Tonya also believes that they should learn from their failures and their mistakes in order to grow and change the security atmosphere at James Martin Manufacturing.

COURSE DISCUSSION QUESTIONS

1. What steps should the security team at James Martin Manufacturing take before they introduce a new security violation reporting and investigating process?

2. How should the security team determine what the appropriate disciplinary measures are that should be applied when there are security violations at James Martin Manufacturing?

3. What approach should the security team at James Martin Manufacturing take to assess the need for additional security training?

4. How would hiring an outside consultant at this point help the security team move forward to continue improving security at James Martin Manufacturing?

COURSE PROJECTS

1. Develop three alternatives ways that James Martin Manufacturing could structure the organization to handle reported security violations. Compare your alternatives to those of your classmates and discuss the differences.
2. Develop a 10-slide PowerPoint presentation to use in a briefing of James Martin Manufacturing employees about reporting security violations. Compare your presentation to those of your classmates and discuss the differences.
3. Draft a one-page memo to James Martin Manufacturing employees that explains the basic steps companies take when there is a security violation. Compare your memo to those of your classmates and discuss the differences.
4. Develop a one-minute elevator speech covering the need to have a security incident investigation process that Tonya can use when discussing the topic with James Martin Manufacturing employees. Compare your one-minute speech to those of your classmates and discuss the differences.

COURSE TEST QUESTIONS

1. Effective prosecution is _____.
2. Gaps in security are _____.
3. Infringement of intellectual property can be _____.
4. The lessons-learned process is _____.
5. Occupational assessments are designed to _____.
6. Progressive discipline is _____.
7. A security violation is _____.
8. In a life-threatening security incident you should _____.
9. Terminations for violations of security policies or procedures or for general misconduct should be _____.
10. A trademark infringement can be _____.

Key Terms

Corrective actions: are those steps that are taken to restore normal operations after an incident and what steps are taken to change an employee's behavior and eliminate further security violations by the employee.

Disciplinary action: is the action taken toward an employee who has violated corporate security policies and procedures or other corporate behavioral policies.

Effective prosecution: is the successful prosecution of intellectual crime perpetrators while simultaneously protecting the trade secrets and other intellectual property of the victim organization.

Gaps in security: are security measures or mitigation methods that are inadequate to protect an asset or do not thoroughly protect the asset that they were deployed to protect.

Individual assessments: are designed to evaluate how well an individual employee is performing a specific task or types of tasks necessary to fulfill job responsibilities.

Infringement of intellectual property: can be the unauthorized reproduction or distribution of copyrighted material, the misappropriation of trade secrets for commercial gain, or the unauthorized use of a trademarked name or logo.

Lessons-learned process: is a structured method of evaluating incidents or events, and determining what individuals or organizations could have done better to deal with the situation, and transforming that lesson into positive actions through employee training, improving procedures, or improving mitigation methods or technology.

Occupational assessments: are designed to examine specific occupational groups to identify gaps in the skills, knowledge, and abilities required to perform their work duties that can potentially result in security violations.

Organizational assessments: are designed to evaluate the level of organizational performance that is required to meet organizational goals and objectives.

Preliminary security violation report: is the first report of a security incident that communicates the basic known facts about the incident including who was involved and the immediate known consequences of the violation.

Progressive discipline: is the application of increasingly severe disciplinary measures to attempt to change an employee's behavior and increase compliance with corporate policies and procedures.

Security violation: is a failure to comply with the policies and procedures established by your organization that could reasonably result in the loss or compromise of sensitive or proprietary information.

Task-based assessments: are designed to evaluate the performance of a wide range of types of employees to determine if there is a gap in the skills, knowledge, and abilities required to perform specific procedures or tasks.

Training gaps: are operational procedures or security methods that employees have not been adequately trained to execute.

12

USING SURVEILLANCE TECHNOLOGIES AND TECHNIQUES

Surveillance technology and its use in conjunction with ID management systems and physical access control systems is a common practice in many organizations, especially in those facilities or buildings that require high levels of security. Although surveillance of facilities is a very good way to detect and prevent security breaches, the technology and the process can be expensive as well as problematic. This chapter covers the basics of managing surveillance systems to prevent insiders from inappropriately accessing secure parts of facilities.

It is important to note that many states in the United States have passed laws or are discussing laws that pertain to video surveillance. Much of the debate about surveillance technology revolves around privacy and the latest antisocial tendency of sexual predators to practice video voyeurism. Many of these laws are well intentioned and are designed to protect individual privacy and safety. Lawmakers and law enforcement officials recognize that it has become an expected norm that a person has "a reasonable expectation of privacy when a reasonable person would believe that he or she could fully disrobe in privacy, without being concerned that the person's undressing was being viewed, recorded, or broadcasted by another, including, but not limited to, the interior of a residential dwelling, bathroom, changing room, fitting room, dressing room, or tanning booth."[87]

The privacy debate and the use of surveillance technologies is moving rather quickly and is expected to continue to evolve. Given the dynamics, it is advisable that all organizations currently using or planning to use video surveillance should consult with their attorneys and keep current on local and state laws that impact their facilities.

12.1 Selecting Surveillance Methods for an Organization

The use of surveillance cameras and other surveillance technology requires careful evaluation and meticulous implementation. In the case of *video surveillance technology*, the placement of cameras is crucial to maximize their effectiveness. Several decisions must be made including whether to use either a *passive video surveillance system*, which relies on the retrieval of previously recorded images that are viewed after the fact, or an *active video surveillance system*, which is monitored in real time usually by security officers. With both systems, those viewing the footage must be trained on the type of activity to watch for, which is why those with law surveillance experience are typically thought to be better suited in these roles. However, regardless of previous experience, all personnel viewing camera footage should have training to help them to learn the process.[88]

In most organizations, the ultimate goal of installing surveillance cameras and other surveillance technology is to reduce property crimes and security violations. The use of surveillance cameras is thought to reduce property crimes and security violations through various dynamics. For instance, by increasing the perceived risk of offending, potential offenders may choose not to offend. By increasing actual detection through surveillance, early intervention may be possible to avert a property crime or security violation.[89]

Typically, surveillance cameras are placed in elevated locations on the perimeters of a facility to provide the greatest possible range and area of surveillance. This placement allows the personnel monitoring the video feed to have the greatest visibility into activities occurring outside the buildings. Surveillance cameras are also usually placed within facilities to monitor specific entry and exit points to areas needing surveillance such as the loading dock, the parking garage, and hallways in the building interiors.

Surveillance cameras used for these types of systems usually contain low-light technology to support detection of unauthorized or suspicious activities at night. The cameras can also use pan/tilt/zoom capability with manual tracking allowing surveillance personnel to adjust the camera in real time to gain the best image of any suspicious or illegal activity that is occurring.[90]

In addition to video surveillance, there are several other types of surveillance methods. These technologies include *audio surveillance systems*, telephone monitoring, e-mail and voice mail monitoring, computer keystroke monitoring, Internet website monitoring, *location tracking* using employee ID cards/badges, and GPS-augmented systems used for tracking vehicles. Organizations can also open and read U.S. Postal Service mail addressed to employees at and delivered to the workplace.

When selecting surveillance systems and methodologies, potential buyers should beware that state laws vary on how the systems can be used and where they can be used. The 1986 Electronic Communications Privacy Act (ECPA) prohibits the intentional interception of any wire, oral, or electronic communication of private citizens, but it includes a business-use exemption that permits e-mail and phone call monitoring. To be on safe ground as an organization, management should have employees sign consent forms and agree to corporate policies when they are hired.[90] At this point it is widely accepted that an employer is generally allowed to monitor workplace communications, such as business phone calls and computer usage, and to access company-owned voicemail and e-mails.[91] Again, it is wise to check state laws that may add some nuances to the situation.[92]

Types of surveillance include the following:

- *Computer use surveillance* is relatively easy and common place, including viewing what is on a user's computer monitor at any given time, e-mail use, Internet use, websites visited, applications used, and keystrokes made. In most cases, employees will be unaware of the surveillance and unhindered by the software installed to conduct the surveillance.
- *Telephone usage surveillance* can monitor an employee's office phone use including which phone numbers were called from the work phone, the duration of the calls, real-time monitoring of conversation, and recordings of actual conversations. In addition, an organization can monitor employee use of a company-issued mobile phone including recording text messages, e-mail, web surfing, contacts, calls made, location information if available on the phone, along with photos and videos stored on the phone. It is also important to note that if an employee brings a mobile phone into the workplace, there

is technology that enables employers to monitor those phones just as they would a company-issued phone.

- In addition to video surveillance systems, there are also audio surveillance systems that can capture voice conversations in an organization's facilities. More advanced systems can monitor both video images and audio conversation simultaneously and follow people as they move throughout a facility.
- Organizations may also use Global Positioning Systems (GPS) devices to track employees in employer-owned vehicles including trucks, automobiles, and self-propelled utility vehicles. The GPS tracking systems monitor where the vehicles travel, how long the transit takes, and how long the vehicle stops at each location visited.

12.2 Why Employee Surveillance and Monitoring Is Important

There are several reasons why monitoring how employees use an organization's technology systems is important. For this analysis, security is the top concern. Insiders have a long track record of stealing proprietary data and sensitive information for a variety of reasons including their own economic gain. There are other significant, although less dramatic, reasons why employee uses of technology should be controlled.

Lost productivity is a very critical issue, especially in unauthorized or inappropriate computer and Internet usage. People love the Internet for shopping, social media, reading, movies, music, and pornography, just to name a few. The economic impact of unauthorized Internet use in the workplace adds up very quickly. The dollar amount of lost wages for a half hour of unauthorized Internet use per employee per year for different wage levels is shown in Figure 12.1. The lost productivity can be very substantial and may easily pay for the software to monitor unauthorized employee Internet use.

In addition to lost productivity, unauthorized Internet use also has an impact on the cost of network bandwidth and data download fees. Depending on the websites visited by employees, there is also the possibility of downloaded malware, spyware, and malicious code of all sorts. Likewise, unauthorized use of e-mail, mobile phones, and

Economic impact of unauthorized internet use				
Number of employees	Average hours of unauthorized use per day per employee	Average hours of unauthorized use per year company wide (based on 200 workdays per year)	Average hourly wage plus benefits	Wages lost per year
50	0.5	5,000	$25.00	$100,000
100	0.5	10,000	$25.00	$200,000
500	0.5	50,000	$25.00	$1,000,000
500	0.5	5,000	$40.00	$200,000
100	0.5	10,000	$40.00	$400,000
500	0.5	50,000	$40.00	$2,000,000
500	0.5	5,000	$60.00	$300,000
100	0.5	10,000	$60.00	$600,000
500	0.5	50,000	$60.00	$3,000,000

Figure 12.1   Economic impact of unauthorized Internet use.

landline phones can increase the costs of these technologies along with the productivity lost during the unauthorized use.

12.3 Using Data from Employee Surveillance Systems

Before investing a lot of money and time in surveillance technology, it is prudent to think through the entire scheme from purchasing, installing, maintaining, and using data from surveillance systems. This includes the time and expense required to extract data from the systems and to constructively use that data to support security efforts.

Just as with surveillance, which can be used either in a passive mode that relies on the retrieval of previously recorded images that are viewed after the fact or an active mode that is monitored in real time, all types of surveillance systems can be deployed in some degree of proactive or reactive modes. Regardless of what mode you deploy, surveillance technology in your organization will not maximize the value of the technology unless it is properly used and used to it highest potential. After reviewing the history of several surveillance technologies, it was found that there are several things to keep in mind when purchasing any form of surveillance hardware or software:

- Surveillance technologies are constantly evolving with more features being added to products every year.
- Some surveillance technologies can provide considerable data on activities that take place in your enterprise, whereas others provide very limited data.
- The effectiveness of surveillance technologies vary considerably, and determining just how effective one specific product is compared to other products can be a challenging, time-consuming process.
- Some surveillance products claim to be very easy to use, whereas others appear to be rather complicated.
- Most surveillance products will require some training for security or information technology (IT) staff to install, maintain, and use on an ongoing basis.
- Deploying several different surveillance products in your facilities will likely take additional security or IT staff to install, maintain, and use on an ongoing basis.
- Many PC-based products for website blocking require access to a PC where the software is installed to extract data about web usage.
- Server-based software can be easier to work with because it is possible to monitor many PCs from one server.
- All surveillance products have some weaknesses, and it is doubtful that an organization can find any perfect surveillance products.
- When purchasing surveillance products, organizations will need to assign a staff person to evaluate and recommend products using methods similar to those discussed in Chapter 6.

Once an organization has selected, acquired, and deployed surveillance technologies and they are properly functioning, then the surveillance staff needs to establish a structured process to extract data from the surveillance systems. However, the work does not stop there. Now that the security team has data, what is it going to do with the data? The surveillance technologies installed will probably always provide some level of deterrence value. However, to maximize the effectiveness of the systems, there needs to be a place and process for surveillance technology-generated data to be analyzed and put to use as a security tool.

Analyzing data generated by surveillance systems is a time-consuming and often boring process. If some time goes by and there has not been a security incident, there may be a tendency to place analyzing this data at a low priority. If this occurs, then an organization may have ended up wasting a great deal of money and time.

Assuming an organization manages to establish an effective process to extract and analyze data from security systems, then the next step is to use that data in a manner that improves security. This could include changes in security procedures or disciplinary action being taken with security violators, as discussed in Chapter 11.

The bottom line on surveillance technologies is that they will not make an organization any more secure if the capabilities of the systems are not fully utilized. In fact, if security staff does not analyze the data the systems can generate and act upon those analyses, employees will soon figure that out. Upon the realization that the organization is not fully utilizing the technologies, insiders with crime on their minds will be far less deterred by the presence of the technology than security planners hoped they would. Once again, organizations are heading down the path of just having wasted time and money and not improved security.

12.4 Blocking and Deterring Unauthorized Use of Assets by Employees

Computer use in the workplace has been increasing steadily over the last two decades. As early as 2003, there were 77 million workers who used a computer at work, and accessing the Internet or using e-mail was among their most frequent activities.[93] Also over the last two decades, more people are doing at least some of their work from home, which has increased the need for telecommuting capabilities, including remote access to corporate computers. In 2015, 38% of workers in management, business, and financial operations occupations, and 35% of those employed in professional and related occupations did some or all of their work from home on days they worked.[94]

One way to prevent unauthorized use is to deploy technologies that prevent behaviors rather than just monitor behaviors. One of the fundamental elements in preventing unauthorized use is to constantly remind employees about what is authorized and the consequences for unauthorized use. Many organizations now employ an *authorized use warning statement* for computer systems access that appears on a computer monitor every time an employee logs into the system. An example of a warning statement is shown in Figure 12.2.[95]

Another method of preventing unauthorized use of computers and the Internet is to deploy website-blocking software. There is a wide variety of website blockers, and many have been heavily scrutinized for their effectiveness in nearly three-quarters of the tests run by a variety of testing organizations. That, combined with the widespread

---

**Sample authorized use warning statement
for computer access**

This ORGANIZATION NAME computer is for authorized users only. By accessing this system you are consenting to complete monitoring with no expectation of privacy. Unauthorized access or use may subject you to disciplinary action and criminal prosecution.

The following disclaimer is a policy statement which requires concurrence from all users of ORGANIZATION NAME information systems: Unauthorized use of the computer accounts and computer resources to which I am granted access is a violation of ORGANIZATION NAME security policies and constitutes theft; and is punishable by law.

I understand that I am the only individual to access these accounts and will not knowingly permit access by others without written approval.

I understand that my misuse of assigned accounts and my accessing others' accounts without authorization is not allowed. I understand that this/these system(s) and resources are subject to monitoring and recording and I will have no expectation of privacy in my use of and content on these systems and the computer equipment.

I further understand that failure to abide by these provisions may constitute grounds for termination of access privileges, administrative action, and/or civil or criminal prosecution.

Figure 12.2 Sample authorized-use warning statement for computer access. (From United States National Aeronautics and Space Administration, Security of Information Technology— Chapter 4: Technical Controls, May 19, 2011, retrieved July 17, 2016, from http://nodis3.gsfc.nasa .gov/displayDir.cfm?Internal_ID=N_PR_2810_001A_&page_name=Chapter4.)

adoption of filters and a growth in the industry, indicates that filters are here to stay.[96]

Other blocking methods that can be deployed are restrictions on telephone access. Many telephone systems designed for office use require employees to enter a numeric code that serves as their ID when making calls. The telephone systems create logs of all calls, and usage reports can be generated by user ID number as well as telephone numbers called. The telephone systems' user ID works like a computer access ID and can restrict usage such as long-distance calling.

Many organizations utilize a policy approach to deter unauthorized use of organization assets by employees by putting policies in place that prohibit unauthorized use. These policies can cover computer systems, telephone systems, photocopiers, tools and equipment of all sorts, corporate vehicles, and more. Using policies without surveillance, monitoring, and enforcement diminishes the impact of policies on authorized or unauthorized use. The policies may be effective in deterring honest people from misusing corporate assets but will probably have little or no impact with people who intend to misuse assets until they are caught and disciplined. Many of those organizations that have strict policies on unauthorized use have historically been lax when it comes to taking timely disciplinary actions.[97]

12.5 Deploying Advanced Sensor-Based Surveillance Systems

There have been scores of advances in surveillance and monitoring system technology through the development and deployment of networked sensors that can be used to detect and warn on a wide variety of conditions and events. The capabilities that these advance sensor-based systems provide go way beyond the video and acoustic surveillance capabilities that security has long relied upon.

A sensor is any device that can take a stimulus, such as heat, light, magnetism, or exposure to a particular chemical, and convert it to a signal that can be transmitted over a network to a control or surveillance system. Recent developments include devices to sense light (photocells), sound (microphones), ground vibrations (seismometers), and force (accelerometers), as well as sensors for magnetic and electric fields, radiation, strain, acidity, and many other phenomena. The modern sensor is smarter, smaller, and easier to deploy than the previous generations of surveillance devices.[98]

The many advances in sensing technologies have been made possible through the miniaturization of sensors, wireless communications to network sensors, and the integration of sensors with microprocessing capabilities to support applications that help better understand the conditions and performance of buildings. These sensors can certainly assist in building or facility management but can also make buildings and facilities safer and more secure. One thing most feared about insiders is their ability to sabotage physical assets, and advance sensors are not only able to detect the presence of unauthorized intruders but will be able to warn of any changes in the environment to which the intruder has gained access.[99]

Occupancy sensors that can detect human presence are capable of enabling control of building components, and they can modulate light output and initiate other systems. For example, when a room is unoccupied, the lights automatically either turn off or dim to a low state to conserve energy. Depending on the control strategy, lights may either turn on automatically when occupancy is detected and will be able to lock and unlock doors. This cannot only provide greater overall energy savings but can control insider movement in a building.

The deployment of wireless systems can help overcome many of the traditional barriers to wired controls. They permit installation in buildings with minimal alterations to the building. They can also reduce installation costs by eliminating the need for extensive wiring through walls. In addition, wireless systems can provide better coverage for larger spaces, such as hallways, warehouse, stairwells, and lecture halls. Finally, calibration and commissioning can be easier compared to wired sensors.

If building codes require that certain spaces, such as stairwells, not go completely dark even when not in use, then light fixtures in these spaces can be deployed with bilevel dimming. In other cases, such as mechanical rooms, manual overrides can be installed for safety considerations.[100]

12.6 The Surveillance Technology of the Future

Surveillance technologies will continue to evolve and gain more sophisticated features as technology becomes available. For example, through the use of video analytics technology, analysis of the overwhelming amount of stored surveillance video can be automated, which will accelerate the review of stored surveillance video to identify threats or security breaches. Other intelligent software will analyze movement in live and recorded video to enhance security officers' situational awareness and alert them to suspicious behavior. Eventually this smart technology will be able to interpret the intent and predict the behavior of monitored subjects.

Smart surveillance technology will help in securing crowded environments by estimating crowd and group size, crowd density, and group speed and direction. This will include the analysis of patterns of following, chasing, fast movement, group formation, and dispersion. Eventually, smart technology will automatically assess social group network structure, number of groups, and leadership structure in small communities.[101]

Through-the-wall surveillance (TWS) technology will be able to detect motion through interior or exterior building walls. TWS can penetrate brick, reinforced concrete, concrete block, sheetrock, wood, plaster, fiberglass, and common building material. It will enable security officers to locate and track individuals inside a building during crisis situations as well as normal day-to-day operations.[102]

Biometrics is the science of using one or more unique physical characteristics or behavioral traits to identify individuals. The best-known biometric identification method is fingerprinting. Other methods are based on facial, iris, voice, handwriting, and signature recognition. Fast and accurate identification enhances officer safety, detects criminals, and helps to secure facilities and information systems from unauthorized access. Already in use in high-security environments, biometric technology will become more widely available as its deployment increases and cost decreases.

It is expected that biometric technology will assist in the identification of individuals, even if they have altered their appearances, from video and audio surveillance for prevention of unauthorized access to secure areas. It may also expedite capture of latent and rolled-equivalent fingerprints and palm prints for security background checks.[103]

Facial recognition technologies are able to identify suspects, and improve security and security officer safety. These systems use multidimensional imaging techniques to create facial images. Recent breakthroughs in high-resolution imagery show the most potential for improving the accuracy of two-dimensional and three-dimensional facial recognition systems.[104]

12.7 Self-Assessment for Selecting Appropriate Surveillance Systems

Before selecting a new video surveillance system or upgrading or replacing an installed system, it is prudent to step back for a moment to determine what is actually needed in a video surveillance system, just as you would in selecting any security technology. Be careful in the selection and design, and be sure to purchase and install what is actually needed to help secure a facility. Consider the following questions in the self-assessment process:

- Have there been times in the past when a video surveillance system has added to security or could have added to security for the facility?
- Have threats been identified from which a video surveillance system can help protect a facility?
- Does the organization have the necessary staff to properly use and benefit from a video surveillance system?
- Are business partners or customers concerned about video surveillance for the facility?
- Has the organization's insurance carrier suggested a video surveillance system or are there discounts on insurance premiums for the facility if there is a video surveillance system installed?
- Do the environmental or social conditions surrounding the facility warrant the installation of a video surveillance system?
- Has business activity changed at the facility or will it change at the facility in a way that makes a video surveillance system a desirable addition to the security efforts of the facility?
- Does the threat of a security incident at the facility make the investment in a video surveillance system financially viable?

If the answer to most of these questions is yes, then a video surveillance system may be worth the investment. If not, decide if there are other overriding concerns that compel the organization to investment in a video surveillance system. Balancing the cost-benefit for installing a video surveillance system or upgrading an installed system can some-times be rather tricky. At times, if there is not a clear answer as to the benefit of installing a video surveillance system, it may be best to start a discussion based on how management and employees perceive the value of the system and if it would make them feel more secure if a system is installed.

If it has been decided to install a video surveillance system, then the next step is to determine what type of system will best add to the security efforts for a facility. Consider the following questions in the self-assessment of what type of video surveillance system should be installed:

- Is the video surveillance system designed to protect against insider threats, outsider threats, or both?
- Will the video surveillance system under consideration help to protect the most valuable part of the facility, for which it is being purchased?
- Does the facility need a video surveillance system that works in real time to help control access to the facility, or will the video surveillance system merely record a video record that can be accessed at a later date to investigate or identify a secu-rity incident?
- Does the video surveillance system that is under consider-ation require additional personnel to maintain and operate?
- Is the long-term cost of ownership for the video surveillance system under consideration affordable by the organization?

The decision as to what video surveillance system to purchase and install is more complicated than the decision to purchase. If costs are acceptable and the video surveillance system under consideration will, in the perspective of management, help improve security, then that video surveillance system may be worth the investment. If after evalu-ating a video surveillance system there is still uncertainty about the value and effectiveness of the system, then it is worthwhile to consider other video surveillance systems. There are many systems on the mar-ket and it may take a while to find the right fit for a particular facility.

These or very similar questions can be used to help guide decisions about other surveillance systems or control systems for information systems, telephone systems, or even corporate vehicles. In many cases it may not take a great deal of added security technology to improve security or to increase the feeling of security.

The caution being suggested at this point is geared to help buyers make fiscally sound decisions. If new systems are inadequate to add to security efforts, then they are probably not worth the investment. Likewise, if new systems are much larger or much more capable than what is actually needed, then the overspending will not increase mitigation efforts and the money will be wasted.

12.8 Summary

This chapter examined how surveillance systems can aid in an organization's security efforts. The complexity of surveillance systems was also discussed along with some of the challenges in achieving a reasonable return on investment from the surveillance system. The chapter also examined potential staffing issues and the long-term cost of ownership of surveillance systems. Key areas covered include the following:

- How to decide to install a surveillance system
- How to select a surveillance system
- The economic impact of employee misuse of an organization's technology
- The need to actually use the data generated by some surveillance systems to determine which employees or visitors have been violating security policies or procedures
- What emerging and future surveillance technology will be able to add to an organization's security efforts
- The need to check on state laws that could restrict the use of certain surveillance systems
- The use of blocking technologies to prevent employees from unauthorized use of technology

COURSE CASE STUDY   THE JAMES MARTIN MANUFACTURING COMPANY (CONTINUED)

Tonya Martin recently became CEO of the James Martin Manufacturing Company, a privately owned company that had been in her family for over 80 years. Tonya assumed the position when long-time manager Harold Smith died a sudden death a few months ago. Upon review, Tonya had discovered that Harold Smith had been embezzling and stealing equipment and supplies from the company for the last decade before his death.

The security team members agreed they needed a more structured approach in dealing with security violations and incidents because they were implementing several new security methods, procedures, and systems, and wanted to be able to handle violations uniformly and fairly. This included establishing a system for reporting security violations, investigating the violations, and responding appropriately. The team suspected that some security violations would occur because employees have not been well trained on security procedures and would end up making unintentional blunders in handling sensitive data.

Tonya was very concerned about being able to protect the intellectual property of the company because long-term sustainability for the company is essential. Tonya also believed that they should learn from their failures and their mistakes in order to grow and change the security atmosphere at James Martin Manufacturing.

The security planning team at James Martin Manufacturing decided now was the time to consider surveillance systems and they are starting to evaluate what types of surveillance systems would best serve the company's security needs.

COURSE DISCUSSION QUESTIONS

1. What are the first three things that the security planning team at James Martin Manufacturing should do to determine what type of surveillance systems they should have installed?
2. What policies should be put into place at James Martin Manufacturing regarding use of the company's computer systems?
3. What should the security team do about monitoring use of the company's telephone system?

4. How should Tonya go about discussing the upcoming installation of a new video surveillance system at James Martin Manufacturing?

COURSE PROJECTS

1. Draft a 10-slide PowerPoint presentation that Tonya can use to brief employees on a new authorized computer-use policy at James Martin Manufacturing. Compare your presentation with that of your classmates and discuss the differences.
2. Create a process to determine what type of video surveillance should be installed at James Martin Manufacturing. Compare your process with that of your classmates and discuss the differences.
3. Create a process to determine where in James Martin Manufacturing the new video surveillance cameras should be placed. Compare your process with that of your classmates and discuss the differences.
4. Since there is only one security person at James Martin Manufacturing, devise a plan to staff the video surveillance system. Compare your plan with that of your classmates and discuss the differences.

COURSE TEST QUESTIONS

1. Active video surveillance systems _____.
2. A process that employs technology such as GPS trackers of RFID chips to monitor the movement and/or location of assets or people is known as _____.
3. The science of using one or more unique physical characteristics or behavioral traits to identify individuals is known as _____.
4. Authorized use warning statements are _____.
5. Sensors that can detect a human presence in a specific space, and are capable of enabling control of building components, and modulate light output and initiate other system responses are known as _____.
6. Smart surveillance technology can _____.

7. A system that records and stores video images of activity at a facility so the images can be accessed and reviewed at a later time is known as a _____.
8. Wireless surveillance systems can help overcome many of the traditional barriers to wired controls including _____.
9. A sensor is any device that can _____.
10. A method of preventing unauthorized use of computers and the Internet is to _____.

Key Terms

Active video surveillance systems: are systems that provide usable real-time images of activity at a facility so security interventions can be made as an incident occurs.

Audio surveillance systems: are designed to monitor and record voices or noises that occur at specific locations in a facility where microphones are placed, and the recordings can be reviewed at a later date or for immediate security intervention into an incident.

Authorized use warning statement: is a statement installed on computer systems that notifies users what is allowed or not allowed when they access an organization's computer systems and which appears on a computer monitor every time an employee logs into the system.

Biometrics: is the science of using one or more unique physical characteristics or behavioral traits to identify individuals.

Computer use surveillance: is a process that tracks and records what users do or attempt to do when using corporate computer systems.

Facial recognition technologies: are technologies that are able to identify human subjects in an idle position or while in motion, and the identification and images are used to improve security and security officer safety.

Location tracking: is a process that employs technology such as GPS trackers of RFID chips to monitor the movement and/or location of assets or people.

Occupancy sensors: can detect a human presence in a specific space, and are capable of enabling control of building components, and can modulate light output and initiate other system responses.

Passive video surveillance systems: record and store video images of activity at a facility so the images can be accessed and reviewed at a later time.

Smart surveillance technology: can help secure crowded environments by estimating crowd and group size, crowd density, and group speed and direction.

Surveillance technology: is any technology that helps an organization watch what employees or visitors are doing while at the facility.

Telephone usage surveillance: is a process that tracks and records what users do or attempt to do when using corporate telephone systems.

Through-the-wall surveillance (TWS) technology: is able to detect motion or movement of people of machines through interior or exterior building walls.

Video surveillance technology: is a system or components that view, record, and/or store images of activity at a facility.

13

WHAT TO DO WHEN HIRING NEW EMPLOYEES

Turnover in the workforce is a natural process, and organizations frequently need to hire new employees. This chapter covers ways to prioritize what to do when hiring various types of employees, including background checks and obtaining references. It is important to recognize that the human resources department is an intricate part of any organization's security effort when it comes to dealing with insider risks. The human resources department is an organization's front line of defense when hiring staff, working on background checks, and working with the training staff to ensure that new hires are appropriately oriented and trained on security requirements.

It is also important to remember that the human resources department can play a key role in administering discipline for security infractions and handling terminations when an employee has made serious security violations or has had repeat infractions. Security staff and the human resources department will always need to work together in efforts to manage security and control insider behavior.

13.1 Addressing Security Concerns Early in the Hiring Process

When hiring new employees, it is important to take security requirements and issues into consideration from the very beginning of the hiring process. *Job analysis* is the first step in the hiring process and a very important step that should not be ignored. Traditionally, job analysis provides an understanding of the tasks performed by workers in the position and the competencies required to perform those tasks as well as the relationship between tasks and competencies.[105]

Now, in the age of heightened concerns about security, a contemporary job analysis will also address security issues related to a specific position that is being created or filled with a new hire.

Security requirements are an essential part of a position description. The human resources department needs to be made fully aware of what, if any, security requirements are essential for a specific position or type of position in the organization. This includes providing enough information about security functions the position may be responsible for and making a joint decision with the human resources department on whether security-related skills should be included on any occupational questionnaires used with applicants for the position. An *occupational questionnaire* typically consists of questions that cover a variety of competencies related to the position.[106]

One early step in the hiring process is a *structured interview*, which helps to measure job-related competencies of candidates. These interviews are very systematic and help probe candidates about their behavior in past experiences and/or their proposed behavior in hypothetical situations. Depending on the position being filled, it may be appropriate to have security-related topics in the structured interview when it is anticipated that the new hire will have some responsibility for executing security-related procedures.[107] During the initial assessment of a potential employee, the human resources staff may discover what job functions the new hire will need to be trained.

13.2 Background Checks and References for New Hires

Background checks have become a standard part of the hiring process for employees who are expected to work with sensitive or classified information. When hiring people for positions that handle sensitive data or assets, many employers try to find out about an applicant's work history, education, criminal record, financial history, medical history, or use of social media. Except for certain restrictions related to medical and genetic information, it is legal to ask questions about an applicant's or employee's background, and even to require a background check. The human resources department is very well equipped to handle these occurrences.

The involvement of the human resources department is important because the department will conduct all of its work in compliance with applicable laws. That includes preventing discrimination based on race, color, national origin, sex, or religion; disability; genetic information (including family medical history); and age (40 or older). These laws are enforced by the Equal Employment Opportunity Commission (EEOC). In addition, organizations must comply with the Fair Credit Reporting Act (FCRA). The Federal Trade Commission (FTC) enforces the FCRA. It is also important to review the laws of the state and municipality where the company is located regarding background reports, because some states and municipalities regulate the use of that information for employment purposes.[108]

It is important for managers in other departments to let the human resources department handle efforts at this stage. Human resources staff knows the laws and will abide by them. Other department managers have been known to just feel good about an applicant and carelessly plow through the early stages of the hiring process. Such behavior can have some very unwelcome consequences and the human resources department can help keep bias and carelessness out of the hiring process.

If an organization gets background information from a company in the business of compiling background information, there are additional procedures the FCRA requires beforehand. First, applicants must be told that the company might use the information for decisions about their employment. This notice must be in writing and in a stand-alone format. Second, if requesting a company to provide an investigative report based on personal interviews concerning an applicant's character, general reputation, personal characteristics, and lifestyle, the applicants or employees must be informed of their right to a description of the nature and scope of the investigation. It is essential to get the applicant's or employee's written permission to do the background check.[108]

Even though background checks can be very helpful when hiring people for positions that require handling sensitive information, it is not a process that should be handled by inexperienced staff. It cannot be overemphasized that department managers should let the human resources department handle the process. Human resources staff will keep an organization out of trouble and they understand that it is essential to apply the same standards in the hiring process to all applicants. There are several sources of information that employers often examine during a preemployment check and many are governed by legal restrictions on how they are used including the following:

- Credit reports—Under FCRA, businesses are required to obtain an applicant's written consent before seeking a credit report. If an organization decides not to hire or promote a person based on information in the credit report, the organization must provide a copy of the report and the applicant has the right to challenge the report under the FCRA.
- Criminal records—State laws vary as to the extent a private employer may consider an applicant's criminal history in making hiring decisions. Companies should consult with their attorney on the laws of the state in which they operate before checking on an applicant's criminal history.
- Lie detector tests—The Employee Polygraph Protection Act prohibits most private employers from using lie detector tests, either for preemployment screening or during the course of employment, except those businesses that provide armored car services; alarm or guard services; or those that manufacture, distribute, or dispense pharmaceuticals.
- Medical records—Businesses can inquire about an applicant's medical background if it can impact the ability to perform specific job duties. However, the Americans with Disabilities Act prohibits discrimination based on a physical or mental impairment, and some states have even stricter laws concerning the confidentiality of medical records.
- Bankruptcies—Although bankruptcies are a matter of public record and they may appear on an individual's credit report, the Federal Bankruptcy Act prohibits employers from discriminating against applicants because they have filed for bankruptcy.
- Military service—Military service records may be released only under limited circumstances, and consent is generally required. However, the military may disclose name, rank, salary, duty assignments, awards, and duty status without requiring the service member's consent.
- School records—Educational records such as transcripts, recommendations, and financial information are confidential

and will not be released by the school without a student's consent under the Family Educational Rights and Privacy Act, and several states have very similar laws.

- Workers' compensation records—Workers' compensation records are public record, and information from a workers' compensation appeal can be used in hiring decisions if an employer can demonstrate that an applicant's injury might hinder the ability to perform required duties.[109]

Most states have some sort of law that requires various types of employers to run criminal background checks before hiring people in certain fields such as caregivers or teachers. As a result of these laws, many state police and local police agencies in the United States can provide some sort of criminal records check services. Many states provide such services online for small fees.

Checking the references that applicants provide is a common practice and is generally handled by the human resources department. The reference check is used to verify information provided by the candidate and to help determine the applicant's potential of success in the job position. Contacting multiple references can help to collect different perspectives on an applicant's skills and abilities.

An applicant's references are more valuable if they are people who were in a position to observe the applicant's work habits, and those references with the most recent contact with the applicant are often considered the most valuable source of information. Applicants should consent to a potential employer checking their references and calling their current employer.

To make the reference check more functional, it is advisable to develop a predetermined list of questions to ask the references. Questions are generally open-ended and cover the behavior and skills that the references are most likely been able to observe. The best way to contact references is usually by phone, and as a courtesy the calls should be kept as brief as possible.

Do not expect all references to happily respond to inquiries, because many companies have policies restricting what type of information they will provide. Although a variety of questions may provide usable information when considering an applicant, it is advisable, in an effort to improve security against insider security infractions, to ascertain what type of security environment current or recent employers have in their workplace.[110]

13.3 Orientation, Training, and Assimilation of New Hires

Providing an initial orientation for a new employee is important because this is the opportunity to inform the new hire of general policies and procedures the company has in place as well as detailed information on expectations and responsibilities regarding security. The human resources department is better equipped to handle this phase more than functional departments in the company. This includes having the new hire sign any agreements regarding authorized use of company assets and confidentiality agreements.

There may be many policies and procedures, especially those related to security, that require more time for training than a brief orientation session provides. Such training should take place immediately or very soon after the new hire comes on board. This is important for the new hire as well as the company. It is not reasonable to expect a new hire to perform security-related procedures for which they have not been trained. At the department level, there may also be a requirement for some orientation that is specific to the department where the new hire will work and that is best handled by the department rather than human resources.

It is usually up to the human resources department in conjunction with the department where a new hire will work to have a well-organized first day. This includes making sure that the new hire has filled out all of the required forms and signed all of the required agreements on security and nondisclosure. If this is not done on the first day, it will require ongoing follow-up until the tasks are completed.

How the new hire is brought into the organization on the first day will make a lasting impression. The tone set on the first day is important in that it will show that an organization is serious about policies and about security issues. The security department should expect the new hire and be prepared for any briefings or orientation provided by the department. In addition, the new hire should be issued an ID card/badge and user ID for computer systems. It is a good idea to have an ID card/badge that indicates that the person is a new hire.

Once the security department has completed the necessary tasks, a representative from the department that the new hire is assigned should escort the employee to the new work location. Once the new hire arrives at the work area, that department should start the necessary orientations and tours covering departmental policies and security requirements.[111]

It is never too soon to assimilate the new hire into the security processes and procedures of an organization, and the departmental level security orientation and training should start as soon as possible. The first few days can serve as a time for on-the-job training on security procedures the new hire will be required to execute.

Upon completion of the initial security and departmental procedure briefings, it is advisable to assign a mentor from the department to work with the new hire for the first few weeks to ensure that the new hire is steadily learning all of the security procedures. The mentor can be available to answer questions and provide guidance and hands-on training.

After a few weeks it is a good idea for security staff or departmental staff, other than the mentor, to follow up with the new hire to determine if there are training gaps in required security procedures. This can be an informal process, but it can also be made more formal by requiring the new hire to complete a questionnaire or a test covering the important aspects of the security procedures that the new hire is required to understand and execute.

13.4 Monitoring the Security Practices of New Hires

Even though the new hire has gone through security orientations, briefings, and trainings, it can be helpful to monitor the new hire's execution of required security procedures and compliance with security policies. It may take a while for some people to learn everything they will need to do in order to be in compliance with security procedures. The more an organization can do to train new employees on security requirements, the less likely they make blunders or careless mistakes that could compromise security. The more formal a *performance management program* can be for new hires, the more likely it is that an organization will get better performance from the employees over the duration of their tenure.

Some companies routinely monitor e-mail and computer usage habits of employees and it may be wise to monitor both the e-mail and computer use of a new hire to determine compliance with authorized use policies. If this is done early in the tenure of an employee, it may be possible to correct the behavior before it continues and increases in severity. This review will are serve as a reminder to the new employee that the company takes security seriously and that the actions of the employee will be monitored. Once counseled on any improper use of technology resources, a later follow-up should take place to determine ongoing compliance with company policies.

The *onboarding* process goes beyond the traditional new hire orientation and training, and can involve a variety of different personnel new employees can benefit from learning about the organization. Peer observation and supervisory monitoring is another approach to assimilating new hires into the workplace and the organization culture. Regardless of the type of program an organization puts into place to assimilate new hires, the goal is to make them more productive and more committed to an organization. From a security perspective, the goal is to quickly indoctrinate new hires into the security culture of the organization and for them to learn and properly execute security procedures. Mentors can also act as monitors.

There are four basic types of mentors. Some mentors will focus on career guidance, counseling, and visibility with new hires, whereas other mentors may just act as an information source. An intellectual mentor promotes collaboration on research projects and provides constructive feedback and criticism. There are also friend mentors who interact socially and provide information about people and the organization.[112] Although it may not be the primary task, each type of mentor can also have a role of monitoring the attitude of new hires toward security and their compliance with security requirements and procedures.

Employee resource groups (ERGs) are also a way to help assimilate new hires into the organization as well as to observe their attitudes toward security. ERGs are usually organization-supported groups of employees that are drawn together by shared characteristics, which could include anything from liking sports to wanting to learn new computer programming languages. Just as mentors can play a role in monitoring, new hires can also be monitored by group leaders as part on organization's security vigilance efforts.

13.5 When Monitoring Can Go Wrong

Monitoring new employees and providing guidance and mentoring to assimilate them into the security culture of an organization can be very helpful for the new employees and for the hiring organization. However, monitoring and mentoring efforts are not without their problems.

The most serious problems can arise when the mentors or monitors are overbearing know-it-alls who have not been properly trained for their roles. Overbearing is unfortunately an exaggeration. But it also may be one of the least of many potential problems for mentoring programs. Mentors, and usually monitors, are by the nature of the role older than most of the people they could potentially be assigned to in their role. Age can certainly help foster and enhance wisdom, but age can also bring with it old mind-sets and prejudices.

The United States is split when it comes to tolerance and inclusiveness. There is a predominate belief that younger people are more tolerant of cultural diversity than older people. In addition, younger people are more accepting and accustomed to people with different lifestyles, religions, gender identifications, and gender preferences in personal or romantic relationships.

The long-held belief that people who are different cannot be trusted is slowly eroding away, but it has a strong foothold in many places and corporate security may be one of those places. Just as many younger companies openly embrace same-sex marriage and seek to have a diverse workforce, there are many older companies that have not yet broken down the high walls and strong barriers to inclusion and acceptance.

In the United States, there are many people desperately clinging to their outdated, white, Christian, homophobic, paranoid, isolationist attitudes and beliefs. There was a time not long ago that even being suspected of being homosexual would get people fired, and many times resulted in them not being hired in the first place. It is so unfortunate that many people still cling to those dysfunctional beliefs.

Racial differences are also a factor. In the United States, white people generally do not like, and in fact many hate, people of any color other than white. The depth and breadth of racial discrimination in the United States is almost so severe that it is unbelievable. Again, as unfortunate as it is, racism is alive and well in the United States of America.

Likewise, religious differences are also a basis of discrimination in the United States and the group that most Christians love to hate in the 21st century is Muslims. As disgusting as it is, this hatred is rather rampant at this point. Bear in mind that the author acknowledges that the United States is not the only nation that thrives on hatred, prejudices, and discrimination.

Perhaps someday all of the hate and prejudices will diminish, but for now it remains a major problem. The point of this discussion is to prevent these deeply rooted prejudices from tarnishing the relationships that are necessary for mentors to be successful. The same can be said for people who are primarily in monitoring roles. If mentors and monitors are bigots, then they might as well not even try to attempt to mentor in modern cultural settings, and if they do, they could do considerable harm to those who they are assigned to mentor.

All mentors should go to diversity training. Although easily said, it is probably not incredibly effective to expect diversity training to change people to any great extent. If an organization's mentoring cadre does not already embrace diversity, then it is advisable that mentors and monitors play limited roles when it comes to assimilating new diverse hires into the organization.

One final note on the use of friendship mentors in the assimilation of new hires into an organization: The mentor of friendship mentors should work to make sure that friendship mentors clearly understand their role in the assimilation process. There have been cases where mentors can do more harm and push new hires out of an organization rather than pull them into an organization. This often happens when the friendship mentor has biases or puts his or her own social agenda ahead of the goals of the organization.

13.6 Hiring Interns and Cooperative Educations Students

Internship programs and cooperative education have been an element of the corporate landscape in the United States for several dec...

When security is not an issue in an organization, hiring interns and placing cooperative education students in positions does not present any particular dangers. However, at least part of the information and data of all organizations is sensitive if not confidential. Thus, integrating interns and cooperative education students in environments where security is an issue can present several challenges.

Internship programs and cooperative education placements provide students or recent graduates with unique opportunities to apply classroom skills and theory to real-life work situations. Most programs take a hands-on approach for participants to develop the confidence and skills that can help prepare them for future employment and can benefit the sponsoring organizations by infusing new talent and diversity into an organization. Participants are generally expected to employ their skills and abilities to contribute to the objectives of the sponsor.

Internship and cooperative education placements can be for a variety of term lengths depending on the need of the sponsors as well as the participants. Most programs require participants to work a minimum number of hours per week for the entire term of the program. Participants' responsibilities and tasks will vary from organization to organization and may include conducting research, plan development/review, attending meetings, training and exercise development, or grant administration.[113] This means that typical program participants will be in and out of a facility many times during the length of their program and that has implications for security.

Organizations that do recognize that security is important for their mission will require participants to have a background check prior to placement. Because background checks can take six months or longer to process, many programs must plan well into the future in order to secure the necessary paperwork to fill the position.

The references of internship and cooperative education program applicants should be checked just as when hiring regular part-time or full-time employees. Likewise, other steps in the recruiting process are very similar to those taken when hiring permanent employees. There may be some difference in interview questions or occupational questionnaires to accommodate recruits who probably have very little work experience.

One key difference in the process of bringing interns or cooperative education students on board is that they may not be granted the same access to sensitive materials as full-time employees even though the intern has had a background check. Reasons vary for this practice, but it usually comes down to security vigilance. Interns or cooperative education students may be more careless in their handling of sensitive information and may be so excited about their position that they share sensitive information with family and friends.

It is important to remember that if interns or cooperative education students perform the same type of work that a permanent employee performs, they must be compensated for their work. Interns in the for-profit private sector organizations who qualify as employees rather than trainees typically must be paid at least minimum wage and overtime compensation for hours worked over 40 in a workweek. Compensation requirements will not apply to an intern if the following six criteria are met:

1. The internship, even though it includes actual operation of the facilities of the employer, is similar to training that would be given in an educational environment.
2. The internship experience is solely for the benefit of the intern.
3. The intern does not displace regular employees but works under close supervision of existing staff.
4. The employer that provides the training derives no immediate advantage from the activities of the intern, and on occasion its operations may actually be impeded by the prescience of an intern.
5. The intern is not necessarily entitled to a job at the conclusion of the internship.
6. The employer and the intern clearly understand that the intern is not entitled to wages for the time spent in the internship.[114]

13.7 Summary

This chapter examined how to integrate security concerns in the process of hiring new employees. The importance of background checks was discussed as well as legal issues about the use of sources of material in background checks. The chapter also examined potential issues with mentoring programs for new hires to assimilate them into the security culture of a company. Key areas covered include the following:

- The use of occupational questionnaires to screen applicants
- Conducting background checks for new hires and various ways to do background checks
- Checking the references of potential hires with some emphasis on security issues
- Using mentors to assimilate new hires into the security culture of an organization
- Using monitors to check on compliance of new hires with security procedures

COURSE CASE STUDY THE JAMES MARTIN MANUFACTURING COMPANY (CONTINUED)

Tonya Martin recently became CEO of the James Martin Manufacturing Company, a privately owned company that had been in her family for over 80 years. Tonya assumed the position when long-time manager Harold Smith died a sudden death a few months ago. Upon review, Tonya had discovered that Harold Smith had been embezzling and stealing equipment and supplies from the company for the last decade before his death.

To improve security, Tonya has been working with Ronald Thomas, the new director of security (DOS), and Samuel Davis, a newly hired supervisor. They had become the security planning team for the company. The team has made considerable progress in getting other people involved in promoting and improving security.

The three security team members suspected that some security violations would occur because employees have not been well trained on security procedures and would end up making unintentional blunders in handling sensitive data.

Tonya was very concerned about being able to protect the intellectual property of the company because long-term sustainability for the company is essential. Tonya also believed that they should learn from their failures and their mistakes in order to grow and change the security atmosphere at James Martin Manufacturing. The security planning team at James Martin Manufacturing has started to evaluate what types of surveillance systems would best serve the company's security needs.

Tonya has been expecting some new contracts to be signed soon and feels she needs to prepare the company to bring on several new hires during the next six months. All departments will need additional staff to deal with the new contracts, and Tonya wants to start planning for succession in some key positions because many of the older employees are getting ready to retire. Tonya has met with the lone human resources staffer and they jointly decided one of the first hiring priorities will be two additional staff members for the human resources department.

Tonya wants to take the new hiring opportunity to introduce some cultural changes into James Martin Manufacturing. First, she wants to bring diversity to the company, which she has considered a bastion of bigotry and prejudice built and defended by her family's male lineage and the middle-level managers they put into place. She also wants a college internship program and to start hiring local high school students for summer work and part-time work during the school year in the school's vocational education program. Hiring more women for the company has long been on her mind, especially women who have served in the military. She hopes by hiring more women she can shake off some of the male chauvinism that has dominated the company culture for far too long.

COURSE DISCUSSION QUESTIONS

1. Should employers have background checks done on all potential employees? Discuss the pros and cons of having background checks done on all potential employees.
2. How should companies structure their mentoring programs for new hires?

3. How should companies go about monitoring new employees to determine if the security-related orientations and trainings have been effective?
4. When companies transition their workforce into a more diverse workforce, what potential security issues might the transition cause?

COURSE PROJECTS

1. Design a security-focused occupational questionnaire for James Martin Manufacturing to use with new applicants for positions at the company. Compare your questionnaire to those of your classmates and discuss the differences in the questionnaires.
2. Draft a set of security-focused questions to ask the references of applicants for positions at James Martin Manufacturing. Compare your questions to those of your classmates and discuss the differences in the questions.
3. Design a structure for a mentoring program that focuses on security for new hires at James Martin Manufacturing. Compare your design to those of your classmates and discuss the differences in the designs.
4. Design a program to help recruit female veterans of the U.S. Armed Forces for open positions at James Martin Manufacturing and provide some emphasis on security. Compare your design to those of your classmates and discuss the differences in the designs.

COURSE TEST QUESTIONS

1. A prescripted interview designed to be uniformly administered with all potential hires and to collect the same information in an unbiased manner from all potential hires is known as _____.
2. A performance management program is _____.
3. An occupational questionnaire is designed to _____.
4. An employee resource group is _____.

5. A standard part of the hiring process for employees who are expected to work with sensitive or classified information is a _____.
6. During preemployment screening, the Employee Polygraph Protection Act prohibits most private employers from _____.
7. Checking the references that applicants provide is a common practice and is generally handled by the _____.
8. An applicant's references are more valuable in helping make a hiring decision if they are _____.
9. Even though the new hire has gone through security orientations, briefings, and trainings, it can be helpful to _____.
10. There four basic types of mentors focus on _____.

Key Terms

Employee resource groups (ERGs): are usually organization-supported groups of employees that are drawn together by shared characteristics, which could include anything from liking sports to wanting to learn new computer programming languages.

Job analysis: provides an understanding of the tasks performed by workers in the position and the competencies required to perform those tasks as well as the relationship between tasks and competencies.

Occupational questionnaires: typically consist of questions that cover a variety of skills and competencies related to the position for which it is being administered.

Onboarding: is a structured process covering all aspects of a new hire's job responsibilities, administrative processes of the hiring organization as well as security procedures. The onboarding process also integrates the new hire into the social and cultural aspects of an organization.

Performance management program: is a structured training and competency development approach designed to continuously improve an employee's performance on current job responsibilities and to expand competencies to logical areas beyond current responsibilities.

Structured interview: is a prescripted interview between a potential hire and a representative of the hiring organization designed to be uniformly administered with all potential hires and to collect the same information in an unbiased manner from all potential hires.

14

CYBER ISSUES AND THE INSIDER

While much of the world focuses on hackers and malicious forces attacking corporate information systems, many people forget that it is the insider that most frequently does damage to computer systems, cripples applications, and steals data. There are around 4 million people in the United States working in computer occupations[115] who are employed by over 100,000 companies.[116] This chapter examines cyber issues and the insider, and how to minimize damage that insiders can do to information assets, information systems, and computer networks.

14.1 The Nature of Insider Crimes against Computer Systems

There are three major types of crimes that insiders can accomplish using an organization's computer systems. First are crimes against the company, such as embezzlement, that are enabled by the computer systems. Second are crimes that involve harm to an organization's computer systems. Third are crimes against others outside the organization using its computer systems to facilitate the crime. It is difficult to estimate just how much economic damage these three types of insider crimes cause since investigative agencies all have some peculiarities as to how they collect and compile data, but the damage or loss is certainly in the billions of dollars per year.

When it comes to crimes against or crimes using an organization's computer systems, two groups or insider culprits are responsible for various types of crimes. First is the educated information technology (IT) professional who actually works supporting an organization's computer systems and networks. Second are non-IT professionals who include all other employees in an organization who use the computers to the best of their ability to commit crimes against the organization or its computers. According to headlines from the Federal Bureau of Investigation (FBI) website on July 25, 2016, examples of insiders using their employer's computer systems to commit crimes the FBI helped to investigate and prosecute include the following:

- Former police department employee sentenced for computer intrusion in connection with stolen identity refund fraud
- Former employee of Silicon Valley company pleads guilty to damaging ex-employer's computers
- Former Economic Development employee sentenced for receiving child pornography
- Former State Department employee sentenced to over four years in extensive computer hacking, cyberstalking, and sextortion scheme
- Former software company employee sentenced to 30 months in prison for sending damaging computer code to company servers
- Former U.S. Nuclear Regulatory Commission employee sentenced to prison for attempted spear-phishing cyber-attack on Department of Energy computers
- Former baseball St. Louis Cardinals official sentenced to prison for Houston Astros computer intrusions
- Former United States government employee charged in computer hacking and cyber stalking scheme
- Former Tesla engineer charged with computer intrusion
- Jury convicts former Fox 40 web producer for conspiring to hack into and alter Los Angeles Times servers
- Eight people charged in a bank fraud scheme that allegedly used information stolen by Wells Fargo employees to access accounts
- National Weather Service employee indicted for allegedly downloading restricted government files
- Man sentenced to 30 months in federal prison for hacking into computer system of his former employer
- Former Parkland Hospital employee admits stealing patient information to market his home health agency in Garland, Texas
- Man arrested for theft of valuable source code from former employer

- Former IRS employee sentenced for $326,000 fraud scheme, identity theft
- New Hampshire company pleads guilty to hacking into a competitor's computer system for commercial advantage
- President of higher education software provider pleads guilty to conspiring to hack into competitors' computer systems
- Former Miami-Dade College employee sentenced in identity theft tax fraud scheme
- Former employee of global financial services company charged with unauthorized access of supervisor's e-mail account on approximately 100 occasions
- Former employee charged with theft of trade secrets
- Bank employee charged in fraud and identity theft case
- Computer professional sentenced to four years in prison for defrauding Catholic Health system
- Former employee sentenced to nearly five years in prison for stealing $4.1 million from the company

These examples show that employees who can get access to an organization's computer systems will commit a wide variety of crimes. This tendency presents a significant challenge to security efforts. All of the offenders in the aforementioned cases had some level of access to the computers of their employers. They were trusted insiders, not outside hackers.

14.2 Preventing Insider Abuse of Computer Access

The deployments of access control systems, authorized use statements, and monitoring of employee use of corporate computer systems have been discussed in other chapters. All of those methods can help reduce unauthorized use of computer systems, but they are not always effective, as is demonstrated by the long string of computer misuse that insiders have committed and for which they have been prosecuted.

Since crimes using corporate computers and crimes against corporate systems will continue, it may be time for organizations to rethink ways to prevent these occurrences and doing so from the ground up. Over the last 20 years, organizations of all types have expanded their use of computers in the workplace and provided more employees with computer and Internet access. This started in an effort to make employees more productive and to facilitate communications in the workplace. There certainly have been some benefits in terms of employees being able to perform self-service for many human resources activities such as accessing benefit processes and submitting online time reports and leave requests.

The increased connectivity has not always worked out for the better because the expanded connectivity has added to the vulnerabilities of corporate systems. The increased connectivity has also paved the way to computer misuse, especially when it comes to Internet access.

However, effectiveness of computer security is improved when employee access is limited to only those systems and applications for which they really have a business need. Thus, allowing employee access beyond job responsibilities can create unnecessary opportunities for unauthorized access to the misuse of data and applications.[117] There are several questions that organizations should address regarding employee use of computer systems:

- Do all of the employees in an organization that have access to computer systems really need access?
- Do all of the employees in an organization that have access to computer systems really need as much access as they have?
- Are there ways of reducing employee access to computer systems and still providing for use of human resources functions and other applications that reduce paperwork and time spent on management tasks?

It is likely that all employees do not need access to computer systems, and it is also likely that employees who do have access do not need the level of access that they have to computer applications. It is also likely that organizations can do more to restrict unnecessary access to computer systems. If all of this is true, then what is the root of the problem? There are two trends that have resulted in excess employee access to an organization's computer systems. First is the trend regarding expanded computer access, which has unfortunately become slowly instilled in corporate culture supported by the belief that computers will make people more productive. This has been a hotly debated topic, and far too often good security practices have lost out to the lack of common sense on the part of management. Employees in many organizations have come to believe that they should be able to check their personal e-mail, play computer games, post to social media, and shop online while at work. Again, unfortunately, many organizations have allowed these attitudes and behaviors to creep into the workplace. The organizations that have done so also face difficulty in reversing the creep and forcing such habits out of the workplace. The second trend is a bit simpler; both complacency and laziness have become pervasive in many organizations. Rather than putting up with employees squawking that they are overworked and need to take care of family matters while at work, many organizations have just given up the fight and accepted lax security and misuse as commonplace as an evil necessity in the age of connectivity. Employee-use monitoring is not effectively performed in many security-soft environments, and discipline for violations of computer-use policies seldom occurs. Meanwhile, employees are abusing computer systems on a daily basis.

These trends will persist unless management makes the decision to reverse the trends and follow more effective security procedures. No magic bullet is going to change the situation. Only management can make the necessary changes to adhere to better computer security procedures. If management does not, then the poor state of computer security is its fault.

14.3 Controlling Actions of Information Technology Staff

Although IT staffs are only a small part of an organization's work-force, they have been known to do considerable damage to computer systems and networks. The level of access that IT workers have to corporate systems far exceeds that of non-IT staff. This certainly has enabled IT specialists to perform their job responsibilities, but it has also allowed them to do considerable damage.

Disgruntled technology workers have stolen data, planted soft-ware time bombs, locked users out of systems for ransom purposes, exposed sensitive information to unauthorized parties, and a long list of other crimes and misdemeanors. In the case of controlling IT staff, both economic and cultural trends are winning out over good security practices.

Economics has had a very negative impact on the ability of the less than super rich organization to hire, manage, and monitor information technology workers. The last two recessions have had a very negative impact on many organizations as revenue went down and cost reduction programs were implemented. Organizations of all types reduced head count through attrition or layoffs, and information technology staff members were not exempt. As head counts were reduced, internal department security suffered and in many cases almost became nonexistent.

It has long been observed that IT work can at times be overwhelming and very demanding. The hours can be long during normal conditions, and when system upgrades are in progress, new technology is being installed, or application platforms are being migrated, the hours and work schedule can be very disruptive to personal lives. As a result, far too many organizations overwork the IT staff they have, and pay increases have been kept at a minimum. Thus, workers would become disgruntled and many just moved on to other jobs in order to keep pace with current pay levels and professional development opportunities.

Hiring IT workers in some geographical locations has become more difficult as well. Workers migrated to more affordable locations seeking higher wages and more opportunity to pursue their careers. There is also the very untalked about trend of the long hours and stressful work burning out technology workers, resulting in them leaving the field altogether. This has required organizations to spend considerable time and money recruiting new staff.

Many of the IT workers that did not move on because of personal or family reasons felt exploited even more by their employers. Some of those workers snapped and did considerable damage on their way out. Again, the solutions are there and it is up to management to implement those solutions. Monitoring and close supervision as well as reviewing computer logs to determine what workers are doing is essential for reducing vulnerabilities.

14.4 Improving Insider Password Management Habits

The guidelines for computer *password management* have been the same for a very long time. Getting people to following those guidelines has been a challenge for just as long as there have been guidelines. Many organizations try to have password discipline by requiring *strong passwords* that are long and complex and thus more difficult for system intruders to guess or crack. Most password policies focus on preventing the exploitation of weak passwords and the reuse of compromised passwords. Requiring strong passwords can help thwart *guessing attacks* such as *brute force attacks* and *dictionary attacks*.

A review of password policies and procedures of several organizations shows a high level of consistency in policies. Users are informed that they can change their password as many times as they would like but are required to change it at least once every 90 days. In general, passwords are required meet all of the following requirements:

- At least eight, but no more than 32 characters
- At least one uppercase letter
- At least one lowercase letter
- At least one special character: ~ ! @ # $% ^ * () _ - + = {} [] |:; ", ?. Do not use < > & or '.
- At least one number[118]

As wise as it is to adhere to the principles of password management, it also creates another set of problems including the likelihood of the passwords being written down and stored insecurely. Outside intruders seldom have physical access to a building or facility and rely on their skills to hack into systems. Insiders who want to access computer systems and improperly use the system or steal data or other sensitive information do not face the challenges of outside intruders and do not need hacking skills to access computer systems. All they need to do is watch their coworkers or walk around the workplace to find where users store the passwords they have written down.

Insiders get to know their territory and have time to observe the work habits of their fellow employees including how and where they write and store their passwords. They get to know who does what type of work on the computer and can guess what type of access they may have. For the employees who do not write down their user names and passwords on a sticky note and mount them on their computer monitors, the favorite places for end users to store their passwords are in one of their top desk drawers or under a desk pad or mouse pad. This is a behavior that can be difficult to extinguish. It is also a behavior that also creates an incredible vulnerability.

There are steps that organizations can take to help protect the written user name and passwords. First, organizations can establish policies and procedures on how users should handle their user names and passwords. Second, they can reinforce those policies and procedures through training, and enforce the policies and procedures through disciplinary actions. This approach does take considerable time and effort, and must be executed consistently for the policies and procedures to be effective. But no matter how strict an organization tries to be with employees, a tour of executive offices will probably reveal that even the highest-level managers do not properly execute password protection procedures.

14.5 Issues of Extreme Misuse of Computers in the Workplace

Beyond the everyday things that employees do on their workplace computers, such as online shopping, checking personal e-mail, and playing on social media websites, there are very serious misuses that have implications for computer security as well as other workplace issues. These misuses include the viewing and storing of pornography, online gambling, purchase or sale of contraband or illegal substances, involvement with hate groups through websites or chat rooms, and posting threatening messages on discussion groups or social media sites. All organizations need policies restricting such activities, and those policies should be enforced.

If an organization utilizes a computer monitoring system to track employee computer use, extreme misuse activities are easily detectable. It is also advisable to have a procedure where employees can report such behaviors on the part of their fellow workers. However, security staff or managers must act to stop these types of online activities and do so very quickly.

There are certainly computer security consequences for extreme misuse, because illicit websites have a reputation for being hosts for malware, spyware, and other malicious code. There are also legal implications for the organization whose computers are used for these types of activities. If crimes are committed during this type of computer use, the next knock on the door could be law enforcement agents that specialize in fighting child pornography, illegal drug dealing, human trafficking, and hate crimes. Once the investigations start there may be frequent law enforcement visits.

If the case is prosecuted, then the organization owning the computers used in any illegal activity may need an attorney, and representatives may need to make court appearances or provide affidavits. Computers can also be taken into custody as evidence or to give law enforcement computer forensic staffs time to collect more evidence. The media will also want to ask managers and security staff lots of questions.

14.6 Controlling Remote Access and Telecommuting

Internet connectivity has made it possible for many people to work from home on a frequent or even permanent basis. Often the employees who have jobs that require thinking, writing, and data analysis, or focus solely on computer-oriented tasks such as data entry, word processing, or computer programming may be good candidates to telecommute. Remote workers may use a company-issued computer or their privately owned computers and network connectivity. Company-owned computers are relatively easy to control in terms of software configurations and security measures. However, employee-owned computers present an entirely different situation and can create security vulnerabilities.

Because of the complex interdependencies between hardware, software, configuration settings, and telecommunication settings, privately owned computers can be a significant challenge and expense to configure and maintain. This involves optimizing systems for performance and protecting the company data on the computer or data that is transmitted over public networks. Security vulnerabilities of the privately owned computer may create unacceptable vulnerabilities to company computers and networks in the office or used by telecommuters.

Organizations that are utilizing telecommuting work arrangements with employees or contractors should establish clear policies on computer maintenance and support. Those policies should make it clear that the employee must install vendor-recommended security patches to the operating system and applications software. In addition, all computers used for telecommuting should be required to be protected by at least a software firewall.

Policies should also make it clear to employees who perform any work on a privately owned computer on behalf of the organization that the work performed and data and information used to perform the work are the property of the organization. An organization should maintain the right to perform security scans on the privately owned computers used for organization business that connect to the organization's network.

Company policies should clearly state that if a privately owned computer has software installed that is licensed to the employer or if the organization pays for any portion of the telecommunications service used to connect a privately owned computer to organization computers, then the organization has the right to inspect the privately owned computer. It should also be made clear to employees that their privately owned computers could be subpoenaed or subject to court-ordered action.

Employees should be notified that if the employer's IT staff provides any hardware or software support for a telecommuter's privately owned computer, it is possible that support staff may encounter illegal software, storage of pornography, or evidence of criminal activity on the computer. Policies should clearly state what actions the organization support staff will take as a result of the discovery.

Company policies should also clearly state what happens if the computer support staff accidentally damages a privately owned computer when attempting to configure the computer for company work. In addition, configuration requirements for connecting to an organization's network or computer systems may not support other activities the computer owner may be pursuing, and employees should be forewarned of this possibility. Finally, policies should clarify when and where computer support staff will work on a privately owned computer.[119]

14.7 Controlling Mobile Computing and Communications Devices

One of the weakest links in computer and communications system security is mobile computing and communications devices, and the employees who use them and misplace them, leave them behind in airport security lines, or leave them unattended so they can be stolen. All the encryption, secure passwords, and tracking chips on the devices cannot make up for the carelessness of employees in protecting the devices. Passengers going through U.S. Transportation Security Agency check points at airports, for example, leave thousands of items behind each year including laptops and smart phones as well as money, cameras, and other valuable items.

Estimates vary but somewhere between 500,000 and 700,000 laptops are lost or stolen every year with a value over $1 billion. There are also over 100 million lost or stolen smart phones every year in the United States alone. In addition to the monetary value of a laptop, when a mobile computing device is stolen so is any stored log-in data, which makes it easy for a thief to access online services and data. The impact and frequency of lost or stolen mobile computing devices is great. Examples of cases and incidents include the following:

- Stolen laptops lead to important Health Insurance Portability and Accountability Act (HIPAA) settlements between the U.S. Department of Health and Human Services and private health care providers.[120]
- A $750,000 HIPAA settlement emphasizes the importance of risk analysis, and device and media control policies.[121]
- Between October 1, 2005, and May 31, 2006, there were 95 computers belonging to the U.S. Department of Agriculture that were stolen.[122]
- Internal Revenue Service employees reported the loss or theft of at least 490 computers between January 2, 2003, and June 13, 2006.[123]
- The U.S. Department of Justice had 400 laptops reported lost, stolen, or missing between October 1, 1999, and January 31, 2002.[124]
- On May 3, 2006, the home of a U.S. Veterans Affairs employee was burglarized and a personally owned laptop computer was stolen, which was reported to contain unauthorized personal information on approximately 26 million veterans and military personnel.[125]
- From January 2001 until September 2006, the U.S. Census Bureau reported 672 lost/missing/stolen laptops.[126]

Unfortunately, employees need to be trained to not leave laptops and smart phones unattended in public places or visible in an unattended car. Organizations issuing mobile devices should keep a detailed inventory of equipment and records of manufacturers, model numbers, serial numbers, and other identification numbers. Law enforcement agencies will need this information if the device is stolen or lost.

Depending on the manufacturer of the mobile device, there are a variety of tracking and locator applications as well as applications that can shut down the device or otherwise render it inoperable so thieves cannot extract data from the device. Encryption software is available for laptops and can be set to require strong passwords to access data files. There are also add-on applications or services that can help keep track of mobile devices. These capabilities vary from manufacturer to manufacturer and are evolving over time. Mobile technology managers should keep current with the available services and security software and decide the best way to secure their brand of devices.

14.8 Summary

This chapter examined computer usage and access issues of insiders, including the types of crimes that insiders commit using their employer's computers and networks. The importance of specific policies covering telecommuting was also covered. The chapter also examined potential issues with employees using personally owned computers to remotely access an organization's central systems. Key areas covered included the following:

- The loss and theft of mobile computing devices
- Information needed to report the theft of mobile computing devices
- The importance of monitoring what information technology staffs are doing on company systems
- Password management problems with insiders
- Potential problems in configuring privately owned computers to access company systems

COURSE CASE STUDY THE JAMES MARTIN MANUFACTURING COMPANY (CONTINUED)

Tonya Martin recently became CEO of the James Martin Manufacturing Company, a privately owned company that had been in her family for over 80 years. Tonya assumed the position when long-time manager Harold Smith died a sudden death a few months ago. Upon review, Tonya has discovered instances of embezzlement, and equipment and supply theft from the company. This included several laptops.

Tonya is very concerned about being able to protect the intellectual property of the company because long-term sustainability for the company is essential. She is now more concerned about this because she is expecting some new contracts to be signed soon and feels she needs to prepare the company to bring on several new hires during the next six months.

All departments will need additional staff to deal with the new contracts, and Tonya wants to start planning for succession in some key positions because many of the older employees are getting ready to retire. Tonya has met with the lone human resources staffer and they jointly decided one of the first hiring priorities will be two additional staff for the human resources department.

Tonya wants to take the new hiring opportunity to introduce some cultural changes into James Martin Manufacturing. First, she wants to bring diversity to the company, which she has considered a bastion of bigotry and prejudice built and defended by her family's male lineage and the middle-level managers they put into place. Hiring more women for the company has long been on her mind, especially women who have served in the military.

The security team at James Martin Manufacturing decided to look deeper into how they could prevent insider violations of computer security. The company was down to only one information technology employee, and on her list of things to do Tonya either planned to hire two new people to help with the computer systems or considering how the company could benefit from cloud computing applications.

COURSE DISCUSSION QUESTIONS

1. How would you go about training employees on how not to misplace their laptops and how to prevent them from being stolen?
2. How would you go about monitoring the work activities of the information technology staff to ensure that they are only working on authorized and assigned projects or tasks?
3. How would you go about training executives on caring for their company-issued laptops and smart phones?
4. Have you or somebody you know ever had a laptop or smart phone lost or stolen? What did you or your acquaintance do about the loss or theft? Discuss your experiences.

COURSE PROJECTS

1. Draft a remote computer-use policy for James Martin Manufacturing. Compare your draft with those of your classmates and discuss the differences in the draft policies.
2. Create a 10-slide PowerPoint presentation that Tonya can use when talking with employees at James Martin Manufacturing about how to manage their computer passwords. Compare your presentation with those of your classmates and discuss the differences in the presentations.
3. Draft a memo describing how cloud computing could help James Martin Manufacturing. Compare your draft with those of your classmates and discuss the differences in the drafts.
4. Design a method to inventory all of the computers and mobile devices at James Martin Manufacturing and decide what information should be included for each computer and mobile device. Compare your design with those of your classmates and discuss the differences in the designs.

COURSE TEST QUESTIONS

1. The process of repeatedly attempting to guess passwords by using default passwords, dictionary words, and other possible passwords that may be relevant to an organization is known as a _____.

2. An attack where an attacker tries all possible combinations of characters from a character set for passwords up to a specified length is known as a _____.
3. What methods can be used to reduce insider violations of security policies and procedures?
4. What should determine an employee's level of access to an organization's computer systems?
5. What type of crimes have disgruntled technology workers committed against their employers?
6. Users should be required to change their passwords at least every _____.
7. When required to use strong passwords, users often _____.
8. Extreme misuse of company computer systems by end users can include _____.
9. If computer-related or computer-facilitated crimes committed by an employee are prosecuted, a company may be required to _____.
10. The use of employee-owned computers to access company systems and work from home can _____.

Key Terms

Brute force attacks: are a variation of a password guessing attack where an attacker tries all possible combinations of characters from a character set for passwords up to a specified length.

Dictionary attacks: are a variation of a guessing attack where an attacker attempts to guess a password using a list of possible passwords.

Guessing attacks: use the process of repeatedly attempting to guess passwords by using default passwords, dictionary words, and other possible passwords that may be relevant to an organization.

Password management: is a structured process of establishing, implementing, and maintaining password policies and procedures throughout an organization.

Strong passwords: are a required length with a required mix of numbers, letters, and special characters, and do not have common words or user names as part of the password.

Appendix: Course Test Questions and Answers

Chapter 1

1. The industries and business sectors that provide essential infrastructure support for the economic activity that enables a country to function economically, politically, and socially are known as *critical industry sectors*.

2. The various devices or protective systems that can be installed to prevent unauthorized movement and monitor movement of people, materials, products, supplies, or data in a facility are *mechanical security measures*.

3. Barriers, locked doorways, and access controlled doors that prevent entry and access to building areas by unauthorized employees or contractors, and that prevent materials or information from being physically accessed or removed from a controlled area are considered to be *physical security measures*.

4. Structured processes or steps that employees must follow when entering or exiting secure areas, when handling and working with sensitive or proprietary materials, or transferring products or data from one controlled area to another controlled area are called *procedural security measures*.

5. Societal conditions that may impact insider behavior and result in security violations or crimes against an employer include *drug abuse, family problems, and untreated mental illnesses.*

6. People who commit many crimes against their employer are generally *white males in their late 20s to early 30s.*

7. Crimes of embezzlement are generally committed by *females.*

8. Examples of spontaneous or situational security measures that are put into place when out-of-the-ordinary events are taking place at a facility include *special security details, designated escorts, or specialized identification badges.*

9. The role of a security champion in an organization is to *speak up at management meetings and planning sessions about security, advocate budgeting appropriate resources for security, and advocate for security reviews and improved policies and procedures.*

10. The Whole Building Design Guide (WBDG) focuses on how to *design and create integrated security into new building construction and in the remodeling of existing buildings.*

Chapter 2

1. An organization structure that prevents individual employees or agents from having access to, or control of work functions in a manner that would allow them to independently misappropriate corporate assets with little chance of detection is called *appropriate separation of duties.*

2. Two or more people that jointly conspire to act maliciously against an organization with which one of them (the insider) is employed or has privileged access and the other does not have a relationship with the organization is known as *an insider–outsider team.*

3. Radio frequency identification (RFID) tags are *very small electronically detectable and readable marking tags that can be read via radio frequencies when they are in a defined proximity*

of an electronic reader that does not require direct contact with the tag.

4. Any form or type of business process, scientific formula, technical specification, economic data, or engineering designs that the owner has taken measures to protect and which economic value can be derived are known as *trade secrets.*

5. Unauthorized use is *the reading, recording, transmitting, or storing of data that belongs to a specific party and is meant for a specific and restricted use by the owning or custodial organization or its designees.*

6. Audits should focus on *systems or processes where the most is at stake.*

7. List four of the FBI recommended methods to help protect trade secrets.
   a. Recognize that a threat exists and prepare to protect trade secrets from that threat.
   b. Determine what trade secrets you own and determine the value of the trade secrets.
   c. Deploy specific measures to protect and safeguard your trade secrets.
   d. Limit access to and knowledge of trade secrets.
   e. Engage in ongoing employee training on how to protect the trade secrets.
   f. Design and deploy a specific program to protect trade secrets from insider theft or compromise.
   g. Engage with law enforcement and report to the FBI suspicious activity regarding trade secrets.

8. Equipment and related parts and supplies have considerable value to an insider thief because they are *relatively easy to sell.*

9. The insider thief may find finished products have a broader theft appeal because *it is easier to tell what the item is and how it can be used.*

10. Visible security systems such as locked doors, surveillance cameras, and security guards can *serve well as deterrents against insider crimes.*

Chapter 3

1. A set of mitigation mechanisms or steps that can protect against known security threats an organization faces because of its activity, location, or value is known as *appropriate security*.

2. An approach to security planning and management that is piecemeal and has several uncoordinated and unrelated elements is known as *ad hoc security management*.

3. A plan that covers all security needs of an organization from the ground up and is designed to mitigate known security threats is referred to as a *comprehensive security plan*.

4. The purpose of periodic reviews of existing security measures is to *determine if they are adequate to continue to protect from ongoing or new threats*.

5. The benefit of having two people leading the security planning team in a coleader arrangement is *if one coleader leaves the team, then the remaining coleader can maintain some continuity in the planning process*.

6. Why is a structured face-to-face meeting between upper management and the security planning team leaders important? *It is conducive to determining how the security planning project is moving along.*

7. What impact does ambiguous, rambling language have on the clarity of security policies? *It makes the policy difficult to understand, which makes enforcing the policy more challenging.*

8. A security procedure has considerable detail and will most often provide step-by-step instructions on *how to execute a specific security procedure*.

9. A walk-through of a security procedure by one or more employees, using the documented procedure to actually execute all of the steps in the procedure, helps to *determine if the procedure is thoroughly documented and that the procedure actually accomplishes the desired goal*.

10. When a person reads through a draft security procedure to determine the clarity and thoroughness of the procedure, the review is known as *a desk review*.

Chapter 4

1. An organization culture in which security pervades every aspect of daily life as well as all efforts to change, evolve, or realign the organization is known as a *culture of security*.

2. The manners in which an individual or classes of individuals prefer to learn new material, ideas, concepts, and technical skills are known as *learning styles*.

3. Safe harbor standards were jointly developed by the *European Union and United States*.

4. A basic level of understanding of security and recognition of the importance of security by employees or groups of employees in an organization is known as *security awareness*.

5. Individuals in an organization who speak of the benefits of good security whenever they have the opportunity to express their support and encourage others to support security efforts are known as *security evangelists*.

6. Knowing that security exists and is necessary in certain situations but involves little knowledge or understanding of security processes and procedures is known as *security familiarity*.

7. A high-ranking and/or respected person in an organization that supports security efforts on a day-to-day basis as well as in organizational activities such as budgeting, planning, and managing, and speaks on behalf of security efforts when appropriate is known as a *security leader or security champion*.

8. The constant attention given to security during day-to-day operations and contributes to security by encouraging the reporting of security violations and makes suggestions on how to improve security when weaknesses are observed is known as *security vigilance*.

9. The manner in which security presence and security operations are visible or are displayed in a particular environment is known as the *visual appearance of security*.

10. The people in an organization that have the day-to-day responsibility of monitoring employee compliance with security procedures are called *supervisors*.

Chapter 5

1. The purpose of social media policies is to specify *who in an organization is responsible for social media operations; specify when, why, where, and how social media can be used on behalf of an organization; and provide guidance on the inappropriate use of social media by corporate media staff and employees.*

2. An organization's use of social media accounts and applications to communicate to individuals or groups as well as the mention, comments, discussions, and display of any material on any social media application that relates to or depicts an organization is known as *social media presence.*

3. Before you start using a specific tool, you need to evaluate how much control the built-in features provide and decide *if that level of control is sufficient to protect you from damage.*

4. How you assign responsibility for social media in your organization is dependent upon *how your existing communication functions are organized.*

5. When it comes to a company requesting that an employee divulge personal social media activity, state laws generally do not prohibit a private company or any employer from requesting that information if *the employer reasonably believes that the information is relevant to an investigation of allegations of employee misconduct or employee violation of applicable laws and regulations.*

6. By posting their professional information and work experience online, employees are working to better themselves in their careers and in their lives, but they are also *exposing themselves to a world that may well want to take advantage of them as an information source.*

7. A company's public image is an asset that needs to be protected just like *physical assets are protected.*

8. Social media, as we now know it, can be relatively easy to become involved with, but it also brings with it *long-term overhead.*

9. A company's social media policies should address how and who uses social media on behalf of the company and what constitutes *appropriate use.*

10. To help avoid unintended consequences of employee personal use of social media, a company should *establish guiding principles for nonofficial and personal use.*

Chapter 6

1. A process that either allows or disallows individual users to have access to specific computer applications and computer data sets including what the user is allowed to do on the systems with their level of access is known as *access control for computer systems.*

2. A company or organization that performs better than its competitors bringing innovations to its field of endeavor and whose products or services become the industry standard to match or beat in open market competition is known as an *industry leader.*

3. Any computer equipment that can no longer provide any functionality in an organization's current computing environment because of the system's architecture or the inability to run current computer applications in an adequate manner is known as *obsolete computer equipment.*

4. A term that refers to the compatibility of a product or service with its target organization and technology environment is a *right fit.*

5. The key role of technology in security systems is to *control access and allow only authorized individuals to view, manipulate, or use information or gain physical access to facilities or assets.*

6. One of the biggest challenges to effective access management of computer systems is to *ensure that the software products are properly installed, configured, and managed.*

7. The website USA.gov is an interagency product that *provides information on government services.*

8. When evaluating the comments of users about products you are considering for acquisition, it is important to *recognize that there can be some question about the authenticity of the comments because they may have been posted via surrogates by the manufacturers or sellers of the products.*

9. When selecting products for your security efforts that are designed to prevent insider attacks, it is important that you conduct *product evaluations.*

10. Part of the cost of using security products on a trial basis is that you *must pay the cost of installation, testing, and deinstallation if you decide not to use the product.*

Chapter 7

1. The automated and human functions that allow a properly identified person or logical entity access to an organization's facilities or computer systems are known as *access control systems.*

2. Authorized logical access is *the access that an insider is allowed to have to an organization's computer and communications systems that an employee may need to perform their job duties.*

3. The access that an insider is allowed to have to an organization's property, buildings, and areas of buildings that an employee may need to perform their job duties is known as *authorized physical access.*

4. The free Internet-based service of the Citizenship and Immigration Services Division of the U.S. Department of Homeland Security (DHS) used to verify an employee's identity and authorization to work in the United States is called *E-Verify.*

5. An organization's policy that informs employees and visitors as to the organization's requirement for ID card/badge display when on the organization's property is known as the *ID card/badge display policy.*

6. The system that is used to identify a person for the purposes of allowing access to an organization's facilities is known as an *identification (ID) system.*

7. Systems that manage each individual's access rights, allowing access to the computer services they need to perform their duties but prevent their access to other computer services as well as what they can do with computer services to which they do have access is known as a *logical access control system.*

8. Systems that are designed specifically to allow an individual to enter specific areas of a facility and block their access to areas of the facility to which they have not been granted access are known as *physical access control systems.*

9. Generally speaking, an employee will be assigned to work in specific areas of a facility and access is authorized after *appropriate background checks are conducted and security clearance levels are determined.*

10. To have an effective ID system for insiders, first you must *authenticate the ID of the person for whom you are creating ID credentials.*

Chapter 8

1. A comprehensive records management system is designed to *show how all documents and records will be handled, moved, used, stored, and destroyed during their life cycle.*

2. Secure areas of buildings have several characteristics including *strong physical access controls and strong security features even though the building with which they are contained may not be secured and have general public access areas.*

3. Secure buildings have several characteristics including *strong physical access control systems that only allow in people that have authorized access and appropriate security clearances. Secure buildings may also have stronger security for designated floors and areas of the building.*

4. Secure communities have several characteristics including *relatively self-contained special purpose communities such as a military base or research campus. Secure communities generally have perimeter security that can be strengthened on demand, have some public areas without secured access within the perimeter, secure facilities within the outer perimeter, secured buildings, and buildings with secured areas.*

5. Secure facilities have several characteristics including *generally comprised of one to several special purpose secured buildings with strong perimeter security surrounding the entire group of buildings. There are generally no unsecured public areas; buildings have secured access levels based on need; and areas of buildings have higher levels of security based on need.*

6. Secure storage devices are designed to *limit access to their contents with strong locking mechanisms and/or durable construction that cannot be easily dismantled or neutralized.*

7. When designing buildings for security user constraints that need to be addressed, include *constraints on designing and implementing security mitigation methods that arise from local concerns about building appearance, local building codes, and local political dynamics.*

8. An insider becomes suspicious when *they seek higher clearances or expanded access outside their job scope, engage in classified conversations without a need to know, work hours inconsistent with their job assignment or they insist on working in private, or have repeated security violations such as trying to enter areas to which they are not authorized access.*

9. One of the most important things to do to mitigate an insider threat is to *limit access to and knowledge of proprietary information as much as possible.*

10. When deciding if a specific container or storage device is adequate for storing classified material or other valuable items you should keep in mind that *the more sensitive the material being stored, the stronger your storage devices should be and the more strict your protection methods and procedures.*

Chapter 9

1. Business partnerships are *relationships between two or more organizations designed to meet specific goals of one or more of the organizations.*

2. Insider misconduct is *conduct by an employee that is against organization policies or procedures or that otherwise can harm the employing organization.*

3. An insider-outsider threat is *a threat that emerges as a result of a relationship between one of your employees and a person working for an outside organization or who is otherwise not related to your organization.*

4. Describe a nondisclosure agreement. *An agreement between two parties where one or both parties agree not to disclose information or data that has been communicated between the parties.*

5. Describe what personal use means in the context of business relationships. *A gift of an item or service not used for the employing organization and is intended for use only by the recipient.*

6. Describe the purpose of a relationship inventory. *It is a list or database of all the outside organizations a company has a relationship with and who is authorized to represent those organizations to your company and who in your company is authorized to participate in interactions on behalf of your organization.*

7. A value-added supplier is *a supplier that does more than just provide a specific type of equipment or supply but helps your organization better leverage their products or processes in operations or manufacturing activities.*

8. How do color-coded ID badges aid in supporting a company's security effort? *Color-coded badges are an easy way for employees to know the type of relationship their organization has with the person wearing the color-coded ID badge.*

9. What should an employee do if they find that a visitor under their escort tries to wander off on their own to tour a facility? *Report the incident to the security department and company management.*

10. What should managers in an organization do if they find that a representative of a supplier is trying to bribe their employees to buy supplies from the representative's company? *Report the incident to the representative's employer and block the representative from entering the company's facilities.*

Chapter 10

1. What is the chaos factor? *A condition that occurs as a result of unsettled and disrupted routine operations of an organization or facility, and an atmosphere of disorder and confusion prevails.*

2. Explain what an exclusion area is. *Those areas that are under the control of an organization in which activities are limited, construction is prohibited, and any type of occupation is usually curtailed that is maintained in order to establish a buffer of nonactivity around a facility or building as a security measure.*

3. Explain what security threats are. *Conditions, people, or events that can jeopardize the security of an organization, a facility, or any asset belonging to an organization or the employees of the organization.*

4. What is a vulnerability assessment? *A structured process by which you evaluate how secure your facilities are based on your perception of security needs.*

5. What should you keep in mind when you mix new security technology with older security technology? *In some cases, older security technology may not work well when you try to integrate new security technology into your security infrastructure.*

6. Why should you be concerned about changes in the ownership of a contractor or service provider that your organization employs? *The nature of the relationship is that your contractors and service providers will likely have employees who will need physical access to your facilities, and if the employees are new, you do not know if they have had background checks or have been cleared for security in other ways.*

7. When there are a large number of layoffs in a company, what should the security department and the IT security staff do? *Deactivate physical access control security cards and user IDs and passwords that enable employees to access computer systems and network capabilities.*

8. In addition to damage that a climatic event can cause to facilities, a climatic event can be *very disruptive to the normal operating routine of an organization and can lead to breakdowns in security and increased opportunity for the insider to cause or create security breaches.*

9. The best way to prevent security breaches during and after events that change the organization's environment is *to have a plan in place to ensure that security is appropriately maintained during the change events.*

10. When construction projects are in progress, remodeling is being done, or there is considerable relocation of equipment, supplies, or work groups what tends to happen? *During such activity, there can often be temporary changes in human traffic flow or changes in location of security guards*

or security barriers. These conditions provide an extra oppor-
tunity for an insider to gain unauthorized access to a secure
area without being noticed or to remove items from the secured
areas.

Chapter 11

1. Effective prosecution is *the successful prosecution of intel-*
   lectual crime perpetrators while simultaneously protecting
   the trade secrets and other intellectual property of the victim
   organization.
2. Gaps in security are *security measures or mitigation methods*
   that are inadequate to protect an asset or do not thoroughly pro-
   tect the asset that they were deployed to protect.
3. Infringement of intellectual property can be *the unau-*
   thorized reproduction or distribution of copyrighted material,
   the misappropriation of trade secrets for commercial gain, or
   the unauthorized use of a trademarked name or logo.
4. The lessons-learned process is *a structured method of evalu-*
   ating incidents or events, and determining what individuals
   or organizations could have done better to deal with the situa-
   tion; and transforming that lesson into positive actions through
   employee training, improving procedures, or improving miti-
   gation methods or technology.
5. Occupational assessments are designed to *examine specific*
   occupational groups to identify gaps in the skills, knowledge,
   and abilities required to perform their work duties that that
   can potentially result in security violations.
6. Progressive discipline is *the application of increasingly severe*
   disciplinary measures to attempt to change an employee's behavior
   and increase compliance with corporate policies and procedures.
7. A security violation is *a failure to comply with the policies*
   and procedures established by your organization that could rea-
   sonably result in the loss or compromise of sensitive or propri-
   etary information.
8. In a life-threatening security incident you should *immedi-*
   ately call law enforcement.
9. Terminations for violations of security policies or procedures or for general misconduct should be *very thoroughly*

documented and kept on file with any previous warnings and disciplinary action.

10. A trademark infringement can be *the unauthorized sale of merchandise or packaging using a counterfeited trademark.*

Chapter 12

1. Active video surveillance systems *provide usable real-time images of activity at a facility so security interventions can be made as incidents occur.*

2. A process that employs technology such as GPS trackers of RFID chips to monitor the movement and/or location of assets or people is known as *location tracking.*

3. The science of using one or more unique physical characteristics or behavioral traits to identify individuals is known as *biometrics.*

4. Authorized use warning statements are *statements installed on computer systems that notify users of what is allowed or not allowed when they access an organization's computer systems. The statements appear on a computer monitor every time an employee logs into the system.*

5. Sensors that can detect a human presence in a specific space, and are capable of enabling control of building components, and modulate light output and initiate other system responses are known as *occupancy sensors.*

6. Smart surveillance technology can *help secure crowded environments by estimating crowd and group size, crowd density, and group speed and direction.*

7. A system that records and stores video images of activity at a facility so the images can be accessed and reviewed at a later time is known as a *passive video surveillance system.*

8. Wireless surveillance systems can help overcome many of the traditional barriers to wired controls including *they permit installation in buildings with minimal alterations to the building.*

9. A sensor is any device that can *take a stimulus, such as heat, light, magnetism, or exposure to a particular chemical, and convert it to a signal that can be transmitted over a network to a control or surveillance system.*

10. A method of preventing unauthorized use of computers and the Internet is to *deploy website blocking software.*

Chapter 13

1. A prescripted interview designed to be uniformly administered with all potential hires and to collect the same information in an unbiased manner from all potential hires is known as *a structured interview.*

2. A performance management program is *a structured training and competency development approach designed to continuously improve an employee's performance on current job responsibilities and to expand competencies to logical areas beyond current responsibilities.*

3. An occupational questionnaire is designed to *cover a variety of skills and competencies related to the position for which it is being used to test applicants.*

4. An employee resource group is *usually an organization-supported group of employees that are drawn together by shared characteristics, which could include anything from liking sports to learning a new computer programming languages.*

5. A standard part of the hiring process for employees who are expected to work with sensitive or classified information is a *background check.*

6. During preemployment screening, the Employee Polygraph Protection Act prohibits most private employers from *using lie detector tests.*

7. Checking the references that applicants provide is a common practice and is generally handled by the *human resources department.*

8. An applicant's references are more valuable in helping make a hiring decision if they are *obtained from people who were in a position to observe the applicant's work habits.*

9. Even though the new hire has gone through security orientations, briefings, and trainings, it can be helpful to *monitor their execution of required security procedures and compliance with security policies.*

10. The four basic types of mentors focus on *career guidance; proving information about the organization; intellectual*

collaboration and constructive feedback and criticism; interacting socially and providing social connects in the organization.

Chapter 14

1. The process of repeatedly attempting to guess passwords by using default passwords, dictionary words, and other possible passwords that may be relevant to an organization is known as a *guessing attack*.

2. An attack where an attacker tries all possible combinations of characters from a character set for passwords up to a specified length is known as a *brute force attack*.

3. What methods can be used to reduce insider violations of security policies and procedures? *Access control systems, authorized use statements, and monitoring of employee computer use.*

4. What should determine an employee's level of access to an organization's computer systems? *Employees should have access only to those applications they need to perform their job duties.*

5. What type of crimes have disgruntled technology workers committed against their employers? *They have stolen data, planted software time bombs, locked users out of systems for ransom purposes, and exposed sensitive information to unauthorized parties.*

6. Users should be required to change their passwords at least every *90 days*.

7. When required to use strong passwords, users often *write them down and keep them in a handy place close to their computer.*

8. Extreme misuse of company computer systems by end users can include *storing of pornography, online gambling, purchase or sale of contraband or illegal substances, involvement with hate groups through websites or chat rooms, and posting threatening messages on discussion groups or social media sites.*

9. If computer-related or computer-facilitated crimes committed by an employee are prosecuted, a company may be

required to *have an attorney and company representatives make court appearances or provide affidavits.*

10. The use of employee-owned computers to access company systems and work from home can *create unacceptable vulnerabilities to company computers and networks.*

Glossary

Access control for computer systems: is a process that either allows or disallows individual users to have access to specific computer applications and computer data sets, including what the user is allowed to do on the systems with their level of access.

Access control systems: are those automated and human functions that allow a properly identified person or logical entity access to an organization's facilities or computer systems.

Active video surveillance systems: are systems that provide usable real-time images of activity at a facility so security interventions can be made as an incident occurs.

Ad hoc security management: is an approach to security planning and management that is piecemeal and has several uncoordinated and unrelated elements.

Appropriate security: is a level of security and a set of mitigation mechanisms or steps that can protect against known security threats an organization faces because of its activity, location, or value.

Appropriate separation of duties: is an organization structure that prevents individual employees or agents from having access to or control of work functions in a manner that would allow them to independently misappropriate corporate assets with little chance of detection.

Audio surveillance systems: are designed to monitor and record voices or noises that occur at specific locations in a facility where microphones are placed, and the recordings can be reviewed at a later date or for immediate security intervention into an incident.

Authorized logical access: is the access that an insider is allowed to have to an organization's computer and communications that an employee may need to perform their job duties.

Authorized physical access: is the access that an insider is allowed to have to an organization's property, buildings, and areas of buildings that an employee may need to perform their job duties.

Authorized use warning statement: is a statement installed on computer systems that notifies users of what is allowed or not allowed when they access an organization's computer systems and which appears on a computer monitor every time an employee logs into the system.

Biometrics: is the science of using one or more unique physical characteristics or behavioral traits to identify individuals.

Brute force attacks: are a variation of a password guessing attack where an attacker tries all possible combinations of characters from a character set for passwords up to a specified length.

Business partnerships: are relationships between two or more organizations designed to meet specific goals of one or more of the organizations.

Chaos factor: is a condition that occurs as a result of unsettled and disrupted routine operations of an organization or facility, and an atmosphere of disorder and confusion prevails.

Comprehensive records management system: dictates how all documents and records an organization has will be handled, moved, used, stored, and destroyed during their life cycle.

Comprehensive security plan: covers all security needs of an organization from the ground up and is designed to mitigate known security threats.

Computer use surveillance: is a process that tracks and records what users do or attempt to do when using corporate computer systems.

Corrective actions: are those steps that are taken to restore normal operations after an incident, and what steps are taken to change an employee's behavior and eliminate further security violations by the employee.

Criminal groups: are comprised of people who are organized for the purpose of committing criminal activity for economic gain or political clout or dominance in a specific geographical area.

Critical industry sectors: are those industries and business sectors that provide essential infrastructure support for the economic activity that enables a country to function economically, politically, and socially.

Culture of security: is an organization culture in which security pervades every aspect of daily life as well as all efforts to change, evolve, or realign the organization.

Dictionary attacks: are a variation of a guessing attack where an attacker attempts to guess a password using a list of possible passwords.

Disciplinary action: is the action taken toward an employee who has violated corporate security policies and procedures or other corporate behavioral policies.

Disgruntled employees: are individuals who are disenfranchised from an organization and often act out their frustrations or anger in violent or destructive manners.

Domestic antisocial groups: are groups of people or minisocieties that oppose the larger society in which they live and/or work.

Domestic fanatics: are radical groups that are residents or citizens of the countries in which they kill, sabotage, or spread hate and fear.

Effective prosecution: is the successful prosecution of intellectual crime perpetrators, while simultaneously protecting the trade secrets and other intellectual property of the victim organization.

Employee resource groups (ERGs): are usually organization-supported groups of employees that are drawn together by shared characteristics, which could include anything from liking sports to wanting to learn new computer programming languages.

E-Verify: is a free Internet-based service of the Citizenship and Immigration Services Division of the U.S. Department of Homeland Security (DHS) used to verify an employee's identity and authorization to work in the United States.

Exclusion areas: are those areas that are under the control of an organization in which activities are limited, construction is prohibited, and any type of occupation is usually curtailed that is maintained in order to establish a buffer of nonactivity around a facility or building as a security measure.

Facial recognition technologies: are technologies that are able to identify human subjects in an idle position or while in motion, and the identification and images are used to improve security and security officer safety.

Gaps in security: are security measures or mitigation methods that are inadequate to protect an asset or do not thoroughly protect the asset that they were deployed to protect.

Guessing attacks: use the process of repeatedly attempting to guess passwords by using default passwords, dictionary words, and other possible passwords that may be relevant to an organization.

ID card/badge display policy: is the organization's policy that informs employees and visitors as to the organization's requirement for ID card/badge display when on the organization's property and can also cover employees on official business not on company property.

ID card/badge policy purpose and scope statement: communicates an organization's purpose for having an ID card/badge policy and should apply to all people on an organization's property.

Identification (ID) systems: are those automated and human functions that are used to identify a person or logical entity for the purposes of allowing access to an organization's facilities or computer systems.

Indigenous group: is a group or class of people that live in their area of origin.

Individual assessments: are designed to evaluate how well an individual employee is performing a specific task or types of tasks necessary to fulfill job responsibilities.

Industry leader: is a company or organization that performs better than its competitors, bringing innovations to its field of endeavor, and whose products or services become the industry standard to match or beat in open market competition.

Infringement of intellectual property: can be the unauthorized reproduction or distribution of copyrighted material, the misappropriation of trade secrets for commercial gain, or the unauthorized use of a trademarked name or logo.

Insider misconduct: is conduct by an employee that is against organization policies or procedures, or that otherwise can harm the employing organization.

Insider-outsider team: is two or more people that jointly conspire to act maliciously against an organization with which one of them (the insider) is employed or has privileged access.

Insider-outsider threat: is a threat that emerges as a result of a relationship between a company's employee and a person working for an outside organization or who is otherwise not related to the organization.

International fanatics: are individuals, groups of people, or mini-societies that are greatly differentiated from the world around them by a belief system that is totally disconnected from larger realities in which they live and have a tendency to act out those differences in violent ways or politically or economically disruptive manners. They are members of radical groups that cross borders or influence individuals or groups in other countries to kill, sabotage, or spread hate and fear.

Job analysis: provides an understanding of the tasks performed by workers in the position and the competencies required to perform those tasks as well as the relationship between tasks and competencies.

Learning styles: are the manners in which an individual or class of individuals prefer to learn new material, ides, concepts, and technical skills.

Lessons-learned process: is a structured method of evaluating incidents or events, and determining what individuals or organizations could have done better to deal with the situation; and transforming that lesson into positive actions through employee training, improving procedures, or improving mitigation methods or technology.

Location tracking: is a process that employs technology such as GPS trackers of RFID chips to monitor the movement and/or location of assets or people.

Logical access control systems: manage each individual's access rights by allowing access to the computer services they need to perform their duties but preventing their access to other computer services as well as what they can do with computer services to which they do have access.

Mechanical security measures: include all of the various devices or protective systems that can be installed to prevent unauthorized movement and monitor movement of people, materials, products, supplies, or data.

Mitigation efforts: are the processes, procedures, or technologies that an organization deploys to prevent security breaches.

Nondisclosure agreement: is an agreement between two parties where one or both parties agree not to disclose information or data that has been communicated between the parties.

Obsolete computer equipment: is any computer equipment that can no longer provide any functionality in an organization's current computing environment because of the system's architecture or the inability to run current computer applications in an adequate manner.

Occupancy sensors: can detect a human presence in a specific space, and are capable of enabling control of building components, and can modulate light output and initiate other system responses.

Occupational assessments: are designed to examine specific occupational groups to identify gaps in the skills, knowledge, and abilities required to perform their work duties that can potentially result in security violations.

Occupational questionnaires: typically consist of questions that cover a variety of skills and competencies related to the position for which it is being administered.

Onboarding: is a structured process covering all aspects of a new hire's job responsibilities, administrative processes of the hiring organization as well as security procedures. The onboarding process also integrates the new hire into the social and cultural aspects of an organization.

Onsite contractors: are those individuals or organizations a company hires for specific tasks or projects that perform their job duties within the company's facilities.

Open organizations: tend to be more informal and not highly structured; they often lack strict hierarchal communication structures; project teams are fluid; information flows freely; and employees have extensive access to information, systems, and people.

Organizational assessments: are designed to evaluate the level of organizational performance that is required to meet organizational goals and objectives.

Passive video surveillance systems: record and store video images of activity at a facility so the images can be accessed and reviewed at a later time.

Password management: is a structured process of establishing, implementing, and maintaining password policies and procedures throughout an organization.

Performance management program: is a structured training and competency development approach designed to continuously improve an employee's performance on current job responsibilities and to expand competencies to logical areas beyond current responsibilities.

Periodic reviews of existing security measures: are an examination or evaluation of existing security measures to determine if they are adequate to continue to protect an organization from ongoing or new threats.

Personal technologies: include employee-owned devices such as cell phones, tablets, laptops, and digital media that can be used to inappropriately record and remove propriety information from an employer's facilities.

Personal use: means an item or service not used for the employing organization and is intended for use only by the recipient.

Physical access control systems: are systems designed to specifically allow an individual to enter specific areas of a facility and block their access to areas of the facility to which they have not been granted access.

Physical security measures: are barriers that control entry and access to building areas by unauthorized employees or contractors, and that prevent materials or information from being physically accessed or removed from a controlled area.

Preliminary security violation report: is the first report of a security incident that communicates the basic known facts about the incident, including who was involved and the immediate known consequences of the violation.

Premeditated malicious act: is an action that an insider deliberately plans and executes that is intended to do harm to their employer or their fellow employees.

Procedural security measures: are structured processes or steps that employees must follow when entering or exiting secure areas, when handling and working with sensitive or proprietary materials, or transferring products or data from one controlled area to another controlled area.

Product or services evaluation company: is a consulting firm that helps you evaluate products and determine if a specific product or service will perform in your environment to help meet the objectives for which they are designed.

Professional relationships: are relationships between employees of organizations with which there is a business relationship that serves business interests and does not jeopardize or create risks for either side.

Progressive discipline: is the application of increasingly severe disciplinary measures to attempt to change an employee's behavior and increase compliance with corporate policies and procedures.

Radio frequency identification (RFID) tags: are very small electronically detectable and readable marking tags that can be read via radio frequencies when they are in a defined proximity of an electronic reader that does not require direct contact with the tag.

Relationship inventory: is a list or database of all of the outside organizations a company has a relationship with and who is authorized to represent those organizations, and who in the company is authorized to participate in interactions on behalf of the company.

Safe harbor standards: are the joint European Union–United States developed standards for handling data and personal information, which have become the de facto standards around the world.

Secure areas of buildings: are spaces that have strong physical access controls and strong security features even though the building with which they are contained may not be secured and have general public access areas.

Secure buildings: have strong physical access control systems that only allow people in that have authorized access and appropriate security clearances. Secure buildings may also have stronger security for designated floors and areas of the building.

Secure communities: are relatively self-contained special purpose communities such as a military base or research campus. Secure communities generally have perimeter security that can be strengthened on demand, have some public areas without secured access within the perimeter, secure facilities within the outer perimeter, secured buildings, and buildings with secured areas.

Secure facilities: are generally comprised of one to several special purpose secured buildings with strong perimeter security surrounding the entire group of buildings. There are generally no unsecured public areas, buildings have secured access levels based on need, and areas of buildings have higher levels of security based on need.

Secure storage devices: are designed to limit access to their contents with strong locking mechanisms and/or durable construction that cannot be easily dismantled or neutralized.

Security awareness: is the basic level of understanding of security and recognition of the importance of security by employees or groups of employees in an organization.

Security evangelists: are individuals in an organization who, although they are not necessarily directly responsible for security, they speak of the benefits of good security whenever they have the opportunity to express their support and encourage others to support security efforts.

Security familiarity: is knowing that security exists and is necessary in certain situations, but involves little knowledge or understanding of security processes and procedures.

Security leader: is a high-ranking and/or respected person in an organization that supports security efforts on a day-to-day basis as well as in organizational activities such as budgeting, planning, and managing, and speaks on behalf of security efforts when appropriate.

Security performance: is the proper implementation of security procedures and adherence to security policies.

Security requirements: are the levels of and types of security required for an organization by law or because of the nature of the work performed, assets held, or research conducted on behalf of other organizations that depend on security provided by the service organization.

Security threats: are conditions, people, or events that can jeopardize the security of an organization, a facility, or any asset belonging to an organization or the employees of the organization.

Security vigilance: is the constant attention given to security during day-to-day operations and contributes to security by encouraging the reporting of security violations and makes suggestions on how to improve security when weaknesses are observed.

Security violation: is a failure to comply with the policies and procedures established by your organization that could reasonably result in the loss or compromise of sensitive or proprietary information.

Sensitive information: is that information held or created by an organization that, if revealed to the wrong party, would cause harm to the organization owning or creating the information.

Smart surveillance technology: can help secure crowded environments by estimating crowd and group size, crowd density, and group speed and direction.

Social and professional networking websites: are websites that are specially geared for like individuals to communicate with each other as individuals or groups in order to better communicate, facilitate professional connections, seek employment, or hire new staff.

Social media applications: are any existing or future networked computer program that facilitate communication between individuals or individuals and groups.

Social media policies: specify who in an organization is responsible for social media operations and specify when, why, where, and how social media can be used on behalf of an organization and provides guidance on the inappropriate use of social media by corporate media staff and employees.

Social media presence: is an organization's use of social media accounts and applications to communicate to individuals or groups as well as the mention, comments, discussions, and display of any material on any social media application that relates to or depicts an organization.

Souvenir value: is the perceived noneconomic value an item has for a person who steals or misappropriates an item.

Spontaneous or situational security measures: are those that are put into place when out-of-the-ordinary events are taking place at a facility.

Strong passwords: are a required length with a required mix of numbers, letters, and special characters, and do not have common words or user names as part of the password.

Structured interview: is a prescripted interview between a potential hire and a representative of the hiring organization designed to be uniformly administered with all potential hires and to collect the same information in an unbiased manner from all potential hires.

Surveillance technology: is any technology that helps an organization watch what employees or visitors are doing while at the facility.

Task-based assessments: are designed to evaluate the performance of a wide range of types of employees to determine if there is a gap in the skills, knowledge, and abilities required to perform specific procedures or tasks.

Telephone usage surveillance: is a process that tracks and records what users do or attempt to do when using corporate telephone systems.

The right fit: is a term that refers the compatibility of a product or service with its target organizational and technological environment.

Through-the-wall surveillance (TWS) technology: is able to detect motion or movement of people of machines through interior or exterior building walls.

Trade secrets: are any form or type of business process, scientific formula, technical specification, economic data, or engineering designs that the owner has taken measures to protect and which economic value can be derived.

Training gaps: are operational procedures or security methods that employees have not been adequately trained to execute.

Unauthorized use: is the reading, recording, transmitting, or storing of data that belongs to a specific party and is meant for a specific and restricted use by the owning or custodial organization or its designees.

Unprofessional relationships: are relationships between employees of organizations that do business transactions, and those relationships do not serve business interests and can jeopardize or create risks for both sides.

User constraints: are constraints on designing and implementing security mitigation methods that arise from local concerns about building appearance, local building codes, and local political dynamics.

Value-added supplier: is a supplier that does more than just provide a specific type of equipment or supply but helps an organization better leverage its product or processes in operations or manufacturing activities.

Video surveillance technology: is a system or components that view, record, and/or store images of activity at a facility.

Virtual private networks: are computer networks that control access of authorized users and keep unauthorized users from access the network or any computer system on the network.

Visual appearance of security: is the manner in which security presence and security operations are visible or are displayed in a particular environment.

Vulnerability assessment: is a structured process by which you evaluate how secure your facilities are based on your perception of threats and security needs.

References

1. United States Department of Justice, Federal Bureau of Investigation. The Insider Threat: An Introduction to Detecting and Deterring an Insider Spy. October 2012. Retrieved May 16, 2016, from https://www.fbi.gov/about-us/investigate/counterintelligence/the-insider-threat.
2. Barnett, Cynthia. The Measurement of White-Collar Crime Using Uniform Crime Reporting (UCR) Data. February 2002. United States Department of Justice, Federal Bureau of Investigation. Retrieved May 12, 2016, from https://www.fbi.gov/stats-services/about-us/cjis/ucr/nibrs/nibrs_wcc.pdf.
3. United States Department of Homeland Security. Critical Infrastructure Sectors. October 2015. Retrieved May 18, 2016, from https://www.dhs.gov/critical-infrastructure-sectors.
4. The White House. Presidential Policy Directive—Critical Infrastructure Security and Resilience. February 2013. Retrieved May 18, 2016, from https://www.whitehouse.gov/the-press-office/2013/02/12/presidential-policy-directive-critical-infrastructure-security-and-resil.
5. National Institute of Building Sciences. About the WBDG. March 2012. Whole Building Design Guide. Retrieved May 18, 2016, from http://www.wbdg.org/about.php.
6. The Building Security Council. The Building Security Council Handbook. October 2013. Retrieved May 18, 2016, from http://bscp.asce.org.

7. Testimony of Ronald L. Dick, Director, National Infrastructure Protection Center, Before the House Energy and Commerce Committee, Oversight and Investigation Subcommittee Washington, DC. April 5, 2001. United States Department of Justice, Federal Bureau of Investigation. Retrieved May 18, 2016, from https://www.fbi.gov/news /testimony/issue-of-intrusions-into-government-computer-networks.

8. United States Federal Trade Commission. Start with Security: A Guide for Business, Lessons Learned from FTC Cases. June 2015. Retrieved May 24, 2016, from https://www.ftc.gov/tips-advice/business-center /guidance/start-security-guide-business.

9. *Code of Federal Regulations.* Title 16—Commercial Practices, Chapter I, Subchapter C, Part 314—Standards For Safeguarding Customer Information. §314.4 Elements. United States Federal Trade Commission. May 2016. Retrieved May 25, 2016, from http://www.ecfr.gov/cgi-bin /text-idx?c=ecfr&sid=1e9a81d52a0904d70a046d0675d613b0&rgn =div5&view=text&node=16%3A1.0.1.3.38&idno=16.

10. Beesley, Caron. 7 Ways to Protect Your Small Business from Fraud and Cybercrime. May 8, 2013. United States Small Business Administration. Retrieved May 25, 2016, from https://www.sba.gov /blogs/employee-fraud-what-you-can-do-about-it.

11. United States Department of Commerce, Western Region Security Office. Proprietary Information & Trade Secrets. November 2001. Retrieved May 25, 2016, from http://www.wrc.noaa.gov/wrso/security _guide/propriet.htm.

12. United States Patent and Trademark Office, Office of Policy and External Affairs. Trade Secret Protection in the United States. August 2012. Retrieved May 25, 2016, from http://www.nist.gov/mep/upload /marinaslides.pdf.

13. United States Federal Bureau of Investigation. Economic Espionage: FBI Launches Nationwide Awareness Campaign. July 2015. Retrieved May 25, 2016, from https://www.fbi.gov/news/stories/2015/july/economic-espionage.

14. United States Federal Bureau of Investigation, Criminal Justice Information Division. Crime in the United States 2012, Table 24, Property Stolen and Recovered. Retrieved May 27, 2016, from https:// www.fbi.gov/about-us/cjis/ucr/crime-in-the-u.s/2012/crime-in-the -u.s.-2012/tables/24tabledatadecoverviewpdfs/table_24_property_stolen _and_recovered_by_type_and_value_2012.xls.

15. National Equipment Register. Our Services. Retrieved May 27, 2016, from http://www.ner.net/services.html.

16. National Insurance Crime Bureau. 2015 Annual Report. January 2016. Retrieved May 27, 2016, from https://www.nicb.org/about-nicb /annual_reports.

17. United States Customs and Border Protection. Supply Chain Security Best Practices Catalog: The Customs-Trade Partnership Against Terrorism (C-TPAT). January 2006. Retrieved May 27, 2016, from www.cbp.gov/sites/default/files/documents/ctpat_bp_2006.pdf.

18. United States Department of Homeland Security. ISC Facility Security Plan. February 2015. Retrieved May 31, 2016, from www.dhs.gov/publication/isc-facility-security-plan-guide.

19. United States General Services Administration. 2003 Facilities Standards (P100) Section 8 Security Design. October 2003. Retrieved May 31, 2016, from http://www.gsa.gov/portal/content/104806.

20. Organization of Economic Coordination and Development. (Malware): A Security Threat to the Internet Economy. January 19, 2007. Retrieved May 25, 2016, from http://www.oecd.org/general/searchresults/?q=insiderthreats&cx=01243260174851139518:xzeadub0b0a&cof=FORID:11&ie=UTF-8.

21. United States Federal Bureau of Investigation. The FBI and Leadership—Part 1: Helping Employees "Lead Where They Stand." May 13, 2013. Retrieved June 5, 2016, from https://www.fbi.gov/news/stories/2013/may/fbi-helping-employees-lead-where-they-stand/fbi-and-leadership-helping-employees-lead-where-they-stand.

22. United States Department of Homeland Security. Insider Threat Fact Sheet. March 3, 2016. Retrieved June 5, 2016, from https://www.dhs.gov/publication/insider-threat-fact-sheet.

23. United States Federal Bureau of Investigation. Cyber Threat: Planning for the Way Ahead. February 2, 2013. Retrieved June 5, 2016, from https://www.fbi.gov/news/stories/2013/february/the-cyber-threat-planning-for-the-way-ahead/the-cyber-threat-planning-for-the-way-ahead.

24. United States Federal Bureau of Investigation. Economic Espionage: How to Spot a Possible Insider Threat. May 11, 2012. Retrieved June 5, 2016, from https://www.fbi.gov/news/stories/2012/may/insider_051112/insider_051112.

25. Defense Personnel and Security Research Center. Online Guide to Security Responsibilities. 2016. Retrieved June 5, 2016, from http://www.dhra.mil/perserec/osg.html.

26. Organisation for Economic Co-operation and Development (OECD). Reducing Systemic Cybersecurity Risk. January 14, 2011. Retrieved June 5, 2016, from https://www.oecd.org/gov/risk/46889922.pdf.

27. United States Federal Bureau of Investigation. Cyber Task Forces: Building Alliances to Improve the Nation's Cybersecurity. May 13, 2011. Retrieved June 5, 2016, from https://www.fbi.gov/about-us/investigate/cyber/cyber-task-force-fact-sheet.

28. Dhont, Jan, María Verónica Pérez Asinari, and Yves Poullet. Safe Harbour Decision Implementation Study. April 19, 2004. European Commission. Retrieved June 19, 2016, from ec.europa.eu/justice/data-protection/document/studies/files/safe-harbour-2004_en.pdf.

29. United States Department of the Interior. Social Media Policy. September 2015. Retrieved June 9, 2016, from https://www.doi.gov/notices/Social-Media-Policy.

30. United States Federal Trade Commission. The FTC's Endorsement Guides: What People Are Asking. May 2015. Retrieved June 9, 2016, from https://www.ftc.gov/tips-advice/business-center/guidance/ftcs-endorsement-guides-what-people-are-asking.

31. United States National Labor Relations Board. Report of the Acting General Counsel Concerning Social Media Cases. January 2012. Retrieved June 9, 2016, from https://www.nlrb.gov/news-outreach/news-story/acting-general-counsel-releases-report-employer-social-media-policies.

32. United States National Labor Relations Board. The NLRB and Social Media. 2012. Retrieved June 9, 2016, from https://www.nlrb.gov/news-outreach/fact-sheets/nlrb-and-social-media.

33. National Conference of State Legislatures. State Social Media Privacy Laws. April 6, 2016. Retrieved June 9, 2016, from http://www.ncsl.org/research/telecommunications-and-information-technology/state-laws-prohibiting-access-to-social-media-usernames-and-passwords.aspx.

34. Assembly Bill No. 1844, Employer Use of Social Media. State of California. 2011–2012. Retrieved June 9, 2016, from http://leginfo.legislature.ca.gov/faces/billNavClient.xhtml?bill_id=201120120AB1844.

35. Revised Code of Washington 49.44.200, Personal Social Networking Accounts—Restrictions on Employer Access—Definitions. State of Washington. Retrieved June 9, 2016, from http://apps.leg.wa.gov/RCW/default.aspx?cite=49.44.200.

36. Texas Workforce Commission. Internet, E-Mail, and Computer Use Policy. Retrieved June 9, 2016, from http://www.twc.state.tx.us/news/efte/internetpolicy.html.

37. Illinois Government News Network. Governor Quinn Signs Legislation to Protect Workers' Right to Privacy: New Law Makes Illinois One of the First States to Prevent Employers from Demanding Social Network Passwords. August 12, 2012. Retrieved June 9, 2016, from http://www3.illinois.gov/PressReleases/ShowPressRelease.cfm?SubjectID=2&RecNum=10442.

38. United States National Institute of Standards and Technology. The Systems Security Engineering Capability Maturity Model. 1999. Retrieved June 15, 2016, from http://csrc.nist.gov/nissc/1998/proceedings/tutorB5.pdf.

39. USA.gov. About the Website USA.gov. Retrieved June 16, 2016, from https://www.usa.gov/history-of-website.

40. National Institute of Standards and Technology (NIST), Computer Security Division. Federal Information Technology Security Assessment Framework. Prepared for Security, Privacy, and Critical Infrastructure Committee. November 2008. Retrieved June 18, 2016, from http://csrc.nist.gov/publications/secpubs/Federal_IT_SAF_2000.pdf.

41. United States Government Accountability Office. Insider Threats: DOD Should Strengthen Management and Guidance to Protect Classified Information and Systems. June 2015. Retrieved June 28, 2016, from http://www.cdse.edu/documents/toolkits-insider/insider-threat-gao-jun-2015.pdf.

42. Combating Terrorism Technical Support Office (CTTSO). Evaluation Criteria. Retrieved June 20, 2016 from http://www.cttso.gov/?q=evaluation_criteria.

43. New York State, Department of State, Division of Licensing Services. Security Guard Training Requirements. Retrieved June 20, 2016, from http://www.dos.ny.gov/licensing/securityguard/sgtraining.html.

44. New York State, Department of State, Division of Licensing Services. FAQ: Security/Fire Alarm Installer Industry. Retrieved June 20, 2016, from http://www.dos.ny.gov/licensing/alarminstall/alarm_faq.html#1.

45. U.S. General Services Administration, National Customer Service Center. Federal Identity, Credential, & Access Management. June 16, 2016. Retrieved June 20, 2016, from https://www.idmanagement.gov/IDM/s/article_content_old?tag=a0Gt0000000XNYG.

46. U.S. General Services Administration, National Customer Service Center. Modernizing Federal Physical Access Control Systems (PACS). June 16, 2016. Federal Identity, Credential, & Access Management. Retrieved June 24, 2016, from https://www.idmanagement.gov/IDM/s/document_detail?Id=kA0t00000008Of8CAE.

47. U.S. General Services Administration, National Customer Service Center. Modernizing Federal Logical Access Control Systems (LACS). June 16, 2016. Federal Identity, Credential, & Access Management. Retrieved June 24, 2016, from https://www.idmanagement.gov/IDM/s/document_detail?Id=kA0t00000008Of1CAE.

48. United States Citizenship and Immigration Services. E-Verify. United States Department of Homeland Security. June 24, 2016. Retrieved June 24, 2016, from https://www.uscis.gov/e-verify.

49. United States Citizenship and Immigration Services. How E-Verify Works. United States Department of Homeland Security. June 24, 2016. Retrieved June 24, 2016, from https://www.uscis.gov/e-verify/what-e-verify/how-e-verify-works.

50. NASA, Office of Security and Program Protection. NASA Security Procedure Requirement NSPR-1600-2: Photo Identification Color-Coding Requirements. September 6, 2006. Retrieved June 26, 2016, from http://nodis3.gsfc.nasa.gov/policy_letters/NM_1600-50_.pdf.

51. New York City Police Department. Guidelines on Access Control, Screening & Monitoring. June 17, 2006. Retrieved June 27, 2016, from http://www.nyc.gov/html/nypd/downloads/pdf/counterterrorism/engineeringsecurity_050_guidlines_on_access_control_screening_and_monintoring.pdf.

52. Organisation of Economic Co-operation and Development. Proceedings of the OECD Workshop: "Information Security in a Networked World." September 13, 2001. Retrieved June 6, 2016, from www.oecd.org/internet/ieconomy/2387671.pdf.

53. United States Immigration and Customs Enforcement (ICE), Department of Homeland Security. Secure Communities. July 2015. Retrieved June 29, 2016, from https://www.ice.gov/secure-communities.

54. United States Department of Defense, Defense Security Service. Checklist for a New Facility Clearance. Retrieved June 29, 2016, from http://www.dss.mil/isp/fac_clear/fac_clear_check.html.

55. United States Department of Defense, Defense Security Service. Information and Services: CDSE Supports the Security Community's Readiness through Education, Training, and Certification. Retrieved June 29, 2016, from http://www.cdse.edu/index.html.

56. United States Department of Defense, Defense Security Service. Physical Security Planning. Retrieved June 29, 2016, from http://www.cdse.edu/toolkits/physical/planning.html.

57. United States Army Corps of Engineers. Unified Facilities Criteria (UFC): DOD Security Engineering Facilities Planning Manual. September 11, 2008. Retrieved June 29, 2016, from https://pdc.usace.army.mil/library/ufc/4-020-01/.

58. United States Department of Agriculture, Office of Procurement and Property Management. Security in the Workplace—Informational Material. Retrieved June 29, 2016, from http://www.dm.usda.gov/physicalsecurity/workplace.htm.

59. United States Department of Defense, Defense Security Service. Student Guide—Short: Classified Storage Requirements. Retrieved July 4, 2016, from http://www.dss.mil/multimedia/shorts/dss_csr_fy11/common/cw/data/CDSE_CSR_Student_Guide.pdf.

60. North Dakota Information Technology Services. Records Management Definitions. Retrieved July 4, 2016, from https://www.nd.gov/itd/services/records-management-program/records-management-definitions.

61. Association of Records Managers and Administrators (ARMA). Retrieved July 4, 2016, from http://www.arma.org.

62. Defense Security Service, Counterintelligence Directorate. Insider Threats: Combating the Enemy within Your Organization. April 25, 2012. Retrieved July 4, 2016, from http://www.dss.mil/documents/ci/Insider-Threats.pdf.

63. Federal Financial Institutions Examination Council (FFIEC). Vendor and Third-Party Management. April 27, 2016. Retrieved July 5, 2016, from http://ithandbook.ffiec.gov/it-booklets/retail-payment-systems/retail-payment-systems-risk-management/operational-risk/vendor-and-third-party-management.aspx.

64. Ohio Department of Transportation. Purchasing Ethics and Vendor Visit Policy. April 17, 2015. Retrieved July 5, 2016, from www.dot.state.oh.us/policy/PoliciesandSOPs/Policies/15-009(P).pdf.

65. United States Army Combined Arms Center, Army Training Support Center. Contractors in the Workplace. Retrieved July 6, 2016, from www.atsc.army.mil/tcmlive/srp/downloads/ContractorsintheWorkplace.doc.

66. United States Department of the Air Force. Air Force Guidance Memorandum to AFI 36-2909, Professional and Unprofessional Relationships. June 15, 2016. Retrieved July 6, 2016, from static.e-publishing.af.mil/production/1/af_ja/publication/afi36-2909/afi36-2909.pdf.

67. National Renewable Energy Laboratory. Nondisclosure Agreements. January 8, 2016. Retrieved July 6, 2016, from https://www.nrel.gov /workingwithus/nondisclosure-agreements.html.

68. New York City Conflicts of Interest Board. Quick Answers to Common Questions: Plain Language Guide. Retrieved July 6, 2016, from http:// www.nyc.gov/html/conflicts/downloads/pdf2/leaflets/two_pg_guide.pdf.

69. United States Department of Agriculture. Risk Based Methodology for Physical Security Assessments. July 7, 2004. Retrieved July 9, 2016, from http://www.dm.usda.gov/physicalsecurity/riskmanagementapproach presentation.pdf.

70. United States Department of Agriculture Forest Service, Technology and Development. Threat and Vulnerability Assessments. March 29, 2013. Retrieved July 10, 2016, from http://www.fs.fed.us/t-d/phys_sec /threat/index.htm.

71. United States Geological Survey. Physical Security Handbook (440-2-H). August 2005. Retrieved July 10, 2016, from https://www2.usgs.gov /usgs-manual/handbook/hb/440-2-h/440-2-h.html#TOC.

72. United States Nuclear Regulatory Commission. Physical Protection Areas. January 13, 2015. Retrieved July 9, 2016, from http://www.nrc .gov/security/domestic/phys-protect/areas.html.

73. United States Department of State. Vulnerability, Assessment, Climate Change Impacts, and Adaptation Measures. December 16, 2013. Retrieved July 10, 2016, from http://www.state.gov/documents/organization /218994.pdf.

74. Moore, S., L. Grunberg, and E. Greenberg. Repeated Downsizing Contact: The Effects of Similar and Dissimilar Layoff Experiences on Work and Well-Being Outcomes. *Journal of Occupational Health Psychology* 3 (2004): 247–257. Retrieved July 10, 2016, from http://www .ncbi.nlm.nih.gov/pubmed/15279519.

75. Stanton, T.H. Organizational Structure and Government Performance. November 2004. Retrieved July 10, 2016, from www.ncjrs.gov/App /publications/Abstract.aspx?id=150166.

76. United States Federal Emergency Management Agency. Building Design for Homeland Security: Unit IV, Vulnerability Assessment. March 10, 2004. Retrieved July 10, 2016, from www.fema.gov/pdf /plan/prevent/rms/155/e155_unit_iv.pdf.

77. United States Department of Justice, Bureau of Justice Statistics, Office of Justice Programs. Violence and Theft in the Workplace: National Crime Victimization Survey. July 1994. Retrieved 2016, from http:// www.bjs.gov/content/pub/pdf/thefwork.pdf.

78. United States Defense Security Service (DSS), Center for Development of Security Excellence (CDSE). Administrative Inquiry (AI) Process Job Aid. July 2011. Retrieved July 12, 2016, from http://www.cdse.edu /documents/cdse/ai-job-aid-for-industry.pdf.

79. United States Department of Agriculture, Departmental Management. Reporting a Security Violation. August 20, 2007. Retrieved July 12, 2016, from http://www.dm.usda.gov/ohsec/pdsd/ReportSecurityViolation.pdf.

80. United States Department of Justice, Bureau of Justice Statistics, Office of Justice Programs. Intellectual Property Theft. 2004. Retrieved July 12, 2016, from http://www.bjs.gov/index.cfm?ty=pbdetail&iid=998.

81. United States Department of Justice, Computer Crime and Intellectual Property Section. Reporting Intellectual Property Crime: A Guide for Victims of Copyright Infringement, Trademark Counterfeiting, and Trade Secret Theft. March 2013. Retrieved July 12, 2016, from https://www.justice.gov/sites/default/files/criminal-ccips/legacy/2015/03/26/ip-victim-guide-and-checklist-march-2013.pdf#page=21.

82. United States Department of Justice, Computer Crime and Intellectual Property Section. "Checklist for Reporting an Intellectual Property Crime" in Reporting Intellectual Property Crime: A Guide for Victims of Copyright Infringement, Trademark Counterfeiting, and Trade Secret Theft. March 2013. Retrieved July 13, 2016, from https://www.justice.gov/sites/default/files/criminal-ccips/legacy/2015/03/26/ip-victim-guide-and-checklist-march-2013.pdf#page=21.

83. United States Internal Revenue Service. Part 6: Human Resources Management, Chapter 751: Discipline and Disciplinary Actions, Section 1—Discipline and Disciplinary Actions: Policies, Responsibilities, Authorities, and Guidance. Retrieved July 13, 2016, from https://www.irs.gov/irm/part6/irm_06-751-001.html#d0e195.

84. United States General Services Administration. CPO (Revalidated) Maintaining Discipline. May 2, 2003. Retrieved July 13, 2016, from http://www.gsa.gov/portal/directive/d0/content/523318.

85. United States General Accountability Office. Federal Real Property Security: Interagency Security Committee Should Implement a Lessons-Learned Process. September 2012. Retrieved July 13, 2016, from www.gao.gov/products/GAO-12-901.

86. United States Office of Personnel Management. Training Needs Assessment: Training and Development Planning & Evaluating. Retrieved July 13, 2016, from https://www.opm.gov/policy-data-oversight/training-and-development/planning-evaluating/.

87. 2016 Florida Statutes, Chapter 810.145, Video Voyeurism. Retrieved July 17, 2016, from http://www.leg.state.fl.us/Statutes/index.cfm?App_mode=Display_Statute&URL=0800-0899/0810/Sections/0810.145.html.

88. United States Department of Justice, National Institute of Justice, Office of Justice Programs. Program Profile: Public Surveillance Cameras. February 11, 2014. Retrieved July 14, 2016, from https://www.crimesolutions.gov/ProgramDetails.aspx?ID=338.

89. United States Department of Justice, National Institute of Justice, Office of Justice Programs. Program Profile: CCTV in Five English Cities. August 31, 2011. Retrieved July 14, 2016, from https://www.crimesolutions.gov/ProgramDetails.aspx?ID=196.

90. United States Department of Homeland Security, Immigration and Customs Enforcement. Privacy Impact Assessment for the Security Management CCTV System. August 4, 2011. Retrieved July 14, 2016, from https://www.dhs.gov/xlibrary/assets/privacy/privacy-pia-ice-smcctv.pdf.

91. Beesley, Caron. Email, Phone and Social Media Monitoring in the Workplace—Know Your Rights as an Employer. June 27, 2012. Blogs: Starting a Business. United States Small Business Administration. Retrieved July 15, 2016, from https://www.sba.gov/blogs/email-phone-and-social-media-monitoring-workplace-know-your-rights-employer.

92. State of California Department of Justice, Office of the Attorney General. Workplace Privacy. Retrieved July 15, 2016, from http://oag.ca.gov/privacy/workplace-privacy.

93. United States Department of Labor, Bureau of Labor Statistics. Most Common Uses for Computers at Work. TED: The Economics Daily. September 2, 2005. Retrieved July 17, 2016, from http://www.bls.gov/opub/ted/2005/aug/wk5/art05.htm.

94. United States Department of Labor, Bureau of Labor Statistics. American Time Use Survey Summary—2015 Results. June 24, 2016. Retrieved July 17, 2016, from http://www.bls.gov/news.release/atus.nr0.htm.

95. United States National Aeronautics and Space Administration. Security of Information Technology—Chapter 4: Technical Controls. May 19, 2011. Retrieved July 17, 2016, from http://nodis3.gsfc.nasa.gov/displayDir.cfm?Internal_ID=N_PR_2810_001A_&page_name=Chapter4.

96. Burt, David. The Facts on Filters: A Comprehensive Review of 26 Independent Laboratory Tests of the Effectiveness of Internet Filtering Software. N2H2. March 12, 2002. Retrieved July 15, 2016, from https://www.ntia.doc.gov/legacy/ntiahome/ntiageneral/cipacomments/pre/aclj/ExhibitA.pdf.

97. United States Department of Justice, Office of the Inspector General. Review of the United States Marshals Service Discipline Process. Report No. I-2001-011. September 28, 2001. Retrieved July 17, 2016, from https://www.oig.justice.gov/reports/USMS/e0111/results.htm.

98. United States National Science Foundation. Sensor Technology: A Convergence of Forces. Retrieved July 17, 2016, from http://www.nsf.gov/news/special_reports/sensor/convergence.jsp.

99. United States National Institute of Standards and Technology, Engineering Laboratory. Advanced Sensing Systems for Building Energy Monitoring. October 1, 2015. Retrieved July 17, 2016, from http://www.nist.gov/el/building_environment/advsensingsystems.cfm.

100. United States Department of Energy, Office of Energy Efficiency & Renewable Energy. Promising Technology: Wireless Lighting Occupancy Sensors. Retrieved July 17, 2016, from http://energy.gov/eere/femp/promising-technology-wireless-lighting-occupancy-sensors.

101. United States Department of Justice, National Institute of Justice, Office of Justice Programs. Video Analytics for Criminal Justice Uses. August 18, 2012. Retrieved July 17, 2016, from http://nij.gov/topics/technology /detection-surveillance/enhanced-surveillance/Pages/video-analytics .aspx.

102. United States Department of Justice, National Institute of Justice, Office of Justice Programs. Through-the-Wall Surveillance. January 23, 2015. Retrieved July 17, 2016, from http://nij.gov/topics/technology/detection -surveillance/enhanced-surveillance/pages/through-wall.aspx.

103. United States Department of Justice, National Institute of Justice, Office of Justice Programs. Biometrics. September 15, 2011. Retrieved July 17, 2016, from http://nij.gov/topics/technology/biometrics/Pages/welcome .aspx/.

104. United States Department of Justice, National Institute of Justice, Office of Justice Programs. Facial Recognition Technology. September 15, 2011. Retrieved July 17, 2016, from http://nij.gov/topics/technology /biometrics/Pages/facial-recognition.aspx./

105. United States Office of Personnel Management. Job Analysis Assessment & Selection. Retrieved July 21, 2016, from https://www.opm.gov /policy-data-oversight/assessment-and-selection/job-analysis/.

106. United States Office of Personnel Management. Occupational Questionnaires Assessment & Selection. Retrieved July 21, 2016, from https://www.opm.gov/policy-data-oversight/assessment-and-selection /occupational-questionnaires/.

107. United States Office of Personnel Management. Structured Interviews Assessment & Selection. Retrieved July 21, 2016, from https://www.opm.gov/policy-data-oversight/assessment-and-selection /structured-interviews/.

108. United States Equal Employment Opportunity Commission. Background Checks: What Employers Need to Know. Retrieved July 21, 2016, from https://www.eeoc.gov/eeoc/publications/back ground_checks_employers.cfm.

109. United States Small Business Administration. Pre-Employment Background Checks, Starting & Managing. Retrieved July 21, 2016, from https://www.sba.gov/starting-business/hire-retain-employees /pre-employment-background-checks.

110. United States Office of Personnel Management. Reference Checking, November 20, 2008. Retrieved July 21, 2016, from https://www.opm .gov/policy-data-oversight/assessment-and-selection/other-assessment -methods/referencechecking.pdf.

111. United States National Aeronautics and Space Administration. Employee Orientation. Retrieved July 21, 2016, from http://employee orientation.nasa.gov/main/FirstDayExperience.htm.

112. United States Office of Personnel Management. Best Practices Mentoring. November 12, 2008. Retrieved July 21, 2016, from https:// www.opm.gov/policy-data-oversight/training-and-development/career -development/bestpractices-mentoring.pdf.

113. Colorado Division of Homeland Security and Emergency Management, Department of Public Safety. Internship Program. Retrieved July 24, 2016, from http://dhsem.state.co.us/budget-finance/internships.

114. United States Department of Labor, Wage and Hour Division. Fact Sheet #71: Internship Programs Under the Fair Labor Standards Act. April 2010. Retrieved July 24, 2016, from https://www.dol.gov/whd/regs/compliance/whdfs71.htm.

115. United States Bureau of Labor Statistics. May 2015 National Occupational Employment and Wage Estimates. Retrieved July 25, 2016, from http://www.bls.gov/oes/current/oes_nat.htm#15-0000.

116. United States Census Bureau. Number of Firms, Number of Establishments, Employment, and Annual Payroll by Enterprise Employment Size for the United States and States, Totals: 2013. February 8, 2016. Retrieved July 25, 2016, from http://www2.census.gov/econ/susb/data/2013/us_state_totals_2013.xlsx.

117. United States Treasury Inspector General for Tax Administration. Managers and System Administrators Need to Limit Employees' Access to Computer Systems. July 2005. Retrieved July 25, 2016, from https://www.treasury.gov/TIGTA/auditreports/2005reports/200520097fr.html.

118. United States Food and Drug Administration. FDA Industry Systems: Password Management Step-by-Step Instructions. July 27, 2015. Retrieved July 27, 2016, from http://www.fda.gov/Food/GuidanceRegulation/FoodFacilityRegistration/ucm091108.htm.

119. United States Geological Survey. Guidance for Support of USGS Employees and Contractors Using Government Computers at Private Residences and/or Privately Owned Computers to Perform Government Duties. January 3, 2003. Retrieved July 27, 2016, from http://water.usgs.gov/admin/memo/policy/wrdpolicy03.03.html.

120. United States Department of Health and Human Services. Stolen Laptops Lead to Important HIPAA Settlements. April 22, 2014. Retrieved July 27, 2016, from http://www.hhs.gov/about/news/2014/04/22/stolen-laptops-lead-to-important-hipaa-settlements.html.

121. United States Department of Health and Human Services. $750,000 HIPAA Settlement Emphasizes the Importance of Risk Analysis and Device and Media Control Policies. September 2, 2015. Retrieved July 27, 2016, from http://www.hhs.gov/about/news/2015/09/02/750,000-dollar-hipaa-settlement-emphasizes-the-importance-of-risk-analysis-and-device-and-media-control-policies.html#.

122. United States Department of Agriculture, Office of the Inspector General. Information Technology—Stolen Computer Equipment Containing Sensitive Information. February 27, 2007. Retrieved July 27, 2016, from https://www.usda.gov/oig/webdocs/50501-8-FM.pdf.

123. Treasury Inspector General for Tax Administration. The Internal Revenue Service Is Not Adequately Protecting Taxpayer Data on Laptop Computers and Other Portable Electronic Media Devices. March 23, 2007. Retrieved July 27, 2016, from https://www.treasury.gov/tigta/auditreports/2007reports/200720048fr.html.

124. United States Department of Justice, Office of the Inspector General. The Department of Justice's Control Over Weapons and Laptop Computers Summary Report. August 2002. Retrieved July 27, 2016, from https://oig.justice.gov/reports/plus/a0231/losses.htm.

125. Department of Veterans Affairs, Office of Inspector General. Review of Issues Related to the Loss of VA Information Involving the Identity of Millions of Veterans. July 11, 2006. Retrieved July 27, 2016, from http://www.va.gov/oig/pubs/VAOIG-06-02238-163.pdf.

126. United States Department of Commerce, Office of Inspector General. Census Has Improved Accountability for Laptops and Other Personal Property, But Additional Improvements Are Needed. September 2007. Retrieved July 27, 2016, from https://www.oig.doc.gov/OIGPublications/IG-18387-1.pdf.

Index

Page numbers followed by f and t indicate figures and tables, respectively.